Capital Women

Capital Women

The European Marriage Pattern, Female Empowerment, and Economic Development in Western Europe, 1300–1800

JAN LUITEN VAN ZANDEN, TINE DE MOOR,
and
SARAH CARMICHAEL

OXFORD
UNIVERSITY PRESS

OXFORD
UNIVERSITY PRESS

Oxford University Press is a department of the University of Oxford. It furthers the University's objective of excellence in research, scholarship, and education by publishing worldwide. Oxford is a registered trade mark of Oxford University Press in the UK and certain other countries.

Published in the United States of America by Oxford University Press
198 Madison Avenue, New York, NY 10016, United States of America.

Library of Congress Cataloging-in-Publication Data
Names: Zanden, J. L. van, author. | Moor, Tine de, author. | Carmichael, Sarah G., author.
Title: Capital women : the European marriage pattern, female empowerment and economic development in Western Europe 1300–1800 / Jan Luiten van Zanden, Tine De Moor and Sarah Carmichael.
Description: New York, NY : Oxford University Press, [2019] |
Includes bibliographical references and index.
Identifiers: LCCN 2018031083 (print) | LCCN 2018048442 (ebook) |
ISBN 9780190847890 (UPDF) | ISBN 9780190847906 (EPUB) |
ISBN 9780190847883 (hardcover)
Subjects: LCSH: Women—Europe, Western—Economic conditions. |
Marriage—Economic aspects—Europe, Western. | Married women—Europe, Western—History. | Women—Europe, Western—History—Middle Ages, 500–1500. |
Women—Europe, Western—History—Modern period, 1600– | Human capital—Europe, Western.
Classification: LCC HQ1587 (ebook) | LCC HQ1587 .Z36 2019 (print) |
DDC 305.4094—dc23
LC record available at https://lccn.loc.gov/2018031083

How good to be a woman, how much better to be a man!
Maidens and wenches, remember the lesson you're about to hear
Don't hurtle yourself into marriage far too soon.
The saying goes: "where is your spouse? Where's your honour?"
But one who earns her board and clothes
Shouldn't scurry to suffer a man's rod . . .
Though wedlock I do not decry;
Unyoked is best! Happy the woman without a man

—Poem by Anna Bijns (1493–1575), on the benefits of celibacy and late marriage[1]

[1] Wilson 1987, 382.

CONTENTS

LIST OF FIGURES

LIST OF TABLES

ACKNOWLEDGMENTS

We owe debts and gratitude, both intellectual and practical, to a number of people who made this book possible.

Intellectually we are, of course, indebted to the anonymous reviewers of the book who provided much useful feedback. Furthermore, we must thank our co-authors who worked on earlier versions of articles that have been reworked into the chapters of this book: Jaco Zuijderduijn, Annemarie Bouman, Anita Boele, Sandra de Pleijt, Selin Dilli, and Auke Rijpma.

Winny Bierman assisted in putting together an earlier version of the manuscript. Liesbeth van Kuijk did an excellent job in ensuring all the references were correct and consistent. Thanks also to Linda de Veen who assisted with the proofs of the book. Finally, however, we owe a great debt of gratitude to René van Weeren, who helped out with dotting a lot of the final i's.

Parts of the results presented in this book are based on research funded by the European Research Council under the European Union's Seventh Framework Programme (FP7/2007–2013)/ERC Grant agreement no. 240928 as part of the project '"United we stand". The dynamics and consequences of institutions for collective action in pre-industrial Europe' (awarded to Tine De Moor), and by the Netherlands Organisation for Scientific Research (NWO) via the VIDI-Grant (276-53-008) for the project 'Nature or nurture? A search for the institutional and biological determinants of life expectancy in Europe during the early modern period'(awarded to Tine De Moor).

Capital Women

1

The Broader Picture

Global Determinants of Female Agency and Economic Growth

> If we are going to see real development in the world, then our best investment is WOMEN
>
> —Desmond Tutu

Describing Female Agency

Economic development is often considered to be a male affair, engineered by male entrepreneurs, male politicians, and male managers. Economic historians trying to analyze long-term economic change have generally also concentrated on men as the main carriers of the processes they try to understand. In this book we make the point that women matter, and in our specific case, that women matter for understanding economic change in preindustrial Europe, as well as for economic development generally, both in the past and today. One of the unfortunate consequences of the increasing specialization among academics is that the study of women's history has become a separate specialism, part of gender studies, and therefore has become isolated, to some extent, from the mainstream of economic history. Much of the work of gender historians is focused on calculating women's "invisible" contribution to the economy, via their activities in the household economy. Regardless of the necessity of this particular quantitative exercise, it does not help us unravel the mechanisms that contribute to or discourage female empowerment more broadly construed. Moreover, the processes we describe in this book go back so far in time that putting figures on them is hard enough, let alone identifying the degree to which women have contributed to those developments. As a result, economic historians have not devoted much time to integrating new ideas and approaches that concentrate on the role of women in their analyses of long-term change.[1] We think, however, that based on insights from development economics and Unified Growth Theory, there are reasons to pay much more attention to the role played by women as engines of economic change.

Women represent roughly half the world's population and are therefore a significant economic resource; however, throughout history and around the world, the *fairer* sex has been discriminated against and frequently left without a voice, on both political and domestic fronts.[2] This goes hand in hand with the fact that male dominance has been a near universal phenomenon, although the degree to which it is practiced has varied.[3] Intrinsically, this is unfair from a social justice, human rights perspective, and improving the lot of such a large share of the population should be a goal in its own right. However, equality between men and women has more wide-ranging effects than those experienced by women alone. This implies that there is also an instrumental importance to focusing on achieving gender equality.

The case for the instrumental role of women in economic development has repeatedly been made convincingly by development economists. The seminal paper on this dates back to 1992, from the then chief economist of the World Bank, Lawrence Summers (1992), who gave a concise overview of the reasons why development requires "investing in *all* the people." He concluded that "education of girls may be the highest return investment available in the developing world."[4] He gave a number of reasons for this. First, he pointed out that women are overrepresented among the poor, and that, in particular in South Asia, there exists a "more general pattern of female deprivation" resulting in the infamous phenomenon of the millions of "missing women" noted by Amartya Sen.[5] This is the result of the fact that fewer girls are born—or are registered at birth—than would be expected on the basis of the normal ratio between girls and boys. They are missing from the birth records because they have been aborted or die shortly after birth (due to infanticide or neglect).

Such practices are usually related to the patriarchal traditions of these societies, where girls leave the household of their parents after marriage, and therefore do not take care of them during old age. Boys, on the other hand, continue to live with their parents. Their wives move to live with the groom's family and are then supposed to care for their in-laws. This gender bias leads to a vicious cycle

[1] Important exceptions to this rule do exist, such as Jan de Vries's (1994) work on the "Industrious Revolution." However, recent syntheses such as Clark (2007b), Landes (1998), Pomeranz (2000), and Allen (2001) do not expand on this issue.

[2] Inglehart, Norris, and Welzel 2002.

[3] Todd 1985.

[4] Summers 1992, 1.

[5] Sen 1990.

of "underinvestment in girls." Summers noticed that "increasing educational opportunities for girls offers the best chance of breaking the vicious cycle. . . . Among other things, women spend more of their income on children than their husbands do, and educated women are more likely to seek medical care and improve sanitation practices."[6] And perhaps most importantly: "Educated women choose to have fewer children and can provide more for those they do have."

Summers's pioneering paper was symbolic of the changing views on the role of women in economic development that occurred during the 1980s and '90s. It has led to plenty of new research on this issue, demonstrating the key role played by women—and by the education of women.[7] This culminated in the World Bank's World Development Report of 2012, which focuses on gender equality and development. The report presents three main arguments for why gender equality matters for economic development. First, as just mentioned, gender equality matters in its own right. Following Amartya Sen, it argues that development can be seen as a process of expanding freedoms for all people. From that perspective, achieving gender equality is a goal in itself: "just as development means less income poverty or better access to justice, it should also mean fewer gaps in well-being between males and females."[8] The second argument is that it is "smart economics" to improve the position of women: in most developing societies (and in many developed ones, as well) women's skills and talents are underused and misallocated because they face discrimination in markets and institutions that prevent them from completing their education, entering certain occupations, and earning the same wages as men. The economic (and social) losses are huge, and eliminating the barriers that keep them from realizing their capabilities will have strong, positive effects on development.[9] Third, women's endowments, agency (the ability to make meaningful decisions about their life course), and opportunities shape those of the next generation. Women have a large—and usually decisive—say in decisions about reproduction. They play a key role in deciding how many children are "wanted" and how these are "spaced" (of course, given the constraints of nature);[10] as we will see, it is their position and human capital that in most societies will determine the level of fertility and hence population growth. Moreover, women play a key role in raising the next generation in their transfer of values and "human capital" to their children. Improvements in women's education and health have strong positive impacts on these and other outcomes for their children.

[6] Summers 1992, 2.

[7] Klasen 2002; Klasen and Lamanna 2009; FAO 2011; Roxburgh, Lund, and Piotrowski 2011.

[8] World Bank 2012, 3–5.

[9] World Bank 2012, 3–5.

[10] See Hilevych 2015 for an exploration of how couples in two different parts of Ukraine negotiate fertility and abortion decisions.

Summing up, women in practically all societies play a crucial role in steering economic and demographic change, or have the potential to do so; they usually do this from a relatively subordinate position, in that they generally do not own the big companies or dominate politics, but if they did, they might be even more influential than those who currently do.

With this book we intend to give further support to the theory that the position of women in society matters for economic progress, presented on the basis of evidence from long-term European history. The historical situation of Europe can be seen as a case study to determine which parameters really matter for economic growth and female empowerment, allowing for future comparison to other societies. The degree to which women are allowed to play an influential role in the economy and society varies greatly from one society to another. This is largely determined by the power balances within households, between men and women, and between generations. These power balances are embedded in complex ideologies about the desired role of men and women in society, and are influenced by economic opportunities and incentives for both sexes. Access to wage labor, for example, may have a strong emancipatory effect and could strengthen women's position. Even culture—and the cultural ideas about the roles of men and women in family and household—is malleable and subject to fundamental change. But the current world economy is characterized by strong differences in the distribution of power between men and women, which has important consequences for the pace and character of economic change in various parts of the world.[11]

In this introduction we will not as yet address the big question of what the causes of inequalities are between men and women in different societies,[12] but will first briefly sketch the global differences in these power balances between men and women, and demonstrate how these can be applied to evaluate societies in the past. Next, we turn to the question of their consequences, and focus on the role of reproduction and human capital for economic change.

Marriage Ages and the Global Dimensions of Gender Inequality

How can we study female agency and gender inequality that existed in the past? Today, institutions such as the United Nations and the World Economic Forum collect datasets covering diverse dimensions of gender inequality, but for the

[11] Dilli 2017; Duflo 2012; Lagerlöf 2003.

[12] We refer to anthropological literature for this; see, for example, Todd 1985.

more distant past such data are often unavailable. In this book, we have taken a different approach by focusing on marriage—and in particular, on the age at which women and men marry—as reflecting the power distribution between women and men, as well as that between parents and children. This is not self-explanatory, so in this section we sketch the reasoning behind our use of this indicator.

Marriage is a topic that has been analyzed by a wide range of scholars, from economists, to anthropologists, to sociologists.[13] The different ways that marriages are organized around the world reflect the differences in male–female unions. Marriage plays an essential role in family formation, and as such is a key determinant of investments in the next generation. The norms surrounding marriage form part of a wider set of family values that govern the transfer of property, power hierarchies, and the responsibilities of relatives. Together, the various societally prescribed values to do with marriage make up a *marriage system*.

The age of marriage of women is closely linked to the marriage system: when marriage is arranged by the parents (or the broader family), girls are usually married off at a very early age. Societies in which arranged marriage is the norm are, for all sorts of reasons, fundamentally different from societies in which the younger generation gets to choose his or her own partner. The transition from the one system to the other is one of the most fascinating and important changes in our history. In Western Europe, this transition occurred very early on (or alternatively, parts of this region never developed a fully patriarchal system); in some areas, it was already underway in the Middle Ages and resulted in the emergence of the European Marriage Pattern, or EMP (as identified by Hajnal in 1965).[14] Why this was the case and the consequences for societal and economic development belong, in our view, to the big questions of European history that we address in chapter 2. It resulted in a situation in which men and women marry relatively late (often older than 24), with a very small age gap between spouses (one to three years, on average). Normally, marriages would not be arranged; individuals sought their own partners, and this took time. In addition, it was only possible to begin this search for a partner at a certain age. Moreover, the "search process" in the marriage market was targeted at more or less equal partners, resulting in the small age gap.

The example of the EMP illustrates how marriage ages of men and women, and the difference between those ages, can be an indicator of different balances of power—balances between the sexes and between parents and their children. In a system of arranged marriages, there is a tendency to marry girls off at very

[13] Lagerlöf 2003; Goody 1990; Becker 1973.

[14] Hajnal 1965.

early ages—sometimes as young or younger than 12. The influence the bride has on this decision is minimal, if not nonexistent; she has, in other words, (almost) no "agency." The rationale underpinning this system is explained in a rather whimsical fashion in the following answer by the regent of Banten (on Java) to the question of why girls in the region married at such a young age:

> If you allow a girl to grow up freely until she has reached the age when her passions are aroused, you run the risk . . . of her choosing a person with whom she will never enjoy a happy marriage. You can prevent this by compelling her to marry another man, but as they say in North Banten: "[W]hen the heart is baked, don't try to knead it." . . . [Y]ou increase the chance of destroying marital fidelity. . . . It's a completely different story for girls between the ages of seven and ten, who have yet to experience the feeling of love.[15]

The point is that, to a certain degree, the balance of power between (young) women and their parents—their families—can be derived from the marriage age of women. Marriage at an older age can have far-ranging implications, as Claudia Goldin sketches in her 2006 Richard Ely lecture. Women who marry later have a chance to form an adult identity that may include a career or profession, while those who marry very early will likely see themselves as secondary workers, optimizing time allocations to accommodate their husbands' labor-market decisions.[16]

The relationship between husband and wife within a marriage is also, to a certain degree, reflected in the age difference between the partners. In Antiquity, men would often marry only after the age of 30 and wed much younger women (12–17 years old), which suggests a substantial degree of inequality.[17] Results from present-day Bangladesh suggest that smaller spousal age gaps are associated with better status for brides, measured by socioeconomic factors.[18] Contemporary work has also shown that the differences in status that result from a wide age gap between husband and wife can result in increased exposure to domestic violence and a power dynamic that undermines wives' agency.[19] Casterline et al. find that when it comes to the determinants of spousal age gaps across countries, explanations based on shortages of women in the marriage market do not suffice.[20] Rather, they conclude that spousal age gaps seem to be

[15] Gooszen 1999, 147.

[16] Goldin 2006.

[17] Sallares 1991.

[18] Amin and Cain 1997.

[19] Kishor and Johnson 2004.

[20] Casterline, Williams, and McDonald 1986.

a reflection of preferences for a given age gap, which they suggest is in turn determined by family organization and the position of women. The EMP, which evolved during the Middle Ages, was characterized by a relatively small spousal age gap, and as already explained, by a relatively late age at marriage not only for men (comparable to the age in Antiquity) but also for women. Especially, this last aspect is notable: societies with high marriage ages for men are widespread, but societies with high marriage ages for women are much more unusual.

Studying marriage ages, therefore, gives us two measures of the degree of "agency" women have: their absolute age at marriage (the higher, the more "agency") and the spousal age gap (the lower, the stronger the position of women in the household). The combination of these parameters brings together two domains—freedom of choice in whom to marry and equality within marriage—based on hypotheses that we developed earlier regarding the evolution of the EMP.[21] Here, we wish to explore the validity of the hypothesized link between marriage patterns and female agency by turning to contemporary indicators of the position of women.

In the past decade, international organizations, such as the World Bank, have developed indices to evaluate the position of women on a worldwide scale and to enable comparisons internationally. The question that we ask ourselves is whether there is currently a relationship between the position of women in these different parts of the world and their age at marriage. Do women in countries where they have a better position also marry later than those in countries where they cannot decide on their future, where no investment is made in their education, and their health is poor? Can we, in other words, use data on marriage age in the past to gain insight into the "agency" of women in the past?

In order to compare measures of marriage patterns with more elaborate measures of the position of women, we use the Gender Inequality Index, or GII.[22] This index first appeared in the UN Development Program's 2010 Human Development Report, calculated on the basis of data for 2008.[23] The GII examines three different aspects (or dimensions) of gender inequality: participation in the labor market, "empowerment," and reproductive health. It gives an indication of the level of development as it relates to the inequality between men and women, measured along these three specified dimensions. It varies from 0 to 1, where 0 means no inequality between men and women and 1 means total

[21] See, for example, the Girlpower Index as described in De Moor and van Zanden 2006.

[22] In the working paper on which this section is based, we also compared marriage ages with the Global Gender Gap developed by the World Economic Forum, but the correlations with both the SMAM and the Girlpower Index were lower, albeit still positive; see Carmichael, De Moor, and van Zanden 2011a.

[23] In the tables, one can observe that the Netherlands scores highest on the GII.

inequality. The GII report for 2010 demonstrates that the gender aspect with the greatest impact on human development is reproductive health, as measured by maternal mortality during childbirth and the adolescent fertility rate.

Figure 1.1 shows the correlation between the GII and female singulate mean age at marriage (SMAM), and figure 1.2 shows the correlation between the GII and the Girlpower index (the latter calculated by subtracting the spousal age gap from the female SMAM). These correlations are both remarkably high, even though marriage age is not part of the construction of the GII, and therefore

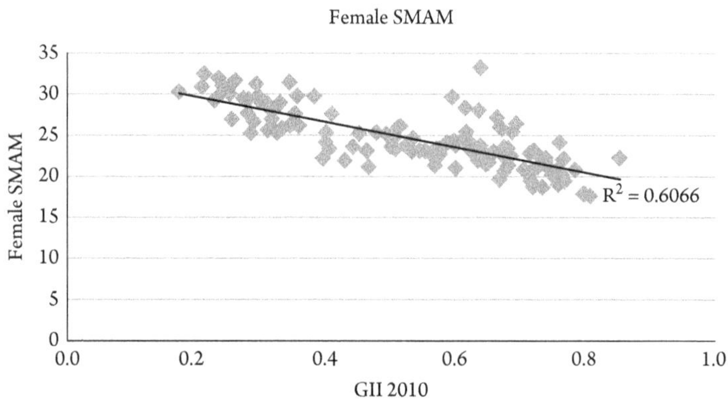

Figure 1.1 Correlation between female SMAM and GII. Source: Dataset from Carmichael 2011 and UN Development Program 2010. Previously published in a different form in Carmichael, De Moor, and van Zanden 2011b, 208–221.

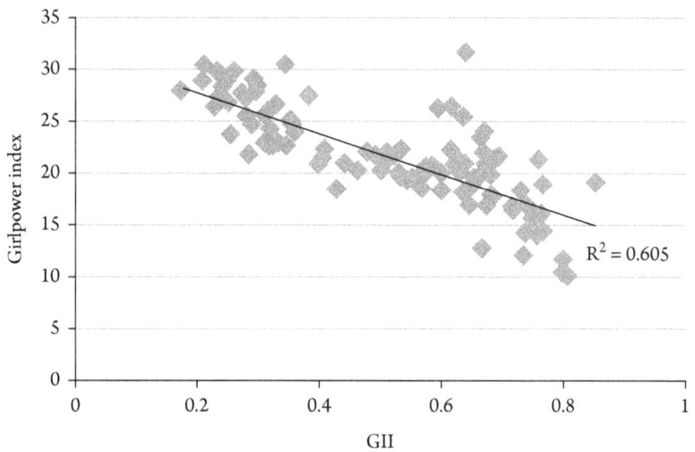

Figure 1.2 Correlation between Girlpower index and GII. Source: Dataset from Carmichael 2011 and UN Development Program 2010. Previously published in a different form in Carmichael, De Moor, and van Zanden 2011, 208–221.

cannot be an explanation for the high level of correlation. Algeria has a higher female SMAM than would be expected on the basis of its GII score. The most extreme outlier is Jamaica; Jamaica was ranked eighty-ninth in the world when the GII is used but ranked first in the world when female SMAM is used.

The high average marriage age of Jamaican women is difficult to explain. It could be related to the phenomenon of "consensual unions," a practice common in Jamaica. In such a system of consensual union, couples live in an unwedded state until they have achieved economic stability, after which they marry. Keith F. Otterbein, in an article on Caribbean family organization, describes the dominant role of women in such a system. Men have, according to a number of authors, a low economic position, which means they must delay marriage and often do not play a significant role in the raising of children.[24]

Empowerment and Economic Development: Reproduction and Human Capital

We approach the topic of female empowerment by studying changing marriage practices, not because we want to suggest that the place of women is in the household; quite the contrary, we think it is a fruitful way to explore the changing role and position of women in general. One of the vital elements in understanding the link between marriage/the household and economic performance is the recognition of human capital. A body of literature suggests that the reproductive activities of women can greatly affect economic development (see Dilli 2017 for an overview). Human capital is at the core of the knowledge economies that have developed over the past centuries in the West, and it is thus of utmost importance that we measure the human capital of the women involved and understand how their empowerment affects the next generation's access to education. The relationship between gender (in)equality and human capital is, then, just another part of the whole cycle from reproduction to production that we study here, but in this section we focus on the role of human capital.

We start by briefly touching upon some debates about these issues so as to provide a theoretical grounding for the historical analysis that will follow. One of the main themes of that analysis derives from the economic analysis of households and demographic behavior, and it concerns the tradeoff between the quantity and the quality of offspring. Given the time constraints in household production—one can do only one thing at a time, and each activity therefore has its opportunity costs—the "production" of children is a costly affair.

[24] Otterbein 1965; Clarke 1957; Smith 1957; Burnard 1994.

A rather crude distinction that can be made (which is also used by biologists to study different reproductive patterns of behavior) is that between a strategy that concentrates on the *quantity* of offspring (thus does not invest much in the raising of the individual child) and a strategy that aims to optimize the *quality* of offspring. In the latter case, only a few children are born, but they receive a lot of attention from their parents. Becker famously argued that economic development requires such a switch from a quantity to a quality strategy.[25] This has since become one of the core ideas of Unified Growth Theory, which tries to explain how an economy can move from a Malthusian equilibrium to modern economic growth.

In a Malthusian economy, people have as many offspring as possible and do not invest in their human capital. Economic growth will, in such a situation, induce more population growth, with the end result being that a population is not able to achieve a level of welfare above subsistence. Such improvement above subsistence is only possible when the quality strategy becomes more important: people then have fewer children and invest more in them.[26] Put differently, economic development requires higher levels of human capital formation; according to Unified Growth Theory, the increase in skills, knowledge, and ideas is the most important source of long-term growth. And this requires investment by parents in the futures of their children. Summing up, there is a demographic cause of the transition from Malthusian stagnation to modern economic growth, which results in strong improvements in general welfare.

Women normally spend more time having (and raising) children than men. Therefore, it is the opportunity costs for women—and not those of men—that really matter here and that will have a large effect on the decision-making process that accompanies reproductive choices. The hypothesis that has received the most attention in this respect is that the human capital of women, which is obviously positively related to their earning power, is negatively related to fertility. This gendered version of the quantity–quality tradeoff has been most clearly developed by Diebolt and Perrin, who also tested the idea for France in 1851.[27] Figure 1.3 gives an overview of this relationship as found in data for developing countries.

In figure 1.3, the average years of education for women are graphed against their "demand for children" (as captured by fertility). These data are for 80 countries (from Algeria to Zimbabwe), for which, for five-year periods between 1950/54 and 2000/04, estimates of the educational attainment of women (and men) are available. The data are then plotted against estimates

[25] Becker 1973, 1991.

[26] For the best overview, see Galor 2011; Galor and Weil 1996.

[27] See the recent contributions by Diebolt and Perrin 2013, 2014, 2016.

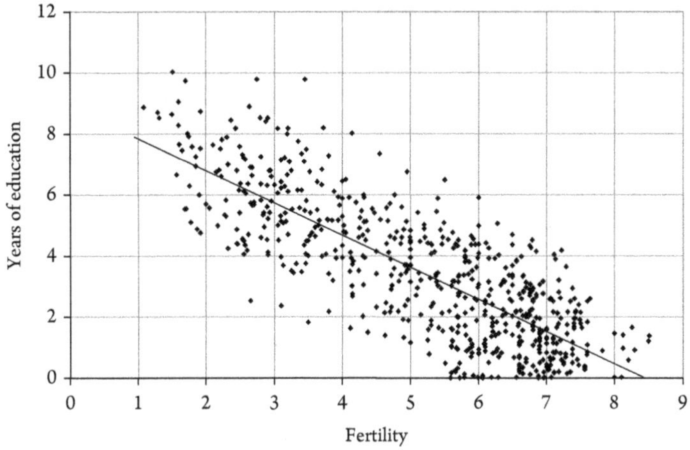

Figure 1.3 Relationship between fertility and average years of schooling for women in 80 countries, taken from five-year periods between 1950/54 and 2000/04. Source: Dataset reproduced from Schultz 1997.

of fertility for the same countries and the same years.[28] The strong correlation between the two variables, which is also confirmed by econometric research,[29] is clearly evident. The levels of educational attainment vary from close to zero to ten years of schooling; women who are not schooled at all have 5.5 to 8 children, whereas highly educated women have fewer children (2.1 is about the level at which a population reproduces itself, a threshold that will be attained with more than six years of schooling).[30] Different countries have different trajectories within this fertility/human capital space, as figure 1.4 shows, where the developments in the Philippines (with a very high level of fertility) are contrasted with those of India (with a relatively low level of fertility) and Kenya (which falls in between).

Figures 1.3 and 1.4 present the classic switch from a situation with low levels of human capital formation and high levels of fertility (the bottom right quadrants of the figures) to one with high levels of human capital formation and low levels of fertility (the upper left quadrants). The point is that the degree to which women have acquired human capital will determine the degree to which they prefer quality of offspring over quantity. Once the process is set in motion—and women begin investing more in their children—there will be

[28] We reproduced the dataset used by Schultz 1997; our discussion is also based on this paper.

[29] Schultz 1997.

[30] In fact, the elasticity of the curve presented in figure 1.3 is close to −1, meaning that one extra year of schooling implies one child less, a rule that also seems to apply to most of the countries when taken separately (see figure 1.4).

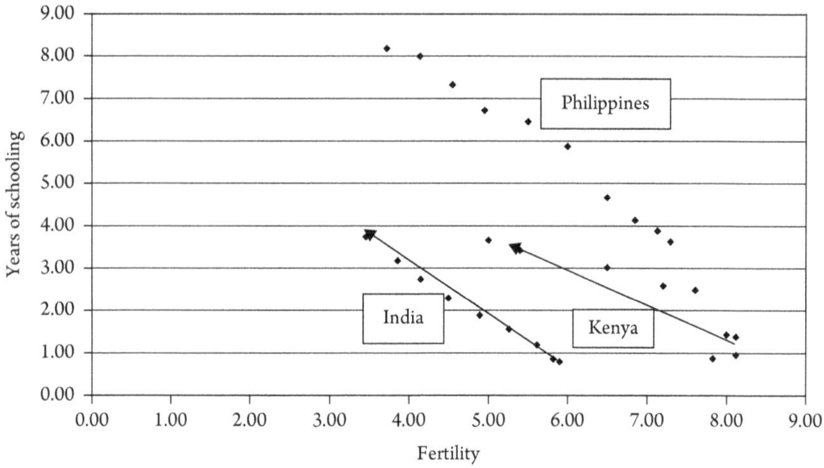

Figure 1.4 Relationship between fertility and educational attainment for women in the Philippines, India, and Kenya, 1950s–1990s. Source: Dataset reproduced from Schultz 1997.

the tendency for every generation to further stress quality over quantity of offspring. Most countries therefore move slowly along the curve shown in figures 1.3 and 1.4.

Econometric research has also demonstrated that men's increased human capital does not have the same effect on fertility. On the contrary, there are strong indications that when men earn more and have more human capital, they tend to demand *more* children.[31] It is the education of women that drives the downward movement. One way to demonstrate this is to show the effect of difference in educational attainment between men and women has on fertility (figure 1.5). It appears that when the gender gap is very large (increasing to 100% difference in education), fertility is also high; an equal distribution of education between men and women seems to be associated with, on average, lower demand for children.

Why is it that well-educated women have fewer, more educated children? A number of mechanisms seem to be at play. As mentioned, economists who theorize about the family and fertility have argued that opportunity costs are involved. When women have higher human capital, their levels of productivity are higher and their wages are higher. In such a situation, it is more "expensive" for women to raise children in comparison to working. The crucial mechanism here is a changing "demand for children," but there are other links as well. It is often suggested that education enhances the degree to which women are open to new ideas, including ideas about birth control.[32] There are direct links between

[31] Schultz 1997.

[32] See, for example, Elgharabway, Saber Ahmed, and Alsuhaibani 2015.

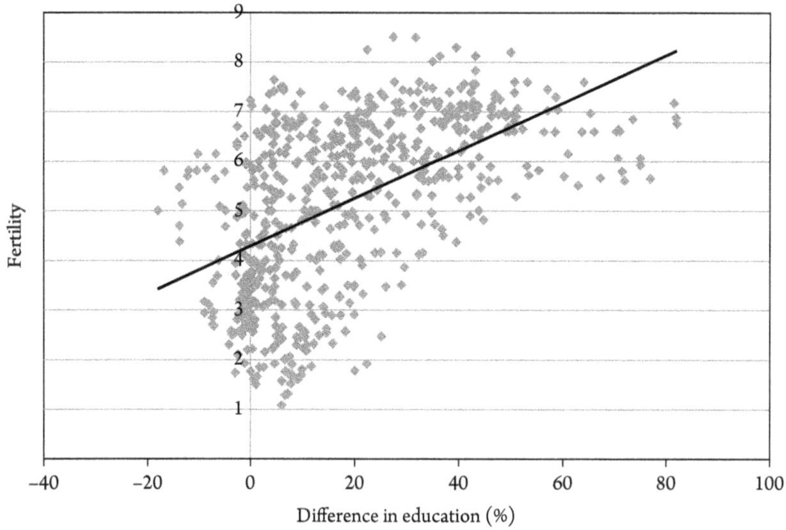

Figure 1.5 The gender gap in education as it relates to fertility. On the horizontal axis is female/male education. As the values move closer to 100, male education approaches double that of women. Note: On the x-axis the percentage difference in men's to women's education is presented. A negative score means that women have more education than men. Source: Dataset reproduced from Schultz 1997.

education and reproduction and age at marriage, which brings us back to the point made at the beginning of this introduction.

Going to school usually conflicts with marrying at an early age—in particular in societies where marriage is tightly linked to reproduction (bearing children as early as possible). A low age at marriage is often a feature of societies in which arranged marriage dominates, in which parents directly control the marriage decisions of their children. Controlling the marriage decision of your children is easier when (in particular) daughters have not acquired too much human capital, which corresponds with a relatively young age. Older children are usually less inclined to obey their parents.[33] So, in a system of arranged marriages, it may not be in the interests of the parents to send their girls to school. Thus, the gap in human capital between men and women may be much larger in societies where arranged marriages dominate, than in systems of consensual marriage. And a low age at marriage will normally lead to high levels of fertility (during the complete life cycle of the women). As Mason has demonstrated, there are many such links between women's autonomy (relative to men) and female age at first marriage.[34]

Female agency, then, not only is linked to human capital but there is also an obvious connection with capital markets. Ever since the microcredit system

[33] See Carmichael, De Moor, and van Zanden 2011b.
[34] Mason 1997.

was developed as a way for the uneducated to rise out of poverty, women's access to financial capital markets has received much attention. The focus of many modern initiatives in this field (such as the Grameen Bank) has been to provide small loans to groups of women that would enable them to set up their own business (see the discussion in chapter 4). Notwithstanding the critique the microcredit system has recently received, connecting women to financial markets is in our view an essential part of the story of female empowerment and economic growth. The most recent, very thoughtful assessment of the microfinance movement by Banarjee and Duflo also concluded that, despite certain limitations (not all men and women have the potential to develop the right entrepreneurial features, and it is unclear how one moves from microfinance to forming an employment-creating firm), it is an impressive movement that is reaching the poor.[35] As we will demonstrate later in the book, the early modern form of economic growth in Western Europe, which led to the Industrial Revolution, could rely upon a well-developed capital market with remarkably low interest rates and a variety of financial instruments used intensively not only by the wealthy classes. Among the participants in those capital markets were a fair number of women who demonstrated an "investment behavior" that was little different from that of their male counterparts.

Another factor concerns female participation in the labor market. That is, the stronger the position of women in society, the more they are able to work outside the household—and vice versa: the more they participate in the labor market, the stronger their position in society. This again has a substantial effect on the age at marriage and on the opportunity costs women bear during marriage. In short, access to labor markets is a strategic link, connecting women's autonomy, level of fertility, and human capital formation—a link that constitutes the focus of this book.

Why This Book?

Nowadays, states implement policies to increase women's access to education, labor markets, and capital markets. Such top-down policies were absent in Europe's past. Still, women participated in labor markets to a remarkable degree, and they gradually built up human capital as a result. As we will explain in this book, they also had a role in capital market activities. Both these developments were, we believe, linked to the rise of a particular form of marriage pattern of which we still see the effects in Europe. The European Marriage Pattern is

[35] Banarjee and Duflo 2012, 181.

characterized by high numbers of single men and women, high marriage ages among men and women, and neolocality, meaning the couple forms a new nuclear household and does not reside with the parents of either the bride or the groom. We argue that the development of the EMP originated in the late Middle Ages and that it was one of the main causes of the gradual move away from a Malthusian state and toward an economy that was able to generate long-term economic growth. This story of female empowerment, therefore, is crucial for understanding the specific developmental path of the Western European economy, which resulted in the Industrial Revolution of the late eighteenth century.

The book relies largely on the work we have undertaken in the past few years exploring various aspects of the topics mentioned here. Much of this work has been published in other versions, but has not been given the global perspective we have sketched here, with clearer identification of the links between various societal processes and the mechanisms governing those processes. We start by bringing our ideas on female empowerment and economic development together in an explanatory framework based on the emergence of the European Marriage Pattern. In chapter 2, we argue that the EMP has played a fundamental role in Western Europe's economic development, and we link this development to other aspects that have been discussed in this chapter. As we will explain, the EMP emerged in northwestern Europe in the late medieval period as a result of teachings of the Catholic Church on marriage based on consensus, the rise of labor markets, and specific institutions concerning property transfer between generations that enhanced wage labor for women. These influences resulted in a demographic regime embedded in a highly commercial environment, in which households interacted frequently with labor, capital, and commodity markets. We also discuss possible long-term consequences of these developments for human capital formation and institution building.

In the following chapters, then, we describe the effects of the EMP on the three areas we have mentioned here: human capital formation (chapter 3), access to the capital market (chapter 4), and participation in the labor market (chapter 5), thereby further testing and developing the central hypotheses as to the EMP's long-term consequences. Dealing with these factors demanded that we develop different methods and use a multitude of sources. In chapter 3 on human capital, for example, we apply a fairly new approach to tracing human capital formation during the pre-statistical era. Instead of using the standard parameter of literacy to trace the development of human capital, we focus on numeracy, which can be retrieved via the age-heaping method. As we demonstrate, this approach yields an entirely different picture of the education of women, whether obtained via the normal schooling system or by a system of learning-by-doing via their activities in the economy. We present new evidence for the development of age heaping of men and women in Flanders and the Netherlands in the late medieval and early modern period so as to test ideas based on previous research on the human capital formation of women and men in the North Sea area. We demonstrate that already in the sixteenth century, age heaping was gradually disappearing in large parts of the Low Countries, that (as we expected) there was almost no gender gap (women even outperformed men at times), and that differences in numeracy between town and country were quite small. This probably points to a very early rise of numeracy (or at least a "number sense") in this region, linked to demographic change and commercial development in both town and country.

In chapter 4, we discuss female (and male) participation in the capital market, principally in regard to the functioning of the private capital market in Holland during the late medieval period. First, we argue that, in the absence of banks' and state agencies' involvement in the supply of credit, entrepreneurial access to credit was determined by two interrelated factors. The first factor was the quality of property-rights protection and the extent to which property could be used as collateral. The second factor was the rate of interest for borrowing money at the time, as well as occurrences of such borrowing compared with the interest rates on risk-free investments.

For our case study, which examines the small town of Edam and its hinterland, De Zeevang, in the fifteenth and sixteenth centuries, we demonstrate that properties were used as collateral on a large scale, and that interest rates on both small and large loans were relatively low (about 6%). This discovery is essential to understanding what made capital so accessible in early modern Europe, while it also links nicely to current forms of microcredit in which women play a central role. As a result of the well-developed capital market in our study area, many households (whether headed by men or women) had financial assets and/or debts, and the degree of financial sophistication was relatively high. Then, in the second part of chapter 4 we demonstrate that women were very active on this capital market and that their choice of financial instruments for investment was not much different from that of male investors.

Chapter 5 focuses on major changes in the position of women participating in the labor market between about 1400 and 1800. We look in particular at wages, and we document that women's wages in the North Sea area were almost on a par with those of men during the late Middle Ages, but then fell to much lower levels during the seventeenth and eighteenth centuries (a result that has recently been confirmed by Humphries and Weisdorf[36]). We try to offer an explanation of this remarkable increase in the wage gap and also speculate about the long-term demographic consequences of this change.

[36] Humphries and Weisdorf 2015.

The next two chapters focus on what we have called the "dark side" of the EMP: the nuclear hardship hypothesis, as formulated by Laslett, that notwithstanding its potential benefits for economic growth, this particular marriage pattern resulted in relatively small households that were more vulnerable to exogenous shocks.[37] We first develop the idea more fully, then argue that Laslett indeed had a point: the degree to which the "resulting" nuclear household could spread risks is limited, not just owing to the small size of families but also to the so-called double squeeze, whereby the older marriage ages of both parents and their offspring mean that the period during which parents and children require help and support in their lives occurs simultaneously (chapter 6). Hence, we would expect a negative impact on the lives—and life expectancies—of people living in early modern EMP areas. However, evidence on life expectancy and the occurrence and effect of famines in late medieval and early modern Europe appear to be inconsistent with this hypothesis: there is evidence that longevity was actually higher in the North Sea area than outside it, and that this region managed to suppress and/or cushion the negative effects of harvest failures more successfully than the rest of Europe.

Addressing this paradox is the subject of the following chapter, in which we look at the "institutional effect" of the EMP. In chapter 7, we concentrate on two examples of institutionalized forms of "solutions" that developed in EMP societies to avoid the hardship Laslett was referring to. We first take a fresh look at servanthood as part of a "commercial household" economy, which may have added flexibility to the EMP household. Whereas servanthood, in the literature, is often approached from the supply side—stressing the large number of single men and women in early modern societies—we view the large presence of servants in EMP areas from the demand side. That is, having a servant in the house could be a solution to the difficulties created by changes in household demographics.

Another phenomenon that may help explain part of the aforementioned paradox is discussed in the second part of chapter 7, which focuses on the Flemish beguinages, a movement of single women who chose to live in communities of equal-minded single women—communities that were in appearance similar to religious convents but in practice functioned quite differently. In their "radicalness," beguinages perhaps illustrate the basic features of the EMP (and the cultural space in which the EMP emerged) even better than the marriage pattern itself. On the basis of a large dataset of these beguinages, we explore the emergence and persistence of this phenomenon in the Low Countries between 1300 and 1900. The explanations offered by the literature (gender imbalances in the

[37] Laslett 1988.

cities and lack of access to convents) are discussed, and an alternative interpretation stressing the voluntary nature of the movement, based on the desire of the women to remain single without entering a strict religious community such as a convent, is advanced.

In the concluding chapter, we enter the debate on how to measure the EMP—via the age of marriage of women or via the underlying institutions—and how to link the EMP with economic development in Europe between 1300 and 1800. We respond to criticism by two scholars, Tracy Dennison and Sheilagh Ogilvie, who have argued that a clear link between the EMP and economic growth cannot be established.[38] To make our point, we broaden the scope of the book by including the whole of Eurasia in our analysis. Finally, we formally test the central hypothesis of this book—that the marriage system of Western Europe, which facilitated a relatively high level of female agency—enhanced economic growth in early modern Europe.

Methodology and Sources

The book is based on a number of papers written by the authors, often together with authors from other disciplines. Annemarie Bouman, an anthropologist, contributed substantially to the analysis of the nuclear hardship hypothesis in chapters 6 and 7; economist and economic historian Alexandra de Pleijt conducted much of the formal testing of the link between the EMP and economic growth presented in chapter 8, and the medievalist Jaco Zuijderduijn (and research assistant Heleen Kole) helped to digitize and analyze the late Medieval sources from the Edam region that form the core of chapter 4. This illustrates the interdisciplinary approach of this project, bringing together ideas and data from economic and demographic history, anthropology, economics, and development studies.

But first and foremost, this is an economic view of a crucial development in European history: the genesis of the EMP in the Middle Ages and its implications for economic development in almost all its dimensions (labor, capital, human capital). The conceptual framework we have developed in chapter 2 to analyze these processes makes intensive use of data and sources related to the Low Countries and England, which together, we think, form the "core region" where the EMP emerged in the late Middle Ages. We not only describe it by using a number of indicators to picture these developments, such as marriage age and spousal age gap, but we also look into the (relatively) short-term and

[38] Dennison and Ogilvie 2014.

(very) long-term effects of the EMP. Given the wide time span covered here, the reader will have to connect the many "dots" we are plotting, using a large variety of historical and present-day sources, with comparisons on different levels, from the very micro level of the individual to the broader macro view of global developments.

Moreover, we introduce and use a wide variety of historical sources to put some "flesh" on the bones of the theories we have set out, but we realize this, too, adds to the challenges we set before our readers. Our databases are based on many different types of sources, and some of them can be considered rather unusual in the field of economic history: from the quite common censuses and population registers, to age references on portraits (which have previously been ignored by historians and art historians alike) as useful sources for reconstructing age awareness and levels of numeracy; and from tediously collected references to women's wages during periods when survival, more than bookkeeping, must have been in the minds of their employers, to data on literacy collected for a wide variety of countries around the world.

Our types of sources are commented upon in the chapters where they are used, so that their applicability for our study becomes clear. For practical reasons, we have mainly used sources related to the Low Countries, or the Netherlands and Belgium taken together, in those chapters where we test the hypotheses about the consequences and implications of the EMP. This is because the Low Countries were part of the core area of the EMP as it emerged in the late Middle Ages. This concentration on the Low Countries, and how it affects our data selection, is most evident in the chapter on numeracy, in relation to human capital formation. When using the age-heaping method to detect levels of numeracy, it's important to use sources at the level of the individual person, not by household. This is because it is never certain whether the age recorded was reported directly by the individual, and in general the recording of ages is something not often found in historical sources. We did, however, find a substantial number of recorded ages for the Low Countries, and therefore we have used these records extensively.

To put this into perspective, for age-heaping data on other parts of Europe, we relied on existing studies and published sources. In contrast, in chapter 5, we paid a lot of attention to developments in the other part of the core area of the EMP—England—to sketch the long-term impact that EMP had on labor markets. The underlying idea is that the countries bordering the North Sea followed a more or less similar development path during the late medieval and early modern period; here, the EMP emerged in its clearest form and a process of long-term economic development began that would, by the late eighteenth century (in England), result in the Industrial Revolution. This "Little Divergence"—in a way, a spin-off of the "Great Divergence" debate, which focused on the separate development paths of Western Europe versus Asia (China, in particular)[39] —has now been established, based on quantitative research into real wages, GDP per capita, human capital, and political institutions.[40] This book contributes to this debate by focusing on the micro dimension of human behavior, its institutions (such as the way in which marriage is organized), and its long-term implications.

We also present readers with a wide variety of methods used to analyze the long-term processes we study here. Which method is suitable depends on the research question we are answering in each chapter, on the causal relationships we are identifying, on the available materials, and on the level of detail needed. Our chosen methods are based on various statistical and econometric standards, but in principle these choices should not detract from our main results. Our biggest challenge was to sketch the important and influential mechanisms governing the behavior of both early modern and present-day Europeans in their daily choices. Many present-day institutions have their roots in changes that go back literally centuries, but we are often unaware how these changes are related to each other, let alone how they interact and may, in turn, lead to new mechanisms or undermine previously established norms.

[39] Pomeranz 2000.

[40] Real wages, in Allen 2001; GDP per capita, in Broadberry, Custodis, and Gupta 2015; human capital, in Baten and van Zanden 2008; political institutions, in Van Zanden, Buringh, and Bosker 2012. For an overview, see de Pleijt and van Zanden 2016.

2

The Patterns Behind Change

Origins and Features of the European Marriage Pattern

The Hajnal Thesis

In 1505, Janne Heyndericx, aged 31, living in the Zeeland village of Kouwenkerke, told a committee investigating malpractice by the local magistrates[1] the following story: Eight years earlier she had promised to marry a young man, Adriaen Jacopsz, and he had also promised to marry her. They slept together and continued to do so without ever officially marrying, as was required by the law of the Holy Church, postponing their wedding until a more mutually convenient time. At that time she was still living with her mother and stepfather, who subsequently refused to maintain her, so that she was forced to find employment elsewhere and left to earn a wage. When she came to work in Kouwenkerke she lived together with another young man by whom she had a child. Four or five years before, Adriaen had tried to be released from his promise to marry her, although they were still in regular contact and were sleeping together. She said she still wanted to marry him, as although they had not been married before the Church, as far as she was concerned they were indeed married before God. Moreover, she reported that it was his fault that she had gone so far (i.e., had a child with another man), because he had kept her waiting for so long.[2]

This story of Janne is strikingly "modern," and when seen from a global perspective, her behavior appears to be exceptional; such an informal "marriage"

[1] These malpractices concerned the levying of arbitrary fines on people living together who had not been officially married by the Church; Bange and Weiler 1987.

[2] Story taken from Bange and Weiler 1987, 404–405. Of course, Janne Heyndricx was not alone in her case of a consensual marriage that went wrong. Similar examples exist for the Netherlands and for England, and have been mentioned by other historians. See examples mentioned by Sheehan 1971. See also Goldberg 1992b, 248–249, and several examples of similar cases in later ages; see Outhwaite 1995, 1–50.

occurring in other parts of the world would have been difficult to imagine. This story is typical, however, of the marriage pattern that emerged in the North Sea area in the late Middle Ages. First, among the elements that make this story so "modern" is that the decision to marry was taken not by parents or other members of an older generation but by the marriage partners themselves. As followers of the Catholic Church, Janne and Adriaen promised to marry each other, and they considered their promise equivalent to being married before God. Second, Janne's mother and stepfather decided that this "marriage before God" should result in the formation of a new household, so they refused to maintain Janne any longer, thus forcing her to leave her parents' household. The third strikingly modern aspect is the fact that Janne was capable of leaving, as she was able to find employment as a wage earner elsewhere. Easy access to the labor market facilitated the adoption of this kind of behavior by both parents and children.

This brief story tells us much about the European Marriage Pattern (EMP) as it emerged in the late Middle Ages and became characteristic for western European society in the early modern period. The existing literature on this topic has focused primarily on typical demographic aspects of this marriage pattern, such as the average age of marriage, the share of the population that never married, and the effects of EMP on fertility and resulting population growth. In this, the literature has followed Hajnal's seminal paper from 1965, in which he stressed these "distinctive features" of the EMP.[3] The main debate that followed Hajnal's paper focused on the question whether the classification of Europe into two distinct demographic regions—east and west of the Hajnal line—was convincing. This, in combination with the approach developed by Laslett to study household structure, led to a proliferation of studies that classified Europe into different demographic regions.[4] It was, for example, proposed that southern Europe had distinct patterns in household structures, which moreover (in particular in Italy) showed large regional variations.[5] And in central Europe, yet another system, the stem family, could be found.[6] A related debate, to which Goody contributed, focused on the issue of whether the "Asian" pattern distinguished by Hajnal was really so different from the EMP.[7]

The debate about the Hajnal thesis mainly focused on the "distinctive features" that were analyzed by Hajnal. Far less attention has been paid to the underlying mechanisms that led to these outcomes, to the underlying causes of the EMP, which can arguably be classed as mysteries of the demographic and

[3] Hajnal 1965, 101.

[4] Laslett 1982; Szoltysek 2008.

[5] See, for example, Curtis 2015; Dalla Zuanna et al. 2012; Beningo 1989.

[6] Berkner 1972.

[7] Goody 1996.

social history of the early modern period. The classic Hajnal paper does allude to these underlying mechanisms. He mentions, for example, that "the conviction that marriage should be decided upon only after the future spouses have got to know each other well" was to be regarded as "a relevant factor which distinguishes modern Western populations from the majority of societies."[8] Hajnal points out that unlike in many other societies where marriage consisted of an arrangement between the heads of households who exchanged marriage partners for gifts, marriage in northwestern Europe meant the establishment of a new household by the spouses themselves, who therefore needed a conjugal fund. This "neolocality" meant that many were unable to marry because they could not afford this "investment."[9] In this chapter, we will attempt to develop these leads in order to explain the mechanisms behind the story of Janne Heyndericx and Adriaen Jacopsz.[10]

Central to our argument is the consideration that a household is a cooperative economic unit aimed at fulfilment of the physical and emotional needs of its members and characterized by certain inequalities (i.e., power imbalances) between generations and sexes. It is based on implicit and explicit contracts between household members, such as the marriage contract and the implicit contracts that exist between different generations. The hypothesis at the core of this book is that the EMP is characterized by power balances between man and wife and between parents and children, which differ from more common forms of marriage and household formation. To be more precise, the most striking feature of the EMP is that the traditional inequalities between the sexes and the generations are caused by socioeconomic, ideological, and institutional factors. The EMP in its purest form appears to be at the rather "extreme" end of the spectrum, as women have a relatively large say in the marriage itself (as based on the consent of both spouses), especially when the women contribute to the income of their households. In a nutshell, it is argued in this chapter that the particular features of the EMP—late and nonuniversal marriage—are the result of its relatively "democratic" character.

Next, we will argue that the EMP was essentially an institutional adaptation to a situation of rapidly expanding employment opportunities and relatively high remuneration in the century or so after the Black Death (although the

[8] Hajnal 1965, 101 and 126.

[9] In his 1982 paper, these thoughts were specified in more detail; see Hajnal 1982, 113–115.

[10] This point was already made by Smith in 1979: "The search for the European marriage patterns as a 'statistical' artefact is intriguing, but it would be unfortunate if, in being so preoccupied with actual ages . . . we failed to detect the wider social structural features that sustained it. Without this, any means of understanding the precise determinants of this unique arrangement will be thwarte" (101–102).

explanation for its appearance is more complex, as we will show later). In brief, it was a reproductive strategy developed by both male and female wage earners that was embedded in a broader institutional framework in which market exchange and trust in the functioning of markets were of fundamental importance. Not only did wage income become a large part of the household income but these households also gained access to capital markets and to markets for consumer goods (a large part of which they did not produce themselves, as their main income consisted of wages). Simultaneously they developed new strategies for survival in the long term, and for enhancing their success and that of their children in the new market environment. Among these strategies were increased investment in formal schooling, in training as apprentices or as servants in others' households, and in social capital to address issues of old age or single parenthood. The result was a society in which between 30 and 60% of the population was partly or completely dependent on wage labor (by men, women, and children); in which markets permeated all aspects of economic life; and in which small, conjugal households became increasingly interwoven with a social infrastructure (of poor relief institutions) that sustained their reproduction.[11] This society emerged in the late Middle Ages in the North Sea area—in England and the Low Countries, in particular[12]—and it was, we claim, the long-term dynamism of this structure that helps to explain the sustained success of this region in the world economy of the early modern period.

The special characteristics and the importance of the EMP is evident when it is compared with situations elsewhere in the world. The more general features of the EMP will be clarified on the basis of comparisons with marriage practices east of Hajnal's line, between Trieste and St. Petersburg,[13] and in particular with China, whenever appropriate.[14] By doing so we hope to complement the current

[11] Kussmaul 1981, 26, estimates that in the 15- to 24-year age group, 60% of the population were servants.

[12] It is possible to distinguish a core area—Flanders, the coastal provinces of the Netherlands, and the eastern counties of England—where we find the features of the system most clearly, and a "larger" North Sea area, including the inland provinces of the Netherlands, Belgium, northern France, and the rest of England, where socioeconomic conditions were often different and the system cannot always be found in its "pure" form.

[13] We follow the line that Hajnal used as a way to divide the marriage patterns of Europe. Within the part east of this line, we compare two of the four sectors that have been discerned by Laslett in his overview of family and household as a work group and kin group in traditional Europe. We consider northwestern Europe, for which we concentrate on the Low Countries and England, and the Mediterranean, where Italy receives (because of source-related reasons) most of our attention. See Laslett 1982; Wall 1983a; and Poos 1986, 228–238.

[14] The scope of this chapter is insufficient to fully treat the differences with China. We refer to the following recent works that could complement our research, at least on the issue of marriage and the position of women in China: Ebrey 2003, Birge 2003, Gates 2001, Bernhardt 1999, Zurndorfer 1999, Goody 1990.

Great Divergence debate with a new approach to explaining the differences in economic growth between East and West, although we realize that we cannot more than briefly touch upon some of the aspects of this complex issue in this chapter. A comparison between marriage practices in southern and eastern Europe and in the North Sea area may shed light on the reasons why the latter had a lead in economic development. According to Hajnal and Reher, there is considerable variety in marriage practices within Europe, and we use their broad geographical subdivisions as our starting point.[15]

Factors of Change: The Emergence of the EMP

The European Marriage Pattern emerged in northwestern Europe because of a combination of three socioeconomic and ideological factors: first, stress on consensus instead of parental authority for the formation of a marriage; second, the position of women in the transfer of property between husband and wife and between parents and children; and third, accessibility of and size of the labor market.

Consensus Versus Parental Authority

The story of Janne Heyndericx illustrates how marriage among wage earners in the late Middle Ages was to a large extent based on consensus between the two spouses, a factor mentioned by Hajnal as distinctive of Europe. This idea is clearly so fundamental to the EMP that the chronology can to some extent be derived from the emergence of this doctrine. In the early Middle Ages, marriage was, according to Peter Biller, basically "a lay and secular matter, whose essentials were the handing over of a girl, by her father, to the groom, the exchanging of gifts, and perhaps the girl's *deduction in domum*, her 'being brought into the house' of the groom or his family."[16] This changed when the Church slowly took over and "established a near exclusive competence over marriage in most regions of Latin Christendom." The gradual change was also symbolized by a change in the location of the marriage ceremony, from the house of the family of the groom to the church.[17] At the same time, the Church was responsible for defining marriage, whether it was based on mutual consent or on *copula carnalis* (physical union), an idea that dates back to Augustine. It is significant that the

[15] Reher 1998, Hajnal 1965.

[16] Biller 2000, 22.

[17] Biller 2000, 22. See also Berman 1983 on the papal revolution.

north and the south had different views on this. Paris, representing the north, emphasized consent, while Bologna, representing the south, focused on consummation.[18] Scholars at the time were aware that this represented contrasting regional customs.[19] Around 1140, Gratian established that according to canon law, the bonds of marriage were determined by mutual consent and not by the consummation of marriage, because "where there is to be union of bodies there ought to be union of spirits."[20] Gratian and his followers frequently pointed to evidence that marriages arranged against the wishes of the partners usually brought about bad results.[21] Gratian's work formed the basis for further theological discussions,[22] and eventually led to inclusion of the doctrine in the decrials of Gregory IX (1234).[23] Thus, boys and girls of a legally marriageable age (14 for boys, 12 for girls) were permitted to perform the sacrament of marriage themselves. Marriages were made by God (which was also the conviction of Janne); a priest only proclaimed his will for the couple after the fact. But this doctrine also led to the problem of secret marriages—marriages that occurred privately, without witnesses and disconnected from any public institution—which was one of the reasons it came under attack during the Reformation.[24] Moreover, whereas the Church doctrine of consensus was not inconsistent with local customs in the north, it was quite different from deep-rooted traditions in the south, and therefore much less generally accepted.[25]

Although it has been shown that the doctrine was not well received among the aristocracy, it did reach the common folk via conciliar and episcopal legislation and sermons.[26] On the basis of an analysis of English pastoral manuals that were increasingly used after the Fourth Lateran Council of 1215 to instruct local pastors on their guidance of the laity, Murray concludes that the doctrine of consensual marriage had spread widely and quickly to the parish level by the middle

[18] Giraudo 2007.

[19] Biller 2000, 53–54.

[20] Noonan 1973, 425; for a more detailed description of how this marriage theory, based on consensus, came into being within the Catholic Church, see the chapter on "Choice of Marriage Partner" in Sheehan 1996, 91–117.

[21] Noonan 1973, 434.

[22] Ozment 1983, 26; and Sheehan 1997.

[23] Brundage 1990, 332–333; see also the discussion in Smith 1992, 18–21.

[24] Ozment 1983, 25–27.

[25] A good example of the tension between canon law (with its emphasis on mutual consent) and local costumes (which implied a much larger role for the family and for the social status of the two spouses) is the story of the relationship between Giovanni and Lusanna, as reconstructed by Brucker 1986.

[26] Sheehan 1978.

of the fifteenth century.[27] The problems that resulted from the application of the new doctrine—such as bigamy and clandestine marriages—were increasingly dealt with in the manuals during the thirteenth and fourteenth centuries, as the new marriage practices had been widely and successfully disseminated.[28]

The fact that both the man's and his future wife's consent was necessary for marriage meant that it was a contract between "equals," since neither could impose consensus upon the other. This means that, in principle, the bargaining position of women in such a situation was relatively strong: she could (try to) select the kind of husband who suited her. In the more romantic interpretation of the EMP, marriage was based on the love between the two partners, which must have had a strong equalizing effect also—assuming that love presupposes a certain degree of equality. This equalizing effect was also visible in the way partners dealt with their property.[29]

As a result, one would expect inequality within marriage to be more common in marriage systems in which the consent of the wife is not required. In China, for example, marriage was a contract not between two individuals but between two families. Eastman cites Mencius, who states that "marriage is a bond between two surnames," a family matter by the family, for the family.[30] Chinese girls often met their husbands for the first time on their wedding day, even though they were groomed from birth for marriage. Marriage partners were chosen by their families by way of a matchmaker who was responsible for making the arrangements.[31]

[27] Murray 1998, 140–144. For the Low Countries, see Bange and Weiler 1987, 399–406; and Hoppenbrouwers 1985, 73–74. The dissemination of the doctrine of consensual marriage went hand-in-hand with the spread of the Church's ideas on the right of widows to (re)marry. In 1160, Bartholomew, Bishop of Exeter, writes a penitential that confirms the Church's doctrine of a widow's right to marry. This type of consent was shortly thereafter extended to all marriages. Some manuals even went as far as to promote clandestine marriage. Murray refers to the work of fourteenth-century English William of Pagula, *Oculus sacerdotis*. See Murray 1998, 131–138.

[28] See for Ghent, Nicholas 1985, 54.

[29] Schmidt mentions that in seventeenth-century Leiden, in more than three-quarters of the testaments, partners named each other as their most important heirs, and in some cases they indicated in the testament that they did this because of "conjugal affection" or "love." See Schmidt 2001b, 186. See also Goldberg 1992b, 273. For an overview of the debate on the emergence of the companionate marriage, see the recent work by Crawford 2007, 13–19. See also Goody 1983, 128–129, on the relationships between age gap, companionate marriage, and monogamy.

[30] Eastman 1988, 24.

[31] Maynes and Waltner 2001; it would, however, be wrong to depict China as fundamentally unchanging in this respect; in fact, some evidence suggests that the patriarchal features here became stronger as Confucianism became institutionalized and part of the official doctrine of the empire, and that during the Sung Dynasty, the position of women was stronger than under later dynasties; cf. Birge 2003.

The power of the male head of the household in Europe was much more circumscribed than in other systems (such as the Chinese marriage pattern), as the EMP was based on the consent of both spouses. David Herlihy is convinced that "The father . . . could neither force a son or daughter into an unwanted marriage, nor prevent him or her from marrying. . . . The Church's doctrine was a damaging blow to paternal authority within the medieval household, and by itself assured that the medieval family could never develop into a true patriarchy."[32] Theo Engelen has stated that the essence of the EMP was that European fathers (and mothers, for that matter) "lacked the means of controlling their adult children. They therefore let them find their own way in the world and hired other people's children to do the work that in China would have been done by their own children."[33] In his view, differences in parental authority—strong in China, weak in Europe—explain why European children were allowed to choose their wedding partners and to set up their own households.[34]

Critics of the idea that marriage based on consent was related to the preachings of the Catholic Church have maintained that this cannot explain the rise of the EMP, because the EMP emerged only in the northwestern part of the continent, whereas "in other parts of Christian Europe, . . . families maintained sturdy patriarchal marriage strategies, often in open defiance of ecclesiastical dictates."[35] This is an important point, although it should also be acknowledged that eventually the EMP, which became the dominant marriage pattern in Europe west of the line from Trieste to St. Petersburg, more or less coincided with the medieval presence of the Catholic Church—and therefore it is highly unlikely that it was completely coincidental. But according to Hartman and others, other factors must have influenced the emergence of the EMP in northwestern Europe, particularly in England and in the Low Countries. In both regions during the fifteenth century, the marriage pattern was dominated by the consensus between the partners, although average ages of marriage were still relatively low at the time.[36]

[32] Herlihy 1985, 81.

[33] Engelen 2005.

[34] These claims are also reinforced when we look at other indicators, such as the relationship between the position in the sequence of children in the household and the age of marriage, or the effect of the father's being alive at the age of marriage. Wrigley et al. (1997) show for England that children born first were not favored over children born later (168–169), and they show that if the father had died before the bride or groom had turned 18, this did not have any effect on their average marriage age (170). In short, family circumstances had no influence on the marriage age of children; see 168–170. See also Laslett 1977, 177.

[35] Hartman 2004, 98.

[36] In his 1965 paper, Hajnal concluded that the EMP was not yet in place in the late Middle Ages, a conclusion largely based on his analysis of the 1377 poll tax; subsequently it has been argued that

We will now focus on the other factors that contributed to the genesis of the EMP, and that may help to explain why it originally occurred in the North Sea area: the transfer of property and access to the labor market.

Transfer of Property Between Generations and Within Households

One of the factors that can contribute to our understanding of the emergence of the EMP in northwestern Europe, and not in southern Europe, is the difference in the systems of property inheritance between generations and between husband and wife in these two regions. The Western inheritance system was distinctive because of women's rights to inherit and the ability to transfer landed property to and through women, as heirs or dowers. Within Europe, both the bride's and groom's sides of the marriage had property rights in their union.[37] But internally there were many differences—in particular, concerning the timing of women's access to their share of the inheritance. Marriage played a crucial role: the bulk of the daughter's share of the inheritance was either transferred to her at the start of her marriage, in the form of a dowry, or at her parents' death. The former was more typical in the south of Europe, while the latter was common in the north, although pre-mortem endowments and dowries were not unusual in the north, either. Essentially, intergenerational property transfer was less related to the event of marriage in the north than in the south.[38]

These differences have been carefully studied for areas at the border between the two regions in France. In the south (of France), in the *pays d'écrit,* or the land of written law, marital property regimes were, for ordinary people as for elites, dotal in form. In the *pays d'écrit* regions, decisions about marital property relations and succession were made in accordance with principles of law derived from Roman law. The rules were written down, commented upon, and authorized by legal scholars, judges, and magistrates. In this system, custom did not govern inheritance, as it did in the north. Individuals had choices about how

he misinterpreted this source, and that the "level of marital incidence is fully compatible with the European type in late fourteenth century England," see the discussion in Smith 1999, esp. 41–42.

[37] Such regimes are referred to as systems of "diverging devolution of property" because in all of them property goes to both sons and daughters ("diverges") as it descends ("devolves"). See Goody 1976, 10–36.

[38] Smith 1986b, 165. It however cannot be denied that there was a substantial difference between the continental part of the North Sea area and England; this difference mainly concerned the somewhat separate question of primogeniture, which was still quite important in England, although in practice this was not always applied; see Spufford 1976, 158. The Low Countries seem to be particularly advanced in their equal division of property between sons and daughters. Cf. Cooper 1976, 224; Leroy Ladurie 1976, 51 and 66; and Schmidt 2001a, 102.

their property was used and transferred, and the owners of family assets were given a degree of control over these decisions. In theory, it was possible for fathers to endow children differently at marriage, for example, because the dowry was part of negotiations with the family of the other spouse. These differences between north and south also concerned the way in which property was held within marriage. The southern European system is often referred to as "separatist" because the property of either spouse brought to the marriage was considered to be distinct, and a conjugal fund was not created at wedlock. The northern European situation is described as "conjugal."[39] The property a bride brought to the marriage was not held separately, as it was in the south, but was instead merged into a communal account that was under the full control of the husband, but to which, in the event of his death, the widow had rights.[40] Wealth accumulated during the marriage also contributed to the conjugal fund.

This created—at least in theory—different incentives for increasing the economic activities of women during marriage. In the north, wives could contribute to their conjugal fund and profit from its growth; in the south, their wealth was more or less fixed, regardless of what economic activities they undertook. This also had implications for their position after marriage: having the right to a share in the accumulated wealth gave greater opportunities for widows to start new businesses and to find new partners. Here again, though, the practice might have been quite different from theory. Couples in the north could, by marital contract, demand a separation of property; Howell writes that the south was not uniform in this practice and was considerably less devoted to the notion of separatism. At least until about 1500, marital property law in the south was similar to northern communal systems in its hybridism and mobility.[41]

The distinction between north and south was perhaps more evident in terms of property transfer from parents to children. Institutions such as the *monti delle dotti,* established in Tuscany during the fifteenth century, are evidence of the continued importance of the dotal regime in the south for all layers of society.[42] Among the Romans, the main purpose of the dowry was to help the groom bear the burden of matrimony (*sustinere onera matrimonii*). In its medieval Italian version, however, the Roman *dos* received a special twist. Unlike original Roman practice, the medieval Italian dowry came to be regarded as the girl's share of the patrimony. This had several important effects. One was that

[39] The principles of marital property law in the south have long been labeled "separatist" because the property either spouse brought to the marriage was considered to be distinct, and no conjugal fund was created by wedlock; Howell 1998, 212.

[40] Taken from Howell 1998, 199.

[41] Howell 1998, 212–213. See also Howell for examples of this flexibility.

[42] Kirshner and Molho 1978, Molho 1988.

girls were excluded from receiving a share in the patrimony (the *exclusio propter dotem*).[43] The *fraterna*, or enduring joint inheritance, was for brothers alone: sisters, provided with dowries, had no further legal part to play in their paternal family's economic life.[44] These *fraterna*, or *frérèches*, were a form of peasant inheritance established in the north of Italy (Tuscany, Lombardy, and Venice) and central France in order to avoid fragmentation of property; they often resulted in an entirely different household structure (i.e., co-residence of several family members and thus a de facto situation of extended families).[45]

In the north (of France), dowries were less important, and the status of heirs and their property rights was determined by birth, not by fiat. In the north, wives did not have the same freedom of choice in terms of endowing at marriage or inheritance when their husbands were deceased. In the few cases where they did have some freedom of interpretation, as in Douai, they owed their freedom to a peculiar interpretation of "community," rather than to general principles that vested absolute ownership rights in individuals.[46]

To an extent, we can only speculate about the potential effects of differences in property-transfer regimes on marriage and on household formation. First, we can claim that there was probably a direct relationship between marriage age and property transfer between parents and children, which influenced the parents' decision to marry off their girls as soon as possible, while also affecting the brides' degree of control over when their marriages would take place. That is, if a women had a right to her parent's inheritance without having to marry, there was no financial incentive for an early marriage. In contrast, the southern dowry system created incentives for both parents and girls to arrange early marriages. Women acquired their share in the estate as a dowry (which was to return to the wife after her husband's death), and the size of her dowry was dependent upon the goodwill of her parents, which created the leverage for parents to control the marriage process. Thus, in areas with partible inheritance, where women were certain about their share of the parent's estate, they could afford to wait before marrying. We may even go as far as to suggest that they used this time to accumulate extra resources in order to make themselves more attractive as potential marriage partners. Women had limited time to do this in those areas where women received only their part of the parents' estate on marriage. One could argue that dowry systems were also more patriarchal. In theory, the presence of

[43] We cannot delve into depth here with the precise evolution of the dotal system. We therefore refer to the works by experts such as Owen Hughes and Botticini; see Hughes 1978; Botticini and Siow 2003.

[44] Chojnacki 1975, 575.

[45] Gottlieb 1993, 215.

[46] Howell 1998, 212.

the Catholic Church in southern Europe meant that women had a right to decide upon their marriage partners. One could argue—on the basis of evidence, for example, from England—that in the north, girls also received endowments without or before getting married.[47] This could only diminish the importance of other marriage-related property transfers and thus make age at marriage even less significant in relation to intergenerational property transfer. Essentially, property transfer in the north (but not the south[48]) may have been unrelated to the event of marriage. This also fits with the notions of the consensus marriage, neolocality, and the high number of single people in the north.

In a dowry system, women had incentives to marry early. Similar incentives were probably created for parents. In fifteenth-century Tuscany, the larger the contribution of the bride to the marital household (in terms of ability to perform household work and to bear children), the smaller the dowry her parents would be obliged to pay to "convince" the groom to accept their daughter. A woman who waited too long before marrying would become too expensive to "sell" in the marriage market. Her parents would have to pay a larger dowry to compensate the groom's household for the smaller net positive contribution the bride would provide to the marital household.[49] The younger the bride, the larger her net positive contribution to the marital household and, therefore, the smaller the dowry her parents had to provide. The importance of the age of the bride is also evident from the fact that—as Molho has shown—many fathers presented their daughters to be younger than they actually were in the *Catasto,* in order to improve their marriage chances.[50]

Moreover, we argue that in the southern system, these elements in combination with the separation of property within the household may have prevented women from becoming active in the labor market (after marriage), because it remained uncertain if they would ever benefit from their efforts after the deaths of their husbands. But even if they had not had such overtly opportunistic ideas before entering into marriage, their early motherhood would probably have prevented them from being as active in the labor market as northwestern European women. In the north, women contributed to their household income in the knowledge that they would eventually receive their share of the conjugal fund. The southern system gave fewer opportunities for widows to take over their deceased husbands' businesses because they did not necessarily get their

[47] Smith 1986b.

[48] See also Leroy Ladurie 1976, 42, on the close relationship between parental authority and intergenerational transfers in southern France.

[49] Botticini 1999, 110.

[50] See Molho 1988, 193–203.

share of the inheritance, nor had they been as actively involved in the business as their northern colleagues.[51]

Our interpretation of the possible links between the inheritance system and their effect on the EMP are, for the most part, tentative. In some cases, it is argued that the lineal marital property regime was devised to control women.[52] Others claim that dotal regimes might have been more advantageous to women than community-property regimes because they protected women from the misadventures or ill will of their husbands, and gave them, as wives, some property of their own in the form of their dowries.[53]

Access to the Labor Market

The preaching of the Church and existing inheritance patterns may have made it easier for young men and women to defy parental authority, decide whom they wished to marry, and set up an independent household. But it was the rise of labor markets in Europe at the time that was most fundamental to the consolidation of western European marriage habits into a recognizable pattern. Before 1348, which marks the arrival of bubonic plague in Europe, a well-developed labor market already existed in many parts of western Europe, from which a significant share of the population earned a living. After 1348, the sudden fall in population levels as a result of the Black Death led to a booming labor market characterized by growing demand for labor—of both men and women—which resulted in a strong increase in real earnings, in particular for women.[54] This accelerated the general acceptance of the EMP in the century after 1348.

Initially, the EMP was the marriage pattern of the poor—wage earners who did not own or rent a farm or have any other substantial property.[55] This is clearly illustrated by Barbara Hanawalt in her analysis of marriage patterns among English peasants. She points out that marriage among the poor was characterized by the (more or less) free choice of the partners themselves:

> Marriage for love has traditionally been assumed to be the dubious privilege of those without property. The lord would not bother to impose

[51] See also the paper by Saito 2005.

[52] See examples given by Howell 1998, 223.

[53] Howell 1998, 224.

[54] In particular as servants in urban households. Mayhew (1990) gives an overview of the number of servants and apprentices in English communities, which complements Laslett's claim that on average between 1574 and 1821, 13.4% of the population in English communities were servants or apprentices (201–203).

[55] For example, Mate 1998, 33–34: "the higher up the social scale one was, the earlier one was likely to marry, with the least freedom of choice."

> a merchet, parents would have no property to bestow and thus have no control, and the Church would not dissolve a marriage even if all the young couple did was to agree to marry while lying together in a haystack. When a young woman, through her initiative and wages, managed to accumulate a bit of chattels and land and paid her a merchet, she could choose her own marriage partner. But the freedom in choice of marriage partner may have been a larger phenomenon, going far beyond those without property.[56]

In the cities, similar developments occurred, as is clear from Goldberg's study of York, for example. A particularly important source of female wage labor (which is often linked to the existence of the EMP)[57] was life-cycle servanthood.[58] Goldberg concludes that in the century after the Black Death, young men and women working as servants in the city of York were able to make marriage choices much more autonomously than were their counterparts in rural Yorkshire.[59] He also compares the reactions of two societies (England and Tuscany) to the consequences of the plague of 1348:

> In England, the labour shortage produced by the huge increase of mortality from the Plague prompted an influx of unmarried women into the towns, a rise in marriage age, and an increase in the proportion of women who never married. In Italy, however, the employment of single women did not increase much in the post-Plague era, nor did women's marriage rate increase. New employment vacancies in Italian cities were filled by men from the countryside, producing high urban male sex ratios, in contrast with low ratios in north-western European cities, where women often outnumbered men.[60]

Although it is claimed that the number of female servants in Italian towns has been underestimated, owing to the particularities of the *Catasto*,[61] it would be

[56] Hanawalt 1986, 202; also Bennett 1981, 193–247, for more evidence on the fact that women did indeed pay their own merchet.

[57] Hajnal 1982, 92–99; also Kussmaul 1981, 26.

[58] Smith 1992; Mayhew 1990, 202; Goldberg 1986b; and Laslett 1977, 44

[59] Goldberg and Riddy 2004, 5; Goldberg 1992b, 236, 243–255, 261–263, 273–275 and Goldberg 1986a. For more data on the importance of servanthood in early modern Europe, and in particular in England, see also Smith 1992, "Geographical Diversity," in particular, p. 36. See also pp. 40–41 on the freedom to move by servants in England versus Italy.

[60] Hartman 2004, 77; Kowaleski, 50–51; and Lynch 2003, 40–41, give additional evidence for the differences in sex ratio and share of single women in the population between north and south.

[61] Molho 1994; Klapisch-Zuber 1985.

hard to find situations—such as in late fourteenth- and early fifteenth-century Yorkshire—where the number female servants outnumbered the number of male servants.[62] The differences between north and south are more apparent in comparing the period during which girls went into service and the average length of their service. Goldberg calculates that Yorkshire female servants entered servanthood in their early teens and often worked until their mid-twenties, after which they married; in contrast, female servants in Florence and Barcelona started work at the age of 8 and left service before they turned 20.[63] Klapisch-Zuber notices that married women and widows far outnumbered unmarried females in service in Florence. It is clear that becoming a servant as an unmarried girl was seen as a last resort, as it could endanger a girl's honor.[64] According to Smith, this is the fundamental difference between servanthood in the north versus in the south: in the north, servanthood was based on free choice and on amassing a "marriage budget," whereas in the south, it was seen as a last resort that would in fact reduce the girl's marriage options.[65]

A number of studies have documented the remarkable depth of the labor market in late medieval western Europe, although there is still discussion about its growth. In the Low Countries, the trend was clearly upward; in sixteenth-century Holland and the Guelders River area, up to 60% of the working population was dependent on wage labor.[66] In England, the estimates range from 25% to more than 50% of the population being (partially) active in the labor market. The most recent estimates by Chris Dyer suggest that there was stability between circa 1300 and 1520, at an extremely high level of about 50%—probably somewhat more than this in the most commercialized eastern counties and less in the west.[67] Or, as Poos argues in a detailed study of Essex in England, being a wage laborer was a normal part of the life cycle of a very large part of the population.[68] These extremely high levels of wage labor can be compared with estimates for Ming China, where perhaps 1 to 2% of the population were wage earners.[69]

We therefore hypothesize that the labor market for women played a key role in the genesis of the EMP. In northwestern Europe, both married and unmarried

[62] Goldberg and Riddy 2004, 12.

[63] See Goldberg and Riddy 2004, 5; Klapisch-Zuber 1985, 173–174.

[64] Klapisch-Zuber 1986, 72–73. See also Molho 1988, 204–217, who gives a large number of interesting examples of the Tuscan's ideas about the ideal age category of a bride: she should still be a *fianculla*, or a young girl in her early/mid-teens. Comparatively, her husband should be anywhere from 20 to 35 years old.

[65] Smith 1992, 45.

[66] Van Bavel 2006.

[67] Dyer 2005, 218–220.

[68] Poos 1991, 183–229, for England (in particular Essex).

[69] See Xu, Wu, and Curwen 1999, 37.

women had access to the labor market, and the increased demand for labor after the Black Death may have set in motion a process resulting in the characteristic features of the EMP. A number of authors have noted the strong increase in nominal and real wages for women after 1348, also pointing out that in some cases women were paid the same as men for the same kind of work. Hilton notes that "around 1400, countrywomen were doing the same manual jobs as men, such as haymaking, weeding, mowing, carrying corn, driving plough oxen, and breaking stones for road mending."[70] We found evidence for a similar absence of a gender gap in Holland from the mid-fourteenth until the mid-sixteenth century.[71] In short, the Black Death brought about a considerable improvement in the labor conditions for women in terms of the number of jobs they had access to and their (relative) remuneration (see chapter 5 for the development of the gender wage gap after 1500). The degree to which European women took advantage of this situation was, however, quite different from region to region. In the North Sea area, these changes led to a marked increase in women's participation in the labor market, while in the south, where the relative wages of women did not increase substantially (see chapter 5), other factors, such as the dowry system, constrained this process.

This expansion of the labor market fundamentally changed the power balance between genders and between generations. In China, and elsewhere, households were organized around the collaborative running of a family farm, and the father's authority was based on his control over productive resources. In contrast, if the household did not own substantive productive resources, as was common in northwestern Europe during the late Middle Ages, the economic basis for parental authority was weakened. If, at the same time, young adults gained access to the labor market, particularly when there was strong growth in wage labor, and there were a variety of options for ways to escape the authority of parents (i.e., becoming a servant, or a day laborer, or migrating to the city), the power balance between generations was fundamentally affected. Adolescents over the age of 16 could earn a considerable surplus over what they needed for subsistence; they worked hard, but their level of consumption was still relatively low and they did not incur the fixed costs that accompany the establishment of a household. In short, it was in the interest of parents to bind their children to the household, as they were net contributors to household income. At the same

[70] Hilton 1975, 102–103; Beveridge 1955, 18–35; see also the criticism by Bardsley 1999.

[71] As per work in progress on a detailed paper discussing the wage gap between sexes in Holland and England; proof for the similarity in wages for both men and women in Holland in this period can be found in Hamaker 1875/1876, 2:423–424, 2:440–465, for data on carrying peat and working at chalk ovens, respectively. The work by Boschma-Arnoudse (2003) shows that the situation in the 1550s was still the same (342–344).

time, those children were attractive to employers, and often found it relatively easy to find jobs in the relatively well-developed labor market. This suggests that the rise of the EMP and the changing power balance between generations may have been caused by the growth of the labor market in late medieval Europe.

One can perhaps go one step further. In the century and a half following the Black Death, young women and men were able to free themselves from parental influence through their high real earnings. In the process, they developed strategies that were oriented toward the labor market; that is, wage labor became a key stage in the life cycle, starting with work as a servant (for girls) or an apprentice (for boys) during their teens, through which they acquired the skills and the savings to set up their own households. A very mobile and flexible labor force developed. Young people migrated to cities at the age of 12 or 14, when job opportunities were growing there, or moved to other regions and/or got jobs when prospects seemed good. And even after marriage and the establishment of a new household, wage labor remained their main source of income. So not only did the booming labor market induce men and women to change their marriage pattern but also the changed marriage pattern resulted in an increased dependence on wage labor. In our view, the co-evolution of marriage patterns and the labor market helps to explain the relatively high levels of waged work that could be found in the North Sea region in the fifteenth and sixteenth centuries.

The increased participation of young women in the workforce allowed women more independence and agency. Traditionally, the father's authority was confined to the household sphere, and when youngsters left the household to become servants before getting married, they also escaped the fathers' authority. This independence is evident in the payment of the *merchet*—the feudal fine levied by the lord upon the marriage of a daughter from a servile family. Judith Bennett has demonstrated that in many cases the daughter was able to pay this sizable sum herself, sometimes without specifying whom she would marry.[72] Women were supported in their decisions to marry by the marriage law, even if their fathers preferred other marriage partners.[73]

Women in this system could also create a substantial amount of social capital for themselves and for their household members. Although it is rather difficult to quantify this social capital and its impact on women's positions, women in the patrilocal system (joint households) experienced considerable disadvantages in terms of social capital; they moved in with their in-laws, often in another village.[74]

[72] Or the equivalent of 25–30 daily wages of an unskilled (female) laborer; Bennett 1981, 202.

[73] As Goldberg (1992b) writes: "Where women achieved emotional and economic independence from parents through service or other paid employment, as was more often true of urban society, they were enabled to exercise greater personal choice and to delay marriage, even to get by without marrying" (263).

[74] Cornell 1987, 146.

In contrast, those who could stay in their family and village benefited more because they were familiar with the local community, its customs, and networks. A girl who left home to get married, however, left behind all that was familiar.[75] To a certain degree, this was also the case for European girls who migrated elsewhere in order to work as live-in maids or servants. However, with their participation in the labor market, they created new social capital—for themselves and for their future spouses.

We conclude that the emergence of the EMP was the result of the interplay of three factors: an ideological contribution (the preaching of the Church), the developing labor market, and a system of intergenerational transfers that did not encourage women into early marriage. Whereas the EMP before 1348 was just one of the possibilities in a variety of alternative modes of family constitution, and mainly "the dubious privilege of the poor," the Black Death—by producing an extraordinary set of circumstances that made EMP the preferred option for large numbers of people—locked into place a self-perpetuating and enforcing system of wage labor and family formation. Only the upper layers of society, where the long-term management of family property was a vital consideration in marriage behavior, were probably to a large extent immune to these changes. In this latter case, parental control remained relatively strong and arranged marriages continued to be rather usual.

Hajnal's "Distinctive Features" of the EMP

Now that we have analyzed the key factors in the emergence of the EMP, and offered an interpretation that focuses on the qualitative aspects of the EMP (consensus of the spouses, weak parental authority, and neolocality), we can revisit its "distinctive features," such as a high average age of marriage and high (female) celibacy, in order to see how they relate.

"Unyoked Is Best": High Celibacy Rates Among Women

The second distinctive feature of the EMP was the relatively large proportion of the female population that remained unmarried. Again, to a large extent this follows from the fact that the search process for a suitable partner started at a relatively high age (i.e., at 18) and only ended when consensus with a partner was reached—or in the more romantic version, when they fell in love with each

[75] Maynes and Waltner 2001.

other. Hajnal has remarked that this individualized search process is a serious limitation of the EMP:

> the conviction that marriage should be decided upon only after the future spouses have got to know each other well . . . may render the finding of a marriage partner very difficult since people often have opportunities to become acquainted only with a few young persons of the opposite sex. If, by contrast, it is possible to arrange a marriage between people who have never met, the circle of potential spouses is greatly widened.[76]

It is therefore only to be expected that for part of the population, the search process was unsuccessful, resulting in a proportion of the population who never married. Kowaleski, with her useful overview of known figures of single women in Europe, concludes that there was a massive difference between the north and the south, and that the number of single women might have been even higher in England than in the continental part of northwestern Europe.[77] This can, as we have suggested, be related to the type of marriage system in place and to the large number of unmarried women who entered into service (a practice uncommon in Italy, where servanthood was not a respected job for unmarried women). In the system of arranged marriages, large numbers of single women appear to have been very uncommon.[78] In this system, marriage was the norm (especially for young women who outnumbered men), as the costs of arranging a marriage were limited while the potential benefits were large, and village and family networks could be mobilized to find a suitable partner.

In short, the two "distinctive features" of Hajnal's EMP are the result of the patterns analyzed. An additional feature is that the differences in age between men and women were relatively small in the "classic" EMP (northern Europe)—again owing to the consensus between (near) "equals"—whereas the age differences in southern Europe were in general much larger.[79] As the poem

[76] Hajnal 1965, 126.

[77] Kowaleski 1998, 46. See also her overview of average marriage ages and percentages of single women; table A1, pp. 326–328.

[78] Only 1 or 2% of women in traditional China remained unmarried at age 30, compared to 15 to 25% in western Europe. See Maynes and Waltner 2001. But see also the literature on the influence of dowry and sex ratio on average marriage age and numbers of single women in medieval and early modern Italy; Molho 1994, 306.

[79] Laslett 1977. Goldberg and Riddy 2004 also gives estimates of age differences for fourteenth- to fifteenth-century Yorkshire, and concludes that couples tended to marry one another at similar ages, which is in accordance with the data found by Razi for the manor of medieval Halesowen (9–11); Razi 1980, 61–63. The mean age difference for urban Yorkshire was 2.9 years and for rural couples, 3.8. Goldberg also noted that in those cases where men were substantially older, these were usually

by Anna Bijns, the epigraph to this book implies, the relative bargaining position of women before (and probably also after) marriage was improved with age at marriage and by a small age difference between men and women.

In contrast to many other societies, in late medieval western Europe, single women were a generally accepted phenomenon. Special institutions—the beguinages—accommodated such a lifestyle, whether made by free choice or *force majeure*. The beguine movement—the rise of a group of single women—started in the late twelfth century, which shows that the roots of this development can be traced back to before the Black Death. Beguines generally came from the middle class and lived in urban contexts. Their exceptional independence from the rest of the world dominated by men was expressed in their way of life: their households excluded males, the beguine communities were only loosely connected with each other, and clerical authorities oversaw them only informally. In chapter 8, we will have a closer look at this institution—arguably the "pinnacle" of the EMP, allowing women a great deal of agency.

Implications of the EMP for Long-Term Economic Development

Labor Market Participation and Human Capital Formation

The EMP as it emerged in the late Middle Ages was characterized by a fundamental adaptation of household structures and marriage patterns to market opportunities. In that sense, it was probably unique: we do not know of comparable earlier examples in history in which households became dependent on markets on such a vast scale. The fact that wage laborers were prepared to develop and carry out a strategy of depending on markets for goods and services is significant: it shows that they had sufficient trust in markets to rely on their functioning, not only for their income but also for consumption. This can be seen as an index of the efficiency of the market economy in the late medieval period in this region: it appears that it generated the necessary trust to make such a transformation possible.

Part of the life cycle that emerged in the later Middle Ages, and which would not change fundamentally before the nineteenth (and perhaps even the twentieth) century, was an extended period of on-the-job training. The EMP was in this way interwoven with the system of apprenticeship that had emerged mainly

widowers marrying women for the first time. See also Wrigley et al. 1981, 151ff., for a discussion on the age gap between spouses in England. Compare with the rather large age difference between bride and groom in early modern Italy, as described by Herlihy and Klapisch-Zuber 1985, and put into its European context by Smith 1992, 33.

in the guilds in medieval Europe, with patterns of "circulating" servants and maids, and traveling journeymen (see chapter 7 for a detailed analysis of the role of servants in the EMP).[80] This all contributed to greatly increasing the proportion of time people spent undergoing training and schooling.

One of these links with broader socioeconomic changes is the supply and demand for domestic services. The distinctive western European servant phenomenon is not found in parts of the world where early marriages are common. Reher confirms this: on the basis of Hajnal's 1965 article, it becomes clear that southern Europe did not fully fit the EMP of late and low levels of marriage, although it was also did not follow patterns found in eastern Europe. In Mediterranean Europe, there were far fewer servants than in central or northern Europe and women married earlier.[81] This led to the phenomenon that is still so typical for Mediterranean countries today: children do not leave their parent's house before marriage, and so leave home far later in Spain or Italy than they do in the North Sea area.[82] And among those who marry, many join their households to that of their parents, thus creating multigenerational households.[83]

Being a servant in another household is an important way of acquiring certain skills. The links between the EMP and human capital formation are more complex, however. In theory, it can be argued that the EMP did not result in increased investment in human capital because the extra income generated as a result of such an investment did not become available to the parents who made that initial investment but, rather, to the new household set up by the couple upon marriage. In short, neolocality is bad for investment in human capital, whereas patrilocality—where the newlywed couple stays within the household of the boy's parents and they profit directly from the extra income he generates—may create better incentives for parents to invest in their children, or at least in the boys.

But there is evidence that notwithstanding the neolocal system, western European parents did invest heavily in their children, and that also from a theoretical point of view, "love marriage" would lead to more investment in human capital than arranged marriage. In a pioneering paper, Edlund and Lagerlöf demonstrate that "a shift from parental to individual consent moves resources in the

[80] On apprenticeship in medieval Europe, see Epstein 1991. There has been some discussion about the importance of servanthood; see Bailey 1996, 7, and the articles by Goldberg and Smith in Goldberg 1992a, and Fox 1996.

[81] Reher 1998, 207.

[82] This is still the case today. See Reher 1998, 208; there is possibly also a link with the dowry system, which was so prominent in southern Europe.

[83] Wall (1983a, 526) claims that the proportion of multigenerational households was high in the south of Europe and very high in the east contrary to the north and west where this proportion was very low.

same direction, favouring young men and young women over old men," because young adults will have more incentives to invest in their offspring than will old adults "who will be around fewer periods."[84] Another part of the explanation is that the new parents who were "freed" from control by their own parents may have had more means to invest in their offspring.

In a way, Chinese and Indian household structures were focused on providing an income for parents during old age, on performing the rites and ceremonies necessary for the well-being of the deceased, and on the continuation of the lineage so that the performance of these ceremonies would be guaranteed forever. Parental authority was aimed at guaranteeing that, during the best years of their children's lives, those children took care of their parents and devoted much of their time, energy, and resources to their well-being. In contrast, in the areas that witnessed the rise of the EMP, children had less interest in taking care of their parents. This created a problem: Who would take care of the elderly in societies where the EMP was developing? Aside from that question, the EMP did, however, create opportunities. It freed up resources that could be spent on the schooling and training of children. That increased investment in human capital should also be seen in light of the the commercialization of the household environment. The measure of success in this new environment was no longer to succeed the father in the management of the family farm (and continuation of the lineage) but, rather, was linked to success in the market economy through a maximization of income from wage labor. In such an environment, investing in the education of children became critical.

Evidence for this is abundant for the Low Countries and England, where levels of literacy rose strongly in the century and a half after the Black Death. In the Low Countries, this is relatively well documented; the spread of new religious movements (the Modern Devotion movement during the fifteenth century and the Reformation after 1517) is clearly connected to this trend.[85] In the sixteenth century, a majority of the male population of Holland could read and write, and these skills were evident in both towns and in the countryside (as the famous Italian traveler Guicciardini from the 1560s testified).[86] In 1585, about 55% of bridegrooms and 32% of brides could sign their names in the marriage registers of Amsterdam, with the differences between immigrants and native Amsterdammers proving insignificant.[87] In England, a similar growth in education and training occurred between 1340 and 1548, as has been documented for York by Hoeppner Moran.[88] In London in the 1470s, the levels of literacy may

[84] See Edlund and Lagerlöf 2006.
[85] See also Derville 1984; Uitz 1990, 71.
[86] Van der Woude 1980b, 257.
[87] Kuijpers 1997, 490–523.
[88] Moran 1985.

have already been as high as that in Amsterdam, although this estimate is less certain.[89] In the same region bordering the North Sea, the premium for skilled labor declined rapidly after 1348 and stayed at an extremely low level during the sixteenth to nineteenth centuries, which points to high levels of investment in this form of human capital as well.[90] Both types of human capital formation were closely linked. Guilds in the Low Countries and in England required their apprentices to be literate, or included training in reading and mathematics in their apprenticeships.[91] In Amsterdam, the poor relief institutions also ensured that orphans attended schools as preparation for apprenticeships.[92] Most strikingly, the gender differences in human capital formation were rather small: parents in western Europe invested in both their sons' and their daughters' education and training. Although men continued to have a lead over women in rates of literacy, for example, this lead was relatively small compared with what we know about other parts of the world, such as China and India.[93] The comparatively high investment in human capital formation in the North Sea area in this period formed the necessary basis for the rapid growth of its economy in the seventeenth and eighteenth centuries (in chapter 3, we refine and test these ideas applying the age-heaping method for calculating numeracy to data for the Low Countries).

Institutions and Trust

The small nuclear families that resulted from the EMP were more vulnerable to the loss of individual members—in particular, the father or mother—than were large extended families, especially when they were largely dependent on wage labor and did not own many resources. Reliance on the strength of family ties—the traditional support network—was not a real alternative. In fact, the EMP was quite individualistic: youngsters left home at an early age, did not take care of their parents, often remained celibate, and set up their own households,

[89] Moran 1985, 20, citing an estimate by Sylvia Thrupp; also Hanawalt 1993, 82.

[90] Van Zanden 2005, 110–112.

[91] Hanawalt 1993, 82.

[92] Kuijpers 1997.

[93] The difference in human capital formation between the sexes becomes even smaller if we look at another parameter—numeracy. Elsewhere we have analyzed a large number of sources to estimate, on the basis of recently developed methods (such as the Whipple index), the degree to which men and women could count and calculate. It appears that in the Low Countries early on in the early modern period overall numeracy levels were already exceptionally high—much higher than in many developing countries today—and that the difference between men and women was exceptionally small. In some areas, women even did better than men in terms of numeracy. Here again we found proof that human capital formation was exceptionally high in the Low Countries and immediate surroundings; De Moor and van Zanden 2008.

frequently outside the place of parents' residence—all factors suggesting that the EMP was one with rather loose family ties.[94] The EMP therefore necessitated the establishment of alternative social support networks, based on solidarity within the community, the city, perhaps even the state, and on the forging of networks of mutual help that were not primarily rooted in bonds of blood (a thought developed more fully in chapter 7).

The elderly were the obvious victims of this decline in parental authority and the trend toward neolocality.[95] Of course, when their children prospered, the parents might have benefited from their prosperity as well. But the transactions, which were in a way "enforced" by parental authority under patriarchal systems, were in the western European system more or less voluntary transfers of money and goods—dependent also on the proximity of parents and on the willingness of their children to contribute to their income.[96] This situation also might have given parents an incentive to invest emotionally in their relationships with their children.[97] More important, however, it gave them clear incentives to start saving for their old age during an early stage of their lifecycle.

Here, the developing capital market began to play a role: saving for the future became increasingly important in this new system, because simply having children was not a guarantee that one would be taken care of during old age. During their teens and early twenties, men and women were expected to save substantial sums of money in order to set up their own households at marriage, then during marriage, they had to save to be assured of an income during their old age. So to some extent, transfers between generations that in patriarchal systems regulated the problem of care in old age and dealt with the establishment of new households were replaced by intertemporal income transfers by the same generation via the capital market. The EMP was therefore not only dependent on a vibrant labor market but also unable to function properly if capital markets were unreliable and inefficient. Fortunately, however, there is strong evidence that the

[94] Hoppenbrouwers 1985 documents the decreasing influence of family and the rise of "individualism" in late medieval Holland in some detail.

[95] Laslett 1988, 156: "he more widespread the nuclear family, and the more strictly neolocal rules are applied, the more important collective institutions will be for the security of the individual." Laslett coined the term "nuclear hardship hypothesis" for this relationship. On the relationship between the European marriage pattern and care of the elderly, see also Kreager and Schroeder-Butterfill 2005, 7–13. For a critical review of Laslett's thesis, see Lynch 2003, 12–14.

[96] Smith 1986a, 199–201. Apart from this type of transaction, it might also be argued that the fact that intergenerational transfers were less important than in the south (see earlier in this chapter) may have had a negative effect on the bond between parent and child. For England, see also Smith 1991.

[97] A review of the debate on emotional bonds between parents and children in the late medieval period can be found in Hoppenbrouwers 1985; on the basis of an impressive collection of evidence related to Holland, he shows the importance of emotional ties between members of the conjugal household.

efficiency of the capital markets greatly improved during the century or so after the Black Death, a topic that we deal with in detail in chapter 4.[98]

In the Low Countries, among the most popular innovations were *renten*, or whole life annuities on which a relatively high interest was paid during the lifetime of the man or women for whom the annuity was established. These annuities became very popular in the late medieval period, and probably were the most important source of urban (long-term) finance in the most commercialized parts of the Low Countries (Flanders, Brabant, and Holland). This was, of course, an ideal means of saving for one's old age.[99] Similar developments can be found in medieval England, where pension contracts performed the same function: the elderly surrendered the use of their lands and resources to family members or non-kin in exchange for individually arranged pension benefits.[100] At the same time, many new types of institutions were being developed and professionalized, as we will explain extensively in chapter 7 of this book. Poor relief institutions were formed, first under the initiative of the Church, and after the Reformation increasingly run by city governments and, in England, by the state. During the Middle Ages, poor relief was primarily the responsibility of the Church, and part of the income of the parish had to be spent on "hospitality"—that is, accommodation of strangers and travelers, and on almsgiving to the poor.[101] In urban centers, this Church-related poor relief was often supplemented by new institutions—some the initiative of pious citizens and some initiated and managed by the cities themselves—to deal with (the excesses of) mass poverty. In the Brabant city of Den Bosch, these late medieval initiatives resulted in an accumulation of capital and land by poor relief institutions, which supplied the funds for poor relief in this city during the following centuries.[102]

In the sixteenth century, the perhaps somewhat uncoordinated character of poor relief institutions that had grown out of the medieval initiatives was increasingly criticized, and attempts were made to reform the "system." In the Low Countries, this led to the first national regulation introduced by the Habsburg monarch Charles V in 1531, but further reform and proliferation of poor relief relied to a large extent on the activities of individual cities and provinces. In England, through the Elizabethan Poor Laws of 1572–1601,

[98] Clark 1988; Epstein 2000, 18–25, 60–61.

[99] Zuijderduijn 2009b; also VerLoren van Themaat and Dokkum 1983. See also Munro 2007.

[100] Elaine Clark shows how in East Anglia about 40% of both men and women received a pension in the last half of the thirteenth century. In the period 1350–1457, about 38% and 23% of women and men, respectively, received pensions; Clark 1982, 316.

[101] The analysis of the foundations of poor relief during the Middle Ages as supplied by canon law, see Tierney 1959.

[102] Prak 1994, 147–170. But see also Lynch 2003 on the emergence of urban institutions for collective welfare.

the state established a national system, which also built on the medieval heritage.[103] These two systems were both considered to be quite generous by the standards of the time.[104] De Vries and van der Woude estimate, for example, that poor relief in the Netherlands may have redistributed as much as 3 to 4% of national income, and they have linked this to "the modest scope of informal, family-based income redistribution practices."[105] Seen in this perspective, the "relatively generous" poor relief of the North Sea area can be considered a by-product of the demographic system that emerged there in the late Middle Ages.[106]

Another vulnerable group was located at the other end of the age spectrum. In China and Europe, there were fundamental differences in the treatment of "unwanted" children. In China and India, female infanticide was quite a normal practice. This was linked to another important difference between the two patterns: the relative appreciation of the two sexes. The Chinese pattern was in essence patrilocal: after marriage, the couple moved in with the parents of the boy, and it was their task to take care of the parents in the years to come. Boys were, therefore, a real asset: a continuation of the lineage and a guarantee that one would be taken care of in old age. Girls were a liability: expensive to raise, requiring a dowry in order to get married, after which they moved to another household to take care of the parents living there. Such a stark contrast between the sexes was absent in the EMP, however. There are indications that although infanticide did happen in the West, child abandonment was a more regular practice than infanticide and it showed an equal sex ratio.[107] Additionally, in the late medieval period, we see the gradual disappearance of the practice of (female) infanticide from western Europe.[108]

Similarly, adoption of foundlings had been encouraged by the Christian Church: during the sixth and seventh centuries. It introduced the principles of *oblatio*, or the donation of children to the service of God through ecclesiastical institutions.[109] This can be considered a rationalization and institutionalization of abandonment. It can also be argued that raising a foundling was not considered very different from raising your own children, since these children were also being raised to become laborers.[110] Around the middle of the thirteenth century, specialized urban institutions for the care of abandoned children

[103] Tierney 1959, 139–133.
[104] Lindert 1998.
[105] De Vries and van der Woude 1997.
[106] Smith 1986a, 199–201.
[107] Lynch 2003.
[108] Hartman 2004, 43–44.
[109] See Boswell 2004, 256.
[110] Tilly et al. 1992.

were increasingly established and spread throughout most of Europe during the sixteenth and seventeenth centuries.[111] The "supply" of foundlings was also closely related to the EMP. That is, poverty was not the only the reason for single and married mothers to abandon their children. In Paris, for example, two-thirds of the unwed mothers who abandoned their children worked as domestics, who were subject to promiscuous situations, far from parental supervision and without a support network.[112]

Strong and weak family ties, and correspondingly strong and weak social institutions, are fundamental to the explanation Reher provides for the differences in marriage systems between northern and southern Europe. He also argues that the two-generation household—in particular, if exclusively dependent on wage work—was much more fragile than the three-generation household characteristic of a patriarchal society, which usually had some access to land or other resources. In southern Europe, vulnerable members of society were helped by the family or by charitable individuals, while in northern societies this was largely accomplished through public and private institutions.[113] There were several ways of dealing with the needy in Mediterranean Europe: co-residence, distribution of the elderly among the households of their offspring, or spatial proximity of the homes of the elderly and those of their children. In England, a smaller proportion of the elderly lived with their children;[114] the community's responsibility for the well-being of the elderly was epitomized in the Poor Laws.[115] It might be presumptuous to argue that it is no coincidence a strong civil society of community institutions developed in the same part of Europe, helping to spread risks in times of hardship. As Reher claims:

> The sense of individual responsibility for collective norms and needs, so essential for the concept of democracy and civil society in the West, is often conspicuously absent from southern European societies. . . . In sum, the countries of northern Europe and North America have well developed civil societies that thrive on individual initiatives, but with a

[111] Boswell 1988, 173, 401, 405–408.

[112] Ransel 1988, 173; Tilly et al. 1992.

[113] This difference is still visible today. Reher explains how a large majority of people older than 65 years in northwestern European countries live in institutions for the elderly, whereas in the south this is only the case for a very small percentage of the elderly. Most are taken care of by their children (1998, 209). See also Thane 2000, 119–124, on the relationship between the EMP and the position of the elderly today.

[114] Reher 1998, 209. See also his note 24 for more references on care of the elderly in Spain.

[115] See also Smith 1981.

dark side shown by their lack of social cohesion and by the desperation and anguish so prevalent in them.[116]

Implications for Intergenerational Support: The Nuclear Hardship Hypothesis

The rise of the EMP had its disadvantages: the smaller nuclear family meant fewer "other" family members and almost no grandparents, which likely made these households more vulnerable for exogenous shocks: loss of employment, harvest failures, wars, and other events that reduced earnings and wealth.

Peter Laslett introduced the "nuclear hardship hypothesis" to explain this aspect of the EMP.[117] Laslett suggests that hardship, stemming from neolocality such as found in parts of northwestern Europe, would have implied greater importance of collective institutions to ensure security for individuals. The idea of a family-to-collectivity continuum, of family and collectivity complementing each other, is central to his argument. The way Laslett puts it, the importance of collective institutions rises as the immediate result of neolocality and the presence of nuclear family households.[118] The "collectivity" in Laslett's description applies to top-down charity organizations that emerged to take care of those who were in need. Laslett furthermore does not confine the nuclear hardship hypothesis to neolocality when he discusses the position of the elderly. He adds the idea of "the life-cycle squeeze,"[119] which arises not only from neolocality but also from high ages at marriage, linking nuclear hardship with John Hajnal's EMP.[120]

High age at marriage causes the life cycles of parents and children to diverge; children tend to marry and have children of their own at the same time as their parents become elderly and needy, and start losing their spouses. Consequently,

[116] Reher 1998, 217. This is difficult to reconcile with the classic study by Putnam of differences in social capital between northern and southern Italy, in which the north figures as the example of a strong civil society; see Putnam 1993.

[117] Laslett 1988, 153–157. Before Laslett, others had used the term, such as J. Smith 1984, 439; and R. Smith 1984.

[118] Laslett 1988, 156; cf. Greif 2006b.

[119] Laslett 1988, 169. Laslett does not, in fact, use the term "squeeze" in this article. The term "life-cycle squeeze" has been employed by sociologists and demographers, who originally focused on the gender aspects of the phenomenon, demonstrating that at some point in the family life cycle at marriage, as well as at the point of children reaching adolescence, a women's income is needed to make ends meet. The idea that this squeeze coincides with that of parents in need was not part of the original hypothesis. Cf. van Dusen and Sheldon 1976; Oppenheimer 1974; Gove et al. 1973.

[120] Three features were central to this EMP: neolocality, a high age at (first) marriage (over 23 for women and over 26 for men), and a large number of singles who never married at all; Hajnal 1965.

both parents and their grown-up children need not only physical assistance (child care, elderly care) but also financial assistance (in the case of the children, to support household formation or to support children not yet able to make an income; in the case of parents, to support themselves when no longer active at the labor market). Combined with neolocality, which causes parents and their married children to live in separate households, diverging life cycles make it more difficult for the elderly to receive the support they might need from their children. A focus on the way in which the elderly cope with this "nuclear hardship" provides insight into the ways the family safety net is replaced.

"Nuclear hardship" also features in articles about family economics. Kotlikoff and Spivak, in a theoretical contribution, claim that "the institution of the family provides individuals with risk-sharing opportunities which may otherwise not be available."[121] Since there is a degree of trust and an exchange of information within the family that is more difficult to achieve with outsiders, problems with respect to "moral hazard, adverse selection, and deception" are less stringent and transaction costs are generally lower.[122] Although Kotlikoff and Spivak do not have historical societies in mind when they discuss these issues, we may assume they hold true for families in the past. Their analysis "indicates that implicit risk-sharing arrangements [within the family] can provide powerful economic incentives for marriage and family formation."[123] Here, they more or less agree with social historians who believe that the family can substitute for insurance institutions (see the discussion in chapters 6 and 7).

This works at a basic level: people who marry and thus combine their assets implicitly create an old-age pension because "for each partner the risk of living too long is hedged by the other partner's potential death: if one partner lives to be very old, there is a high probability that his (or her) spouse has already died leaving him a bequest to help finance his consumption."[124] This form of risk pooling increases with the number of partners. Kotlikoff and Spivak calculate that substantial wealth effects are possible by marrying (ranging from an increase of 11.7% to 43.0%, depending on age and risk adversity) and entering into three-person polygamy (15.8% to 68.7%). They also calculate this for parents with children, for whom creating a pool of wealth on the condition children will support parents during old age also substitutes for insurance. Their theoretical approach lends support to the nuclear hardship hypothesis: "complex" types of

[121] Kotlikoff and Spivak 1981, 372.

[122] Kotlikoff and Spivak 1981, 372.

[123] Kotlikoff and Spivak 1981, 373–374. Cf. their assertion "that the recurrent instability in family arrangements may, to some extent, reflect recent growth in pension and social security public annuities" (388–389).

[124] Kotlikoff and Spivak 1981, 380.

family formation provide better possibilities for security in old age, and hence, nuclear families are more likely to experience problems.

So, a strong case can be made for the EMP's certain negative welfare effects. But do we find evidence for such effects in western Europe between 1400 and 1800? In chapter 6, we will review this hypothesis more fully and see if its predictions hold in reality: Were the regions where the EMP originated more fragile and less able to deal with exogenous shocks?

Conclusions: From Families to Households as the Core Unit of Western Society

The late Middle Ages have been called the "Golden Age of the Laborer," but perhaps, as Barron suggests, it was also a golden age for women who wished to become active in the labor market.[125] In the North Sea region, women's earnings were relatively high and access to the labor market was relatively easy, although they still experienced serious constraints when compared with male members of the labor force.[126] Similarly, during the twentieth century, the same trends—increased relative pay and increased female participation in the labor force—were driving forces for the emancipation of women, which accelerated in times of labor scarcity (during the two World Wars and during the rapid economic growth afterwards). If we continue this line of thought, one might even mention the assumption of economists that increased relative earnings of women leads to lower levels of fertility, because the opportunity costs of rearing children are higher. Perhaps such a link between female labor participation and fertility may also help to explain the low levels of fertility that can be hypothesized for

[125] See Barron 1989, who coined the term "Golden Age of Women" in her study of medieval London; but see also Hilton 1975, 95–110 and Dale 1933, for earlier proponents of the idea that women were better off during the late Middle Ages. It is perhaps also significant that historians of feminism have identified the late medieval period as the "first wave" of feminism; see, for example, Stuurman and Akkerman 1998. According to Joan Kelly (1984), early feminism begins with Christine de Pisan's *The Book of the City of Ladies* of 1406 However, there is also substantial opposition to the idea of a golden age; see, for example, the works by Kowaleski and Bennett 1989 and Bennett 1996, 47 and 120.

[126] Critics of Barron's ideas about a "golden age" of women have rightly pointed out that women were active only in rather limited segments of the labor market and not, for example, in the "specialized crafts" with the highest earnings; and that the range of options for women who wanted to earn a living in this way were "generally quite restricted" (McIntosh 2005, 210 and 250); cf. Bennett 2007, 85–86; Bardsley 1999; and Mate 1998, 193–194.

post-1348 England, when population growth stagnated at the much reduced post-Plague level.[127]

Essentially, we have argued that a rather odd combination of forces—the doctrines of the Catholic Church, the system of intergenerational transfers, the expansion of the labor market, and the effect of the Black Death—lay behind the emergence of the EMP in the late medieval period. This development was characterized by relatively low levels of parental authority over their children and of men over women. The EMP was well adapted to the new commercialized environment that emerged during this period.[128] Wage labor became an integral part of the life of members of the small conjugal household, and other market transactions (such as the use of credit and the accumulation of savings) became part of their survival strategy. This co-evolution of the demographic regime and the emerging labor market helps to explain the strong commercialization of society and economy that occurred in this period, when one- to two-thirds of the population became (partially) dependent on wage labor and working for wages became a normal part of a person's life. In our view, the "deep" penetration of markets in late medieval and early modern European life, and particularly in the region around the North Sea, should be seen in this light.

In this chapter we have focused on the developments occurring during the late Middle Ages. From the sixteenth century onward, however, things began to change for working women in the western European labor market. In this later period, real wages declined sharply, making it increasingly difficult for women and men to survive on labor alone.[129] The wages for women probably fell more than those for men, owing to a female labor surplus, a situation that probably depressed the wages of unskilled workers more than those of skilled workers.[130] As we have seen, the average age of marriage then increased dramatically—to the levels that were considered typical for the system outlined by Hajnal. From our perspective, one can perhaps argue that the fifteenth century's golden days of the EMP in the North Sea region—of self-empowerment of men and women

[127] A critical examination of this hypothesis appears in Bailey 1996; in this chapter, we have not concentrated on the "pure" demographic effects but, rather, on the social and economic consequences of the EMP.

[128] For the opposite situation, in southern France, see Leroy Ladurie 1976, 62.

[129] See Rappaport (1989, 375–387) for a more moderate view on the decline of living standards during the sixteenth century. He claims that Tudor London—contrary to the rest of England—did not experience an enormous increase in social problems and inequality.

[130] Humphries and Weisdorf 2015. Clark (2007), for example, estimated that in England, relative wages of women after 1599 were substantially lower than before (the difference with wages of unskilled men was 31% before and 58% after that date.

as a result of a booming labor market—were over by the sixteenth century.[131] Also, in the ideological arena, a tendency to stress parental authority returned—both among Protestants, following Luther, and among Catholics, following the counter-Reformation.

Nevertheless, the emergence of the EMP during the late Middle Ages had important long-term consequences. We have argued that income transfers between generations changed dramatically as a result. First, the young profited from increased investment in human capital. To some extent, the number of children, limited as a result of higher ages at marriage, can be considered a reproductive strategy that increased the quality (not quantity) of offspring. Investment in human capital (schooling and on-the-job training) became a normal part of life for young men and women, effectively delaying their entry into the marriage market. In short, instead of being backward-looking—for example, taking care of the parents—the household became forward-looking by investing in its offspring.[132] At the same time, the household may have become more fragile and less resilient, as predicted by the nuclear hardship hypothesis.

The elderly were the main victims of the new regime; their authority was undermined and they did not receive the income transfers that were due to parents in patriarchal marriage systems. Saving for old age was one of the options open to them, and we speculate that there are connections between the emergence of the EMP and the strong development of capital markets in western Europe during this late medieval period. Moreover, because households were smaller, the chances that they might "fail"—for example, disintegrate due to the death of one of the parents—was higher. We suggest that, in response, new institutions emerged that formed the safety networks for the old, the very young, and the infirm.

Perhaps the point can also be made that the "industrious revolution"—the changes in the orientation of households during the early modern period toward market opportunities, resulting in an increased labor supply, which, according to Jan de Vries preceded the Industrial Revolution of the eighteenth century—may be interpreted as a continuation of changes that began during the late medieval period. As de Vries has argued, the labor provided by women and teenagers played an important role in the economic transformation that occurred in the

[131] Smith (1992, 38), for example—with Goldberg—shows that the sexual composition of the urban servant labor force in York started to change by the late fifteenth century: female servants were increasingly being excluded from the craft households.

[132] Although the contrast with the Eastern way of life is not acknowledged by him and the meaning of the term is different, Goody (1983, 153) has coined the term "child-oriented" family and sees this as a consequence of the Church's preference for a family that was bound by affectionate ties and created by mutual consent.

North Sea region, resulting in the Dutch Golden Age of the seventeenth century[133] and even more importantly, the British Industrial Revolution of the eighteenth century.[134] The emergence of the EMP and the resulting success of the North Sea region in the post-1600 period was due to the development of and participation in labor markets, increased investment in human capital, and the development of capital markets. Of course, we do not claim that the EMP explains it all, but we hope to have shown that the stubborn behavior of Janne Heyndericx did make a difference.[135]

"Don't Hurtle Yourself into Marriage Far Too Soon": High Average Age at Marriage for Women

Because men and women chose their own partners, marriage under the EMP was mainly the result of a search process that could be undertaken only by young men and women mature enough to select their own partners; hence, the average age at marriage was 18 to 20 years. In contrast, systems of arranged marriages are characterized by much lower average ages, especially for girls. But within the EMP, a lot of variation was possible, depending on the level of real wages and the general state of the economy. The very high average ages at marriage that we find in western Europe in the early modern period is the result of the EMP under restraining circumstances of "high pressure"—that is, low real wages and relatively high population pressure. In the earlier fifteenth century, by contrast, the same EMP could result in a somewhat lower age of marriage, as conditions were more favorable.[136] The data that we have for late medieval Holland and

[133] See also the project "Women's Work in the Northern Netherlands in the Early Modern Period (c. 1500–1815)," at https://socialhistory.org/en/projects/womens-work-early-modern-period.

[134] De Vries 1994. In a recent paper by Voigtländer and Voth (2006), in which they address the question why the Industrial Revolution occurred in England, they distinguish two underlying causes: the EMP and the generosity of poor relief. Both were, as we have demonstrated, interrelated and rooted in the changes in reproductive strategies and labor market orientation of the late medieval period.

[135] The comparison with China may be instructive once more; Goldstone 1996 argues that there existed a stage in the life of European women (between puberty in their early teens and marriage in their mid-twenties or later) during which they were available for the wage labor market, which is different from China. Chinese women did not have such a stage in their lives and were thus not available for the wage labor market, although—as is commonly known—China did have the technical skills available. Factories could not compete with the household laborers who worked for next to nothing. Goldstone claims that the development of cotton spinning was slow in China because of restrictions on the deployment of female labor outside the home, as a consequence of Confucian ethics.

[136] Youngs 2006, 137, discusses some evidence that average age of marriage fell after the Black Death of 1348, and rose in the second half of the fifteenth century as a result of contracting economic opportunities.

Zeeland, for example, point to a relatively low age of marriage. In the sources of 1505—from which we cited the story of Janne—we find a number of married men who are 20 years of age, a man of 22 with a wife and four children, and another man, Adriaen Jansz, citizen of Middelburg, 21 years old, who married his wife Cornelie Adraen Vierloesdochter van Vijkenkercke three years earlier in a ceremony that was "clandestine and in order to get absolution," probably against the will of her parents, who seemed to be of noble descent.[137] On the basis of this evidence, it seems that in 1505 in Zeeland, the marriage age of farmers and craftsmen was 20 or slightly lower. For 1540–41, another rather fragmentary source allows us to estimate the average marriage age of a group of men and women in the countryside around Leiden (the source mainly contains information on proto-industrial households). It appears that women probably married at the age of 20 or 21 ($n = 10$), whereas men were one or two years older (21–22) ($n = 29$); still, a large share of men and women married before they reached the age of 20.[138] These estimates are comparable to those for fifteenth-century England, which show a range between 18 and 23 years (for women). Goldberg suggests, for example, that rural women in Yorkshire married in their late teens and early twenties, but urban women waited until their early to mid-twenties.[139] In both countries, the average age of marriage increased considerably during the sixteenth century,[140] to reach the levels thought to be characteristic of the EMP by Hajnal in the second half of the sixteenth century. In the 1580s and 1590s, the mean age at first marriage for women in Amsterdam fluctuated (according to as yet unpublished research by Hubert Nusteling) between 23.5 and 25 years, and it remained at this level until the 1660s, when it rose still further. The mean age at marriage for men was about 1 to 1.5 year higher, on average. Of 8,052 men who married in Amsterdam between 1578 and 1601, only 118 (1.5%) were younger than 20, and nobody was younger than 18 years, whereas almost half (47.5%) were older than 25.[141] Similarly, in the first decades of the seventeenth century, the average age of (first) marriage in England had increased to more than 25 for women and about 27.5 for men.[142] Whereas Hajnal considered those high marriage ages to be one of the fundamental characteristics of the EMP, we propose that they were to some extent the result of the deterioration of living

[137] On the other hand, the same sources reveal two men, aged 31 and 30, who are still single and living with their mother (and in the first case, with three unmarried sisters).

[138] See van Zanden 1993, 28.

[139] Data are very scarce; see Kowaleski 1998, 41–45, offering the best recent overview; see also Kowalski 1999, app., p. 326; see also Smith 1979 for a discussion of some of the evidence, and Youngs 2006, 135.

[140] Hartman 2004, 39.

[141] Van Nierop 1934.

[142] Wrigley et al. 1997, 134.

standards during the sixteenth century in a system based on consensus and neolocality.[143]

The pattern found in fifteenth-century northwestern Europe is clearly different from that established for the Mediterranean region. Although it is claimed that the ages of women at first marriage in the *Catasto* could have been adjusted downward in order to make them more attractive in the marriage market, women did marry rather young in fifteenth-century Florence.[144] Women married in their late teens (on average, at age 18) while men married much later, and were much more senior than their brides (by 10 to 12 years). Celibacy was virtually unknown among the Tuscan women,[145] and remarriage of widows was rather uncommon. Men, on the contrary, did remarry, but preferably with much younger brides.[146] At the age of 21 (the average marriage age in England), a Tuscan girl could already be considered as having surpassed the marriageable age.[147] The benchmark age was 19: after that, the time to find a husband was running out.[148] Not surprisingly, the work by Herlihy and Klapisch-Zuber shows us that 97% of all Florentine women were married by the age of 25.[149]

[143] Similarly, one finds lower mean ages of marriage in colonial America, where marriage continued to be based on these rules, but the economic conditions were much better than in western Europe; cf. Gallman 1984, 613, who estimates a mean age of marriage of 20–22 years for women and of 24–26 years for men.

[144] See Molho 1998 for an interesting comparison between ages in the *Catasto* and the *Monte delle Doti* (dowry fund, where parents could submit a kind of life insurance that would be paid in full at marriage, for their newborn daughter) for 1480. His analysis shows that the older a girl grew, the lesser concordance there could be found between the—probably correct—ages in the records of the *Monte* and the registered ages in the *Catasto*. But Molho unfortunately does not tell us how much younger the girls were reported to be in the *Catasto*.

[145] For an overview of the figures on single women in Italy and elsewhere, see Kowaleski 1998, 43–45.

[146] More than 95% of the women in their late twenties mentioned in the *Catasto* were married. For the analysis of the *Catasto*, also see Herlihy and Klapisch-Zuber 1985; Smith 1992, 50n44.

[147] In this context one should also consider the importance of marriage as a way to preserve the honor of the bride and her family. References to this are made, for example, by Klapisch-Zuber and Herlihy on medieval and early modern Tuscany, but also, in a more general by Wrigley et al., 124–125:

> To oversimplify in the interests of clarity, it might be said, that in most of the major cultures of the past, marriage, at least for women, was triggered by the approach to or the attainment of menarche. Physiological change provoked individual and family action backed by social sanctions. To avoid shame the family had to arrange a match. In contrast, in England, and in some other parts of western Europe, marriage was triggered by economic circumstances and was accordingly a movable feast.

[148] See Molho 1998, 206.

[149] Herlihy and Klapisch-Zuber 1978, 215.

Much of the literature on the EMP has concentrated on its long-term effects on population growth. Essentially, the first generation of studies that follows Hajnal argued that the EMP used Malthusian preventive checks—that is, postponement of marriage until age 25 to 30, and the fact that a relatively large part of the (female) population remained unmarried—to stabilize population growth.[150] When times were bad, marriages were postponed and population growth slowed. This was contrasted (following Malthus) with the Asian or Chinese patterns, which were assumed to result in unrestricted population growth because these preventive checks were missing. The new interpretation of Chinese population development, however,[151] has shown that within marriage, levels of fertility were much lower than in Europe; this is partially explained by the practicing of infanticide and partially the effect of a lower level of fertility within marriage as such.[152] Again, it can perhaps be argued that the contrasting levels of marital fertility are to some extent the result of the underlying structures already discussed. When marriage is based on consensus—on mutual love—one expects a high "propensity to have sex," even to have sex before the actual marriage ceremony has taken place (increasing the level of marital fertility even more) since once the decision to marry has been taken, one is married "before God." The EMP, therefore, produces high levels of fertility immediately after marriage and during marriage. Arranged marriages may have a lower "propensity to have sex" or, as argued by Kok, Yang, and Hsieh in a comparative study of fertility in nineteenth- and early twentieth-century Taiwan and the Netherlands, "in arranged marriages, a large age difference between husband and wife may have obstructed the process of familiarization."[153] This seems especially true for "minor marriages," which occur in (parts of) China, characterized by the fact that the girl was taken into the household of the boy at a very early age, that they grew up together as brother and sister, and that then they were declared man and wife at a certain age. As Kok, Yang, and Hsieh convincingly show, these marriages are characterized by a low level of fertility, possibly because the spouses found it difficult to develop new sexual modes of behavior (the literature suggests that at

[150] See Wrigley et al. 1997, 479–480, for a detailed comparison with the types of preventive checks used in pre-industrial systems. They claim that in low-pressure England fertility was controlled by the timing and incidence of marriage, whereas in high-pressure France, control was achieved within marriage. For further explanation and refinement of the theory in particular regarding the situation in France, see Weir 1984.

[151] Lee and Feng 1999.

[152] Lee and Feng 1999, 8.

[153] Kok, Yang, and Hsieh 2006, 18. For an interesting discussion on the effect of age difference and marriage age on sexuality in the household in early modern Europe, see Crawford 2007, 22–24.

times they had to be forced to have sexual intercourse).[154] Living under parental authority perhaps also restricted sexual development.[155] More practical reasons that relate to the economic position of the women within the household may offer a further explanation of the lower than expected fertility. As women's work was mostly domestic, mothers were able to breastfeed their children longer than in Europe, thereby extending the period between births, as well as enhancing the survival chances of their children.

The European behavioral patterns were based on a large degree of mutual trust: teenagers from age 10 onwards (and sometimes even younger) were entrusted to the households of other individuals, the search process for a future spouse was entrusted to young adolescents, and women (and men) could actively engage in wage labor and in the social interaction that accompanied it, often in places distant from their homes, without damaging their reputation. Perhaps the best examples of these high levels of mutual trust are the practices of courting and premarital sex that emerged. The EMP as it developed after 1500—with its high marriage age—did not mean that couples who had found each other but who had postponed setting up a household had to abstain from all sexual activity. Whereas in patriarchal societies the spheres of young unmarried men and women are strictly separated—in order to protect the virginity of the girl—in western Europe, practices of courting and premarital sex developed without resulting in high levels of illegitimacy. Hartman summarizes the literature on this as follows: "couples hardly denied themselves all sexual activity. The important thing was to avoid having babies, and evidence on courting practices throughout north-western Europe reveals that couples, especially those already betrothed, often engaged in socially sanctioned sessions of petting and fondling."[156] Jan Kok, in a similar analysis of these practices in the Netherlands, points out that it was based on a remarkable degree of trust in the young people, who were allowed to enjoy these "games"—a degree of trust that in most cases was justified, as levels of illegitimacy were lower than elsewhere.[157]

[154] This is not to suggest, of course, that other factors suggested in the literature to explain the low marital fertility in China did not play a role, such as malnutrition and/or the conscious planning of children (see Kok, Yang, and Hsieh 2006).

[155] Maynes, referring to Lee and Feng. 1999, 90–92.

[156] Hartman 2004, 62.

[157] Kok 1990.

3

The Effects on Human Capital Formation

Measuring Human Capital

The process of economic growth before the Industrial Revolution in the eighteenth century has been a hot issue among economic and social historians for some time now.* The idea that the pre-1800 economy was static has been replaced with a rapidly developing literature that stresses the many forms of dynamic change that were taking place in the European economy, resulting in a relatively slow and spatially uneven process of economic development.[1] One of the factors driving the gradual expansion of the early modern European economies was investments made in human capital. Recent studies have documented the gradual rise of literacy in this period,[2] and new theoretical literature has suggested the central role played by human capital in the transition from the premodern to modern economic growth.[3] As is common among economic historians, the evolution of human capital formation has been quantified, and literacy has long been considered the most important indicator of human capital. The ability of a person to put his or her signature, usually on a marriage contract, has often

* The data on which this chapter was based were collected by several researchers; we would like to thank in particular the following colleagues: Erika Kuijpers (pre-marriage acts, *confessieboeken*, and *justitieboeken* for Amsterdam), Bibi Panhuysen (civic registers [*burgerboeken*] for Amsterdam), Bruno Blondé and Dries Lyna (census year IV), and Guy Dupont (*Doorgaande waarheden* for Brugge). Furthermore, we would like to thank Joerg Baten, Dorothee Crayen, and Peter Solar for their useful advice regarding the applied methods. For the data collection of the census of 1796, we also relied on the help of several other people, including Mr. Vandenbosch, Ms. Servranckx, and the organization Pro-Gen.

[1] A review of this debate is in van Zanden 2002b.

[2] Reis 2005, Buringh and van Zanden 2009.

[3] On growth theory, see among others Lucas 2002, Lucas 1988, and Romer 1986. This literature has led to new research about the determinants of economic growth in the long run, where these concepts are central. Compare with Reis 2005 and van Zanden 2005.

been used as the most trustworthy indicator of literacy.[4] Other forms of measurement have recently received attention as well, such as how many books were produced and/or consumed.[5] What was the price of human capital in terms of, for example, the skill premium?[6] Pioneering work by de Pleijt has also charted the growth in average years of education in England over the very long run.[7]

These alternatives were developed among others because of problems encountered with using literacy as a benchmark of human capital formation. Is a person who puts down his signature on a contract, for example, really capable of reading and writing?[8] And what does having such a capability mean for market exchanges and for saleable skills in the labor market?[9] Is literacy really the proxy for human capital that is so essential for economic development, or are other dimensions more important? Given the limitations of literacy as a measure, therefore, another approach for capturing the development of human capital is required. One such approach focuses on the capability of men and women to count and calculate, or numeracy—skills that are undoubtedly essential for every type of market environment. In most cases, we cannot measure numeracy directly, however; rather, we can build on research that suggests that a method called "age heaping" can be taken as proxy for the degree to which people can count and calculate.[10]

This idea was developed by demographers some time ago.[11] First, they considered age heaping, which is the tendency that people, when asked for their age, round off to a given number, often ending in a 5 or 0. The result of this is that ages ending with a 5 or a 0 are overrepresented, distorting the "true" age pyramids demographers are interested in deliniating. The officials who, for example, put together the Indonesian census of 1930 refused to published the results of their age structure because of the extremely high levels of age heaping they had encountered.[12] Gradually, methods were developed to correct this phenomenon, most recently by the United Nations. For example, by not asking for age but, rather, for the year of birth; or alternatively, by checking their results against existing birth certificates.

[4] Van der Woude 1980b, Kuijpers 1997, Reis 2005.

[5] Compare the estimates of book production and consumption in Buringh and van Zanden 2009.

[6] Van Zanden 2005.

[7] De Pleijt 2016a.

[8] See, for example, Sweden: 100% of the male population wrote their signatures but it turns out that their active knowledge was limited; see Reis 2005.

[9] Nilsson, Petterson, and Svensson 1999.

[10] A'Hearn, Baten, and Crayen 2009; Crayen and Baten 2006.

[11] Myers 1954.

[12] See Volkstelling 1930.

Nevertheless, scholars realized that the degree of age heaping they encounter is an important source of information in itself, and they began to develop measures to establish its levels for certain groups and particular time periods.[13] Most recently, a group of scholars led by Joerg Baten have started collecting this kind of information on a much wider, even global scale. Moreover, A'Hearn, Baten, and Crayen have systematically compared different ways of measuring age heaping.[14] They also researched the relationship between literacy and numeracy, both in present-day and historical societies, and they concluded that these indicators are closely related.[15] This means that age heaping can be used as an alternative for estimating literacy—or human capital, in its broadest sense—whenever the necessary data are lacking.[16] Thus, by measuring the degree of age heaping, we can derive new insights from these "mistakes" in historical sources. In this way, social and economic historians have opportunities for the analysis of previously neglected source material.

In this chapter, we use age heaping to chart and analyze the long-term development of human capital in the Low Countries during the late medieval and early modern periods. We do this because it has been suggested that the Low Countries had an early start in the accumulation of human capital, and that this is one of the factors contributing to the area's strong economic performance during the fifteenth to seventeenth centuries. It has also been argued that the differences between levels of human capital in towns and countryside appear to have been rather limited, possibly related to the fact that the countryside became very market oriented at an early point.[17] We also think that this high level of human capital formation is related to the marriage pattern prevalent in the Low Countries—a pattern that stimulated investment in the human capital of both men and women (a hypothesis we have explained in more detail in another publication[18]).

The literature suggests that the gender gap in human capital in this region was limited because of the relatively equal positions of men and women in marriage and in the household, and because of women's well-integrated position in market activities.[19] Following recent insights gained from development

[13] See Myers 1954 and Bachi 1951.

[14] A'Hearn, Baten, and Crayen 2009; Crayen and Baten 2006.

[15] Crayen came to the conclusion that, for the second half of the twentieth century, there is a strong relationship between illiteracy and age heaping in developing countries. On the basis of an analysis of 270,000 individuals in 416 regions of Latin America to Oceania, the correlation efficient is 0.7. See Crayen 2005.

[16] See, among others, A'Hearn, Crayen, and Baten 2009; for a critical discussion of this approach, see Reis 2008. Another pioneer in this field is Mokyr 1983, 246; also Duncan-Jones 1990, 79–92.

[17] Van der Woude 1980b.

[18] See De Moor and van Zanden 2010a.

[19] See De Moor and van Zanden 2006, in particular chap. 4.

economics, moreover, we can see the economic position of women as a strategic variable in economic development: women's empowerment affects not only demographic behavior (high levels of female human capital formation tend to lead to a decline in fertility) but also human capital formation in the next generation (via the choice for quality versus quantity of offspring).[20] Though these ideas stem from a long and rich historiographical tradition, they have as yet not been tested systematically; we hope to do this here by studying new data for the Low Countries and by viewing the findings from an international comparative perspective.

Literature on gender and human capital is currently dominated by the debate regarding the literacy levels of men and women—particularly that showing a fairly consistent image of men having a (much) higher level of human capital than women. This conclusion is usually based on the fact that a larger percentage of men signed agreements or contracts, the difference often amounting to 20% or more.[21] In this chapter, we show that age-heaping results urge us to revise these conclusions considerably. Furthermore, we evaluate the relationship between numeracy and literacy in several ways. The analyses discussed in this chapter cover from the fifteenth to the end of the eighteenth century, and whenever possible, comparisons are made with other parts of Europe.

Age Heaping: Methods

The method of age heaping can most easily be illustrated on the basis of a number of graphs. The famous *Catasto* of 1427, which is a detailed census of the population of Tuscany, is the basis for figure 3.1.[22] We concentrate first on the population of 23- to 62-year-olds, which is the age group central to age-heaping research. It is clear that the ages reported by people cannot all be correct: there seem to be a remarkable number of people aged 50 or 60, and hardly anyone reported as being 49, 51, 59, or 61. This effect also seems to be somewhat stronger among women than among men, although the differences are fairly limited. Less prominent are the peaks at five-year intervals, though here as well the concentration seems to increase with age. This unnatural heaping of ages has absolutely nothing to do with peaks in fertility, but everything to do with the limited capacity of the population to estimate their own ages accurately.

By measuring the degree of age heaping, one gets an impression of the population's capacity to estimate their ages correctly, which can be shown to

[20] Cf. Schultz 1997.

[21] See, among others, the conclusions by Kuijpers 1997, Derville 1984, and Hart 1976.

[22] The *Catasto* data were taken from Herlihy and Klapisch-Zuber 1978, 656–663.

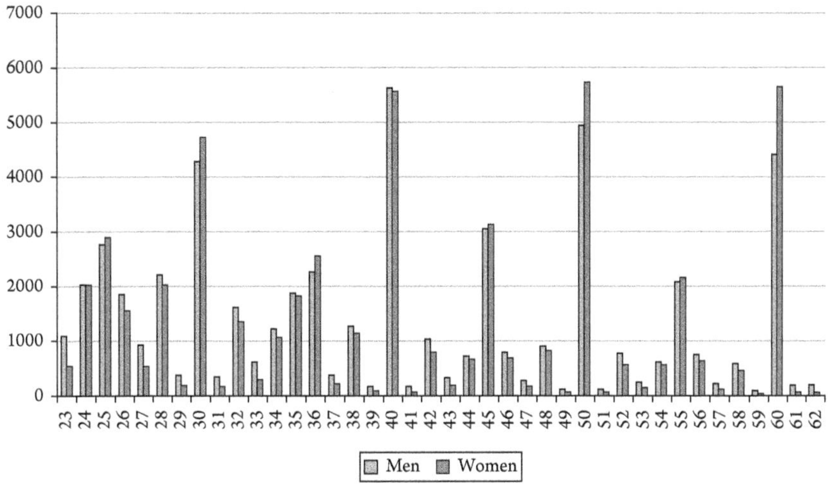

Figure 3.1 Ages of men and women in Tuscany, according to the *Catasto* of 1427.
Source: Based on tables from Herlihy and Klapisch-Zuber 1985 and previously published in De Moor and van Zanden 2010b, 179–208.

relate to a population's numeracy, as well as to its capability to count and calculate.[23] Herlihy and Klapisch-Zuber, on whose data the figures for Tuscany are based, show moreover that age heaping diminishes when the social position of the respondents is higher (richer people "age heap" less than poorer people) and between rural and urban populations (in the city, people are more aware of their ages than in the countryside). This shows that age heaping is not a coincidental phenomenon related, for example, to the carelessness of the surveyor; rather, it has a clear social and economic dimension.[24]

In the literature on age heaping, it is usually assumed that rounding off one's age is an "unconscious" choice, the consequence of a lack of knowledge about one's precise age. It is, of course, not impossible that a person might explicitly *choose* to give a wrong, possibly rounded-off, age; for example, in societies where old age is highly respected, one would expect a systematic tendency to overestimate one's age. But this is not the pattern found in our sources. One gets the impression that when, in 1514, local notables of the Holland cities and villages were interviewed, these often rather young representatives raised their ages to augment their status and authority. Elsewhere, Danneel reports for Ghent that it was not uncommon to increase the age of orphan girls so they could start as apprentices.[25]

[23] See http://unstats.un.org/unsd/demographic/products/dyb/DYBcensus/V1_Notes1c.pdf.
[24] See also Duncan-Jones 1990, 84; Mokyr 1983, 264.
[25] Danneel 1995, 236.

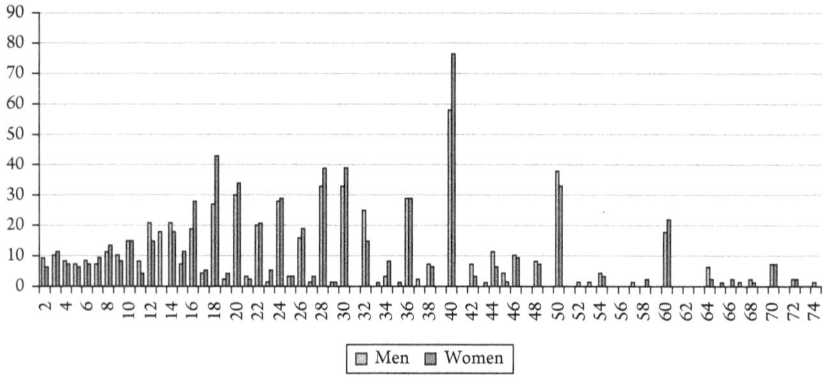

Figure 3.2 Age distribution of men and women in Reims in 1422 (2–75 years).
Source: Based on the "Tableau IX, Données brutes du dénombrement de Saint-Pierre," from Desportes 1966, 497. Previously published in De Moor and van Zanden 2010b, 179–208.

If everyone were to do this (by adding, for example, five years to his or her age), the effect on age heaping would be nil. But in practice, whenever people start rounding off or exaggerating their ages, there will be a preference for ages ending in a 5 or a 0. Similarly, there can be other motives for giving a younger age. For instance, superstition can disturb age pyramids; regarding figure 3.2, the absence of girls aged 13 in 1422 Reims is rather remarkable. Later in this chapter we show the preference for multiples of 12 that appears in our sources, which might be related to religious biases but could also be linked to economic activity. That is, people often counted in dozens; and in the currency system, dozens and their multiples played a significant role, going back to the original pound introduced by Charlemagne, which consisted of 20 shillings (*schellingen*) and 240 dimes (*duiten*). Why is heaping nevertheless most frequent in multiples of 5? The answer is probably biological: we have five fingers on each hand, and the fastest way to count is to use those fingers.[26]

For comparative research, having a method to measure age heaping in a systematic way is an absolute requirement. There are a number of measures available, some of them explicitly linked to the measurement of overrepresentations of 5 and 0 (such as the Whipple's index); other measures take into account all distortions of the expected age distribution (such as Myer's Blended index). The point here is that age heaping is a complex phenomenon, and that the degree of overrepresentation of various numbers may differ from one society to the next. Japanese seventeenth-century sources, for example, show, in addition to the usual overrepresentation of 5 and 0, a certain preference for figures ending in

[26] A discussion on the more general problem of "number sense" can be found in Dehaene 1997.

8, probably because 8 is a lucky number in Japanese culture.[27] In China, to give another example, being born in the year of the dragon is considered particularly fortuitious, and this may have consequences for age heaping.[28] Recent research by the Baten team, which aimed to put together global maps of age heaping, seems to ignore these culturally embedded forms of age heaping, which only come to light with a careful exploration of the sources.

Not just how people's ages are calculated but also whether or not people are actually interested in knowing their ages is culturally embedded. Such "age awareness" clearly changes over time and as such influences the desire of local governments to record ages as "useful" data in their censuses and other studies. As mentioned, for some studies, age was considered vital—for example, to determine the number of minors in a household—but for many others, recording people's ages would not correspond with the purpose of the (written) source. Sometimes, age awareness can lead to the emergence of specific cultural phenomena, which are then not necessarily expressed in written, but, for example, in pictorial sources. Most age-heaping studies make use of censuses or other written sources that state the ages of respondents, but other sources, such as portraits mentioning the *aetatis suae* (in the year of his or her age), can sometimes also be used for this purpose.

In this chapter, we demonstrate the potential importance of age heaping for the detection of levels of numeracy, and have therefore scanned all the sources used for typical heaping patterns. For instance, as mentioned earlier, the frequently used Whipple's index, which studies the age groups of 23- to 62-year-olds, shows the degree to which persons who report their ages as ending in a 5 or a 10 are overrepresented in the population distribution.[29] The total number of persons with an age ending in a 5 or a 10 is then divided by one-fifth of the total number of people in this surveyed age group, because this is the number of persons supposed to actually have that age. This result is then multiplied by 100.[30] By implication, a Whipple's index of 100 indicates that there is no age heaping;

[27] Hayami 2001, 24–25.

[28] A Chinese census of 1990 shows that the Han Chinese (the largest ethnic group in China) show a preference for the ages 38, 50, 62, 74, which are exactly the ages that correspond with dates of birth that fall in the year of the dragon, also the national symbol of China. For further information on the influence of age heaping as a "culturally controlled phenomenon," see Jowett and Li 1992.

[29] The United Nations gives a more complete explanation of the Whipple's index and its application; see http://unstats.un.org/unsd/demographic/products/dyb/DYBcensus/V1_Notes1c.pdf. See also the following publications for a more technical explanation of the possibilities of age heaping for historical research: A'Hearn, Crayen, and Baten 2009; Crayen and Baten 2006.

[30] The formula for the Whipple's index is as follows:

$$H_w = \frac{\sum\left(n_{25} + n_{30} + n_{35} + \ldots + n_{60}\right)}{1/5\sum_{i=23}^{62} n_i}$$

the maximum value is 500, or when all respondents report having an age ending in a 5 or a 10. The Whipple's is used only for the 23- to 62-year-old group, because in demographic terms this range is considered the most stable population group (after 62 there is a higher chance that mortality influences the patterns) and because age heaping among youngsters is less prevalent or manifests itself in other ways (by, for example, heaping more on even numbers).[31]

To deal with other forms of age heaping, we calculated indices that measure the possible overrepresentation of other age groups. For the sources used here, only our Dozen index, which measures the tendency to round off to multiples of 12, gave interesting results. The data for Tuscany, and even more so for comparable material for Reims in 1422 (presented in figure 3.2), show that these effects occur simultaneously.[32]

The Reims data show us the following: up to 12 years of age, there seems to be no clear pattern (this group is clearly underrepresented, but that is owing to other factors), suggesting that parents seem to know the ages of their children with a fair degree of accuracy. Afterwards, however, biases start to creep into the data: there are, for example, no girls aged 13. As girls, according to this source, often married just after turning 12, this absence is even more remarkable—or was no one willing to marry a girl who was 13 years old? Beyond age 13 a pattern that also occurs in other sources emerges: the even years are clearly overrepresented. There are, for example, considerably fewer boys and girls reported as being 17, 19, or 21 years old than one would expect, and this stress on even-numbered ages is continued into older age groups. This contradicts the classic preference for ages ending in 5s: 24 and 26 are more popular than 25, and 36 is preferred over 35. And 40 is the most popular age of all, especially among women.

We can summarize this by noting a few recurring patterns: the classic age heaping (a preference for numbers ending in 5 and 0), a preference for even numbers in comparison to uneven (especially among teenagers and those in

H_w gives the sum for all ages that are multiples of 5, divided by one-fifth of the total sample (of the age group 23 to 62 years old).

31 A slight bias may occur also in the other age groups because of the gradual "thinning out" of older ages, but by taking the cohort between 23 and 62 years of age, one implicitly compares—for example—those aged 60 years with the "surrounding" ages of 58, 59, 61, and 62; the 58 and 59 age groups will normally be larger than those aged 60, the 61 and 62 age groups will be smaller, but on balance, the degree of distortion will be very small. Methods have been developed to check in which age categories there was most age heaping, such as the Myer's Blended index. See A'Hearn, Crayen, and Baten 2009, 789.

32 Desportes 1966. Another striking feature of these data, which will not be discussed here, is the small size of the age groups below age 10, compared with those of teenagers and those in their (early) twenties, which may be related to the fact that immigration concentrated in the latter age groups and/or the fact that the post-1347/48 plague epidemics tended to cause more fatalities among the (very) young than among (young) adults.

their twenties) and, a special version of the latter: a preference for multiples of 12. Thus, we claim that for the study of age heaping, the simple Whipple's index, which considers only preferences for multiples of 5 and 10, does not show us the full picture, as other "mistakes" are excluded from the index. However, it is no problem to design, analogous to the Whipple's index, other indices that do take into account the overrepresentation of even-numbered ages and the popularity of multiples of 12. Those latter indices, named the "Even" index and the "Dozen" index, have been constructed in such a way that they total 100 when there is no particular preference for even-numbered ages or multiples of 12, respectively; and just like the Whipple's index, they are over 100 when a preference for these numbers exists.[33] These indices do not overlap with the Whipple's index nor with each other, as each age preference is taken into account in only one of the indices. To avoid overlap with the Whipple's index, we have not included the multiples of 10 in the other indices; in other words, the Even index takes into account only those numbers that have not been included in the Whipple's or Dozen indices.[34] For technical reasons, the upper limit of the Even index is 320 and 1,333 is the upper limit of the Dozen index.[35]

What does numeracy in medieval Europe look like when explored with these measures? The data for Reims shows rather extreme levels of age heaping for all three indices, with only very limited differences between men and women. Women do slightly worse on the classic Whipple's index than men, but this is compensated for by their better scores on the other indices.[36] It is remarkable that in Reims, all ages ending with a 5 are seriously underrepresented. That is,

[33] To maintain comparability with the Whipple's index, the age group used for both is that between 23 and 62 years (which probably has a more or less balanced age distribution).

[34] In case of the Dozen index, we take into account the ages of 24, 36, and 48. For the Even index, only those ages that have not been taken into account in the Dozen index or the Whipple's index are taken into account, in order to avoid overlap in the results.
Formula for the Dozen index:

$$H_D = \frac{\Sigma\left(n_{24} + n_{36} + n_{48}\right)}{3/40\sum_{i=23}^{62} n_i}$$

H_D gives the total of the ages 24, 36, and 48 (multiples of 12, without 60) divided by 3/40 of the total sample.
Formula for the Even index:

$$H_E = \frac{\Sigma\left(n_{26} + n_{28} + n_{32} + n_{34} + n_{38} + n_{42} + n_{44} + n_{46} + n_{52} + n_{54} + n_{56} + n_{58} + n_{62}\right)}{13/40\sum_{i=23}^{62} n_i}$$

H_D gives the total number of even-numbered ages without those ages already included in the Whipple's and Dozen indices, divided by 13/40 of the total sample.

[35] This follows from the definition given in note 34.

[36] But, of course, one goes with the other: if one scores 500 on the Whipple's index, meaning that all ages are multiples of 5, the score on the other indices is per definition 0.

inhabitants of Reims were age heaping a lot, but did not especially "favor" numbers ending in a 5, preferring instead even numbers and multiples of 12. Of all analyses mentioned in this chapter, we found the highest Dozen and Even indices in Reims. In fact, Reims is the only place where the Even index gives significant results; we have therefore not included this index in the analysis of the Dutch data given later in the chapter.

Adding the other two indices leads to a strong increase in the estimated share of the population unable to give their exact ages. Also, in the English post-mortem figures of the thirteenth and fourteenth centuries (from pioneering work by Russell), we find high Whipple's indices.[37] Lastly, the Tuscan data have been included in table 3.1, split between the city of Florence and the rest of Tuscany, which consists mostly of countryside, though cities like Pisa and Siena have also been included (the age heaping in rural areas must have been even more extreme).

Florentine men were fairly good at counting, but urban women were lagging well behind. The latter did better, however, than men and women in the country. The Dozen index has no high values, and the rural Even index is smaller than 100, owing to the popularity of ages ending with a 5. Thus, the data analysis shows that in Tuscany, ages ending in multiples of 5 contributed considerably to the age-heaping effect (this in contrast to the findings for Reims). Duncan Jones has suggested that the preference of the Romans for these numbers was related to the celebration of lustrums, and one could speculate that this tradition continued in Tuscany.[38] What is also remarkable is the low value of the Dozen index in England compared to that of Reims. We can summarize that in the late Middle Ages, age heaping was still a common practice, with an estimated 35 to 45% of the population reporting a rounded-off age. Only the men in Florence did considerably better. Women usually had a lower level of numeracy than men.[39]

How important are these different levels of age heaping? The ability to count and calculate is without doubt of fundamental importance for the efficient functioning of a market economy. According to Max Weber, rational calculation of profit is even part of the "essence" of capitalism,[40] and he attributed quite a large role to it in the introduction of modern ("Italian") bookkeeping during the rise of capitalism. One does not have to agree with this position to acknowledge that there is likely a link between the ability to make complex calculations—which are necessary for "rational" conduct in the marketplace—and a certain

[37] Russell 1948, 108–111.

[38] Duncan-Jones 1990, 90.

[39] To put these European estimates into perspective: for Cairo in 1848, we found a Whipple's index of 471; see Alleaume and Fargues 1997.

[40] Weber 1978, 334–335.

Table 3.1 **Whipple's, Even, and Dozen Indices for England (Thirteenth to Fourteenth Centuries), Reims (1422), and Tuscany/Florence (1427)**

	England	*Reims*			*Tuscany*			*Florence*		
	Male	*Male*	*Female*	*Total*	*Male*	*Female*	*Total*	*Male*	*Female*	*Total*
N	225	343	362	705	53327	51508	104835	7849	6509	14358
Whipple's (H_W)	256	224	243	234	272	307	289	176	250	209
Even (H_E)	64	163	149	156	78	69	74	104	91	98
Dozen (H_D)	184	253	239	246	130	140	135	146	157	151

Sources: England: Russell 1948. Tuscany: Herlihy and Klapisch-Zuber 1985. Reims: Desportes 1966.

interest in and knowledge of one's own age. In other words, rounding off one's age is probably a sign of being unfamiliar with large numbers and of having a limited level of numeracy.

Age Heaping: Sources

Before we present our results on age heaping for the Low Countries, though, we need to deal with a few source-related issues.[41] In principle, all sources that report ages of respondents can be used for age heaping, but the origins and limitations of the sources need to be taken into account. We are, after all, not looking for an indication of the ages of a population but, rather, we need to find the proof that respondents personally reported their ages rather than their being recorded by another person, such as the head of the household. The latter, of course, may be relevant for the population census of 1796 which we use here; in some cases, the mentioning of "son frère" or "sa mère" gives the impression that these entries were contributed by a relative, not by the persons themselves.

It is not surprising that such notations are found more frequently in regard to women than to men (respectively, 27% and 9% per counted women and men; total population of 540,845). Surprisingly, however, this did not result in a higher level of age heaping among those referred to as such, suggesting that this practice did not lead to significant distortions of the data.[42] Concerning the other sources we have used here, in almost all cases it is certain that the people involved themselves informed the civil servants who prepared the documents of their age; with the exception of the census of 1796, most of our sources regarding the Low Countries are about individuals, rather than households.

A problem may arise when those being registered have a clear interest in the age documented. This interest may result in intentional misreporting and in age heaping when, for example, people might be exempted from military service or be eligible for a pension.[43] Sources for which mentioned ages are less important are, therefore, more suitable for this kind of research, in contrast to militia lists, which carry incentives for cheating. In general, we have used sources that do not have these problems.

We have concentrated on sources for the pre-1800 period. For the nineteenth century, marriage contracts are in principle useful—and widely

[41] To De Moor and van Zanden 2008 we have added an extensive appendix, in which we have described all sources that are also used in this chapter.

[42] Kerstin Manzel and Joerg Baten have both found a similar absence of the "head of household effect" in their studies on Latin America; based on a conversation with Manzel regarding her dissertation research (2008).

[43] Budd and Guinnane 1991.

available—sources for age-heaping analysis, but the introduction of population registers in the period after 1796 makes it more likely that the precise ages of the marriage partners and their parents could be deduced from official documents (rather than by recall of the individuals in question). The introduction of systematic population registers in the Low Countries in these years must have enhanced people's awareness of their precise ages, and therefore changed the conditions under which these registrations were recorded.

An additional problem with marriage contracts is that they are clustered for people around the age of 25, which leads to an overrepresentation of these age groups. Hence, the Dozen index cannot be calculated when working with marriage contracts, as the age of 24 is too common. Sources that do not report the age but do report the year or date of birth pose another problem: they can have strange concentrations of certain ages, owing to a tendency to round off birth dates.[44]

Which sources, then, are suitable for reviewing levels of age heaping? We prefer sources stating the ages of individuals (instead of households, although we also used the latter source for 1796), where the age was asked but did not play an essential role. Following these guidelines, we expect unbiased results. Below we discuss several types of sources, linked to an analysis of the numeracy of the inhabitants of the Low Countries, from the fifteenth century to the end of the eighteenth century. Sources are scarce, but they nevertheless offer enough material to test the ideas discussed in the introduction to this chapter.

Probably the most remarkable of all sources we have used are the registers of *doorgaande waarheid* (literally: "passing truths") of the neighborhood of Oost-Proosse in Bruges and the surrounding countryside, dating from the late fifteenth century and well into the sixteenth century (1475–1575).[45] The information was gathered by the bailiff and aldermen in the form of a sort of questionnaire, with the intention to trace not-yet-prosecuted crimes. Each year the inhabitants of Bruges and the surrounding area were compelled to answer a number of standard questions regarding local crimes, and they had to provide some personal details as well, including their ages and (sometimes) their occupations, which makes this an ideal source for observing age heaping.[46] Moreover, the preserved registers allow us to compare the situation in the country with that in the

[44] See the remarks of the United Nations: "where statistics on age have been derived by reference to the year of birth, and tendencies to round off the birth year would result in an excessive number of ages ending in odd numbers, the frequency of age reporting with terminal digits 5 and 0 is not an adequate measure of their accuracy" (http://unstats.un.org/unsd/demographic/products/dyb/DYBcensus/V1_Notes1c.pdf).

[45] We would like tot thank Guy Dupont for collecting the data on the Doorgaande Waarheden. For a more elaborate description of this source, see Dupont 2001, 137–139; Strubbe 1923.

[46] Boone 1998, 41. See also Dupont 2001, 137.

city, although we had to be content with just one part of the city, Oostproosse. This is a neighborhood of relatively low social status with, for example, large numbers of prostitutes.[47] A clear advantage of this dataset is its balance between male and female respondents, at least for the period until 1525. Strangely, thereafter women more or less disappear from the records. Although these limits were not always respected, the data were collected among inhabitants aged 20 to 60, which is nearly exactly the age group we need for the age-heaping analysis (23–62).[48]

The data, in combination with our knowledge of the social background of the respondents, paints a surprising picture of numeracy during this period. The average levels of age heaping by both men and women, in town and country, had Whipple's indices between 150 and 180, which are relatively low, at least in comparison with earlier mentioned values for Reims and Florence, even if we take into account that levels of age heaping may have dropped slightly in the intermediate period.[49] The absence of large differences in the values for the sexes—in Bruges, women outperformed men—is remarkable, as are the very limited differences in age heaping between those in town and those in the country (though the former value is influenced by the particular population sample for Bruges). The Dozen index is, however, very high, which might be related to the very high age-heaping values we found for Reims, with the same Catholic background (see table 3.2).

How exceptional was the situation in Bruges and its surroundings? For other parts of the Low Countries, it is harder to find comparable data, but we do have some sources, such as the famous *Informacie* of 1514, which contains the names and ages of usually three notables (the mayors or aldermen in case of towns) who reported on the situation in their town or village to the government commission that had organized this inquiry.[50] The quality of their reports is high; they are full of details, with a multitude of precise information about, for example, tax revenues and expenditures of the town or village; this amount of

[47] Dupont 1996, 65–70.

[48] The data used for this chapter concern the neighborhood of Oost-Proosse, within the city walls of Bruges, and the village of Wenduine, outside the walls; we have collected data for the period 1475–1575, but we concentrated on the first half of the period because of the absence of women in the post-1524 period; the level of age heaping by men did not change much between the first and the second half of the period.

[49] Herlihy and Klapisch-Zuber 1978, 64, point to a drop in the number of persons in Prato who let their age end in a 0, from 38% in 1371 to 28% in 1427. In 1470, this number amounted only to 16%.

[50] See Fruin 1866. The *Informacie* can be found online; see: https://socialhistory.org/en/nationalaccounts/enqueste-en-informacie.

Table 3.2 **Whipple's and Dozen Indices for Bruges (city) and Surrounding Countryside, 1474–1524**

	Men			*Women*			*Country*	*City*
	Country	*City*	*Total*	*Country*	*City*	*Total*	*Total*	*Total*
N	1,777	204	1,981	41	188	229	1,818	392
Whipple's (H_W)	158	172	159	171	168	168	158	170
Dozen (H_D)	183	137	178	163	199	192	183	167

Table 3.3 **Whipple's and Dozen Indices for the *Informacie* (1514) and Zeeland/ Holland 1505/1541**

	Informacie *1514*	*1505/1541 Men*	*1505/1541 Women*	*Total*
N	1,285	95	19	114
Whipple's (H_W)	203	168	158	167
Dozen (H_D)	112	154	70	140

detail suggests that the respondents must have had relatively high levels of numeracy and literacy.

Besides this source, there are two others that registered the ages of the more "average" inhabitants of Zeeland and Holland. The first is an ecclesiastical questionnaire of 1505 in Zeeland that contains the names and ages of 37 men and 4 women, and the other is the *Enquête naar de buitenneringen,* held in 1540/41 among the inhabitants of the countryside around Leiden, which has listings of another 58 men and 15 women recording their ages.[51] These numbers are small, but they can nevertheless put the data from Bruges in perspective (table 3.3). They do indeed show that Holland and Zeeland are quite similar to Bruges, especially in terms of Whipple's indices. Strangely, the notables who reported in the *Informacie* turn out to have had a rather high Whipple's index. Might they have had the inclination to inflate their ages in order to gain authority? Again, we find that the differences between men and women are limited, but the number of women included in the analysis is very small ($n = 19$).

[51] Posthumus 1912.

A series of sources from the end of the sixteenth century is available and these have played an important role in our research on population and literacy in the Netherlands. These are the Amsterdam pre-marriage registers (equivalent to the English marriage bans). Although they do not portray a complete age spectrum, and therefore are not suitable for calculating the Dozen index, they do have the major advantage of dealing with all levels of society and include data on literacy (signature) and occupation. The degree of literacy based on these sources has already been analyzed by L. van Nierop and Erika Kuijpers,[52] and it is on the basis of the latter's dataset and additional research into more recent sample that we have calculated the values for the Whipple's index for the 1585–1800 period (see table 3.4).

The numbers for the first sample are small, but a certain pattern does emerge: with values around 150–160, the Whipple's index for 1585 is comparable to what we have found for Holland and Flanders earlier in the sixteenth century. Thereafter, there is a strong decrease to values around 110–120, which is a remarkably low level for a preindustrial society. Again, in all years, the very small difference between the values for men and women is striking, and in some cases, women even do better than men.

The decrease of the Whipple's index from 150–160 to 110–120 runs parallel to what is known about the increase in literacy during this period, but we do find a significant difference between men and women. The percentage of men who signed the marriage contracts increases from 55% in 1585 to more than 70% in 1700; the share of literate women who signed grows in a similar way from 32% in 1585 to 51% in 1700.[53] It seems that in the Low Countries women were as numerate as men, but they still lagged behind when it came to reading and writing. Or is the story more complicated? Can it be that literate women wishing to marry illiterate men did not dare put their signatures down next to the simple cross of their new husbands? Do the pre-marriage registers systematically underestimate the level of education of women that now, via age heaping, finally surfaces? Or should we question the ideas about the parallel increases in literacy and numeracy in general?

The pre-marriage acts represent a wide spectrum of society, probably only excluding the very poor (who might not marry) and married immigrants. Data from criminal records, the *Confessie* and *Justitieboeken*, for the period 1651–1750 can be complementary, as the accused who is mentioned (with age and sometimes also profession) often belongs to those poorer social classes. These data,

[52] See van Nierop 1934 and Kuijpers 2005. The data here are based on the database compiled by Erika Kuijpers.

[53] Kuijpers 1997, 511.

Table 3.4 **Whipple's Indices on the Basis of the Amsterdam Pre-Marriage Registers, 1585, 1600, 1650, 1700, and 1800**

	1585			*1600*			*1650*			*1700*			*1750*			*1800*			*T*
	M	*W*	*Tot*	*M*	*W*	*Tot*	*M*	*W*	*Tot*	*M*	*W*	*Tot*	*M*	*V*	*Tot*	*M*	*V*	*Tot*	
N	81	66	147	242	175	417	192	143	335	261	232	493	245	240	485	171	163	334	2211
Whipple's index (H_W)	154	159	156	103	129	114	125	94	112	142	121	132	135	119	127	114	129	121	124

collected by Pieter Spierenburg,[54] contain nearly 1,500 women and men in the age category relevant to our study.

It is remarkable how many women were actually brought to court: nearly 38% of the persons of whom we know the age were female.[55] As is to be expected, the degree of age heaping in this group is higher than those who were registered in the pre-marriage records for the same period: the average Whipple's index for men is 123 ($n = 928$), and for women, 152 ($n = 558$). At the very bottom of the social pyramid are, thus, clear sex differences in age heaping, although the levels for both men and women are still remarkably low.

A third source, the Amsterdamse *burgerboeken*, the registers of persons who have acquired citizenship, is available for the period 1730–1799, and adds information on ages of the (upper) middle class.[56] The degree of age heaping in this group is very limited: the Whipple's index is 116 for men ($n = 2.146$) and 118 for women ($n = 1.912$). As Amsterdam was a city full of immigrants, their numeracy can be studied using these sources.

None of the sources mentioned here perfectly reflects preindustrial society. The lower classes and migrants are insufficiently represented in the pre-marriage records, though this can be "repaired" by adding data from the criminal records. The *burgerboeken* clearly represent the upper class. Combined, however, they do offer the possibility of comparing the levels of age heaping among Amsterdammers with that of different groups of immigrants.[57] There are two possible ways to calculate the Whipple's indices of these groups: we either add all individuals of all three sources to one dataset and calculate the relevant Whipple's indices per source per group, or we take the unweighted average of the three Whipple's indices that can be calculated on the basis of the three sources (marriage acts, criminal records, and *burgerboeken*). The advantage of the latter procedure is that, considering that the Dutch are better represented in the *burgerboeken*, there will be no bias in the Whipple's index.

Table 3.5 shows the results, subdivided according to a number of regions. Among the immigrants from the northern and southern Netherlands and France,

[54] The data and additional information on the *confessie* and *justitieboeken* are archived by DANS (Data Archiving and Networked Services). See the following persistent identifier for more information: urn:nbn:ui:13-8vl-meg. For a more thorough discussion of the criminal sources used here, see Spierenburg 1984, 208–210.

[55] Currently, about 17% of the people suspected of criminal behavior in the Netherlands are women, but this share is rising slowly; cf. Leers 2003.

[56] The data are based on a database of the *Amsterdamse burgerboeken*, compiled by Bibi Panhuysen and used for Panhuysen 2000.

[57] For a thorough description of immigrants in Amsterdam and their representation in the pre-marriage registers, see Kuijpers 2005, 85–92.

Table 3.5 **Unweighted and Weighted Average Whipple's Indices of the Dutch and Immigrant Population in Amsterdam, Sixteenth to Seventeenth Centuries**

	Country/Region of Origin														
	Netherlands			*Belgium and France*			*Germany*			*Scandinavia*			*Rest*		
	M	*W*	*Tot*	*M*	*W*	*Tot*	*M*	*W*	*Tot*	*M*	*W*	*Tot*	*M*	*W*	*Tot*
N	2055	2222	4277	266	109	375	1274	639	1913	119	76	195	128	39	167
Unweighted	118	120	119	117	128	120	121	137	127	139	151	144	125	141	129
Weighted	119	124	121	113	128	117	123	144	131	144	152	142	133	158	140

age heaping is nearly absent. The Whipple's indices are around 120, and those of women are usually somewhat higher than those of men (an effect that can be explained by the "performance" of women on the *Confessie* and *Justitieboeken*). The degree of age heaping among German immigrants, as well as among "the rest" (especially those coming from central Europe), is slightly higher. Of the men it is the Scandinavian men, who are often unskilled workers coming directly from the countryside, who have the highest incidence of age heaping.

Summary

The strong decrease in age heaping, which happened, according to A'Hearn, Baten, and Crayen in the seventeenth and eighteenth centuries, in large parts of western Europe, had already taken place in the Low Countries a few centuries earlier. Around 1500, we already find Whipple's indices indicating that only 15 to 25% of the population reported an incorrect age, which is considerably lower than the usual age-heaping levels elsewhere in western Europe (35–45%). On the basis of the data for Amsterdam, we notice a further decrease to approximately 5% in 1600, which is a level not attained until the nineteenth century in other parts of Europe. Moreover, the differences between men and women were very limited—in some cases, women even appear to be more numerate than men. The same goes for differences between the cities and the surrounding countryside; these too were surprisingly small.

The Loss of Belgium

To return to Belgium, we include here an analysis of the numeracy of the Flemish (and Dutch Limburg) population at the very end of the eighteenth century, based on the first countrywide population census taken, in the Napoleonic year IV, or 1796. This provides us with a much more complete image of the population than the pre-marriage records or civic registers.[58] The census could, however, have one shortcoming: mentions of "sa femme," "son fille" or "son fils" in the columns provided for listing a person's occupation. This suggests that the

[58] More precisely, we are dealing here with the census taken following the law of 10 Vendémiaire Year IV (October 2, 1795) about the communal police. Many of the sources date from later years, however. Each municipality was obliged to compose a list of all inhabitants older than 12 years, including address, name, age, occupation, and year of immigration. In some cases, the place of origin and the length of residence in the municipality were also reported for immigrants, with a distinction made between male and female children. For a more elaborate discussion of the historical value of this source, see Art and Vanhaute 2003, 125–126.

head of the household might have reported the ages for the whole family, but we have no precise information about this. On the other hand, the different levels of age heaping between men and women are here, again, so small that it is more likely the information was reported by the individuals personally.

The reason we close this chapter with a census dating from the end of the eighteenth century, which is the point at which most age-heaping studies start, has to do with our earlier mentioned criteria for source material. In the southern Netherlands, this 1796 census is the first systematic population survey but also the last one that could not be influenced by official population registration.[59] In fact, this census was used as the basis for later population registration. The 1796 census offers also—as far as the original documents have been preserved—the possibility of comparing the whole of the southern Netherlands and later Dutch Limburg, as the census was executed in a fairly identical way throughout the area.

Unfortunately, the 1796 census held in the northern Netherlands does not report people's ages (or occupations), which hampers a comparison for the whole of the Low Countries. In order to have a representative sample, we collected over 50,000 records, most of which deal with the countryside; the really large cities such as Gent, Antwerpen, Brussels, and Bruges, are not included here (no electronic versions of the source are as yet available), but some smaller provincial towns such as Leuven, Lier, Tienen, and Turnhout are included. Table 3.6 lists the indicators of age heaping according to current province boundaries.[60]

The first striking fact that is clear from the table is the east–west gradient in the degree of age heaping: the province of West Flanders is an area with a very low level of age heaping, followed by the province of East Flanders and Antwerp. The two provinces of Limburg (in the west, Belgian Limburg and in the east, Dutch Limburg) have much higher scores, with Whipple's indices close to 200, whereas the Walloon part of Brabant has the highest index. This east–west gradient, with a decrease in human capital the farther one moves away from the North Sea coast, is even more remarkable, as the data we have for the top-scoring provinces of West and East Flanders are mainly data from rural locations,[61] and it might be supposed that rural numeracy would have been lower than that found in urban locations. A closer look at the underlying data shows that this premise is not a general rule: the city of

[59] Officially, the southern Netherlands started with the "Registers van Burgerlijke Stand" after the French decree of June 17, 1796. In practice, it would take some time before registration really started. See, further, Art and Vanhaute 2003, 143–145.

[60] Ages were noted systematically in the census. In only 1.4% of all the data collected was there no age reported. In total, we collected 51,572 nominative data spread out over 55 villages and cities, of which we had ages for 49,016 persons (25,872 men and 23,145 women). For 33,442 persons, we could also indicate the sex in the age group 23–62 years old. More information on the data used can be found in De Moor and van Zanden 2008.

[61] The data for West Flanders also include the city of Kortrijk.

Table 3.6 **Levels of Age Heaping in the Southern Netherlands, 1796**

	WEST FLANDERS			*EAST FLANDERS*			*ANTWERP*			*FLEMISH BRABANT*			*WALLOON BRABANT*		
	M	*W*	*Tot*	*M*	*W*	*Tot*	*M*	*W*	*Tot*	*M*	*W*	*Tot*	*M*	*W*	*Tot*
N	731	678	1,409	576	521	1,097	3,643	4,049	7,692	9,130	6,155	15,285	782	798	1,580
Whipple's (H_W)	123	117	120	165	156	161	154	141	147	167	151	161	220	193	206
Dozen (H_D)	131	153	142	79	187	130	106	123	115	98	111	103	114	147	131

	BELGIAN LIMBURG			*DUTCH LIMBURG*			*Total*
	M	*W*	*Tot*	*M*	*W*	*Tot*	
N	2,651	2,650	5,301	545	533	1,078	33,442
Whipple's (H_W)	195	176	185	192	200	196	163
Dozen (H_D)	98	111	104	110	133	121	111

Lier does better than the province of Antwerp (Whipple's indices for men/women/total: 126/129/128); similarly, Hasselt (171/163/167) does better than the average for Belgian Limburg, but Leuven (171/175/171) and Tienen (196/164/180) do not perform better than the rest of Flemish Brabant, while Turnhout—situated farther east in a less commercialized and poorer area than Lier—has much higher Whipple's indices (174/150/161) than Lier, which is closer to Antwerp.[62] On average, then, the differences between city and country are quite small.

If we now consider the differences between the sexes, it turns out that women do better in nearly all parts of Belgium on the Whipple's index than men; only in Dutch Limburg is the opposite true. Again, we find proof that the distribution of this aspect of human capital over the sexes is quite different from that suggested by the data on literacy, for which women always have much lower levels than men.[63] The Dozen index suggests that women systematically use more multiples of 12 when reporting their age. Nowhere, except in the very well developed province of West Flanders, do men also have a preference for multiples of 12, whereas women age-heap on 12 nearly everywhere—in some cases, to such an extent that the Dozen index equals "medieval" values. Is this an effect of the different religiosity of women and men? Though it is an interesting phenomenon, we cannot give a clearcut explanation here.

It is difficult to compare these data with our information on age heaping in Bruges and its surroundings during the fifteenth and sixteenth centuries. The 1796 values we find for West Flanders are clearly much lower than the levels of age heaping as presented in table 3.2. The increase in numeracy we found for Holland may also have occurred in Flanders and Brabant, and the levels of numeracy at the end of the eighteenth century are quite high, although only the province of West Flanders can actually match the levels we found for Holland.

This comparison however does show that the data we used for Bruges and its surroundings from the late Middle Ages are probably more exceptional than we initially assumed, considering that this province was the most advanced in the southern Netherlands in 1796. Lastly, the levels of age heaping we found for 1796 for Limburg and the Walloon part of Brabant are not very different from what we find elsewhere in western Europe—at some point between 1500 and 1800, these parts of the southern Netherlands probably lost their advantage over the rest of the continent.[64]

[62] Concerning the analysis of data for Hasselt and more information about the broader context, see Lyna 2005; for Waals-Brabant, we only have data for Waver, which makes it impossible to make the urban–rural comparison.

[63] For more on literacy in Belgium during the eighteenth and nineteenth centuries, see Ruwet and Wellemans 1978.

[64] Van der Woude 1980b.

Literate and/or Numerate?

In their research recent, A'Hearn, Baten, and Crayen examined the relationship between literacy and numeracy in both present-day and historical societies and came to the conclusion that the two are closely related.[65] This suggests that age heaping could also serve as an alternative for estimating literacy when the necessary data for the latter indicator are not available. Can we draw the same conclusions on the basis of our research?

The pre-marriage registers of Amsterdam can help us to make some inferences about the link between numeracy and literacy. Because of the limited amount of data, we have combined the different samples in order to get sufficient critical mass for our analysis. The degree of literacy, or the degree to which one could sign the marital act with a real signature, was quite different between men and women: of the sample studied for the period 1585 to 1800, 71% of the men and "only" 50% of the women signed the contract—figures that, when viewed from an international perspective, are very high.[66] However, the relationship between literacy and age heaping is quite weak, which perhaps follows from our earlier conclusion that the differences in age heaping between men and women were very small (table 3.7). On average, persons able to sign their name have a slightly lower Whipple's index than those who could only mark with an X, but this not really surprising result is only due to the positive relationship between literacy and numeracy among women. Strangely enough, we find a reverse result among men: literate men have a higher Whipple's index than illiterate men!

Calculating the Whipple's index per occupational group gives us a different insight into numeracy as human capital (table 3.8). We conducted this exercise on the basis of the pre-marriage contracts for the years 1600 and 1650, and only for the men (after about 1590, the marriage contracts do not register the occupation of women anymore; after 1700, they stop doing this for men as well). For both years, we have a fairly small sample of men whose occupation is registered (1600: n = 218; 1650: n = 185). Nevertheless, the data confirm our expectations: professionals, including surgeons, doctors, chemists, and merchants, have very low Whipple's values, but their sample is also very small. Craftsmen and small retailers also had low levels of age heaping, and those of unskilled laborers are only marginally higher—again confirming the high levels of human capital for even those persons classified as having no skills (such as sailors and cloth shearers), especially compared with the rest of Europe.[67]

[65] A'Hearn, Baten, and Crayen 2009, 783–808.

[66] Compare the estimates in Reis 2005; and Allen 2003, 403–443.

[67] See, for example, the estimates of literacy and numeracy for European sailors in van Lottum and van Zanden 2014.

Table 3.7 **Whipple's Index for Total Number of Records of Pre-Marriage Contracts, 1585, 1600, 1650, 1700, 1750, 1800) (per sex and per ability to sign name)**

	Literate Men	*Illiterate Men*	*Men Total*	*Literate Women*	*Illiterate Women*	*Women Total*	*Total*
N	847	345	1192	505	514	1019	2211
Whipple's	129	122	127	109	134	122	124

Table 3.8 **Whipple's Index for Amsterdam Pre-Marriage Contracts in 1600 and 1650 (only men), According to Occupational Category**

	Craftsman	*Unskilled laborer*	*Professional*	*Total*
1600: *N*	123	92	3	218
Whipple's (H_W)	102	109	n.a.	103
1650: *N*	105	63	17	185
Whipple's (H_W)	124	127	59	119

We can do a similar analysis for the southern Netherlands in 1796. The census allows us to make more distinctions between occupational categories, and it includes categories that were absent in Amsterdam, such as farmers and the religious. This gives a broader perspective on numeracy for the whole of society.[68] The results are not all that surprising (table 3.9): the men indicated as poor or with an equivalent status, such as beggar or orphan or cripple, are very infrequently able to report their real ages, given the Whipple's index of around 300. All other categories do a lot better. Remarkable here is that unskilled laborers, farmers, and craftsmen do not differ much, which confirms the very small differences we found for Amsterdam between the first and the last group. The professionals, including occupations such as the civil servants and teachers, have a rather high level of age heaping, with a Whipple's index of 151. What is

[68] Craftsmen and small retailers: for this category, we have included persons who were registered as craftsmen, such as baker, sculptor, butcher, decorator, broom maker, inn keeper, brewer, boatsman, salesman/retailer, shoemaker, ropemaker, etc. Wage laborers: this includes persons with as an occupation, such as servant/maid, day laborer, and helpers of craftsmen. Professionals and civil servants: we included occupations such as doctor, notary, lawyer, surgeon, director, and other persons considered as civil servants, such as clerks, officers, mayors, and teachers. Religious persons: this category includes pastors, priests, canon, and curates, but also beguines. Poor: this category includes those registered as poor, beggars, needy, crippled, mentally ill, and orphans. Occupations in agriculture: these include forestry and livestock farming, farmers, ox farmers, foresters, cow and sheep herders, and pig tenderers.

Table 3.9 **Age Heaping in the Southern Netherlands in 1796, According to Occupational Category (men)**

	Craftsman	*Poor*	*Agriculture*	*Unskilled laborer*	*Religious*	*Professional*	*Total*
N	5,002	53	3,060	5,382	193	529	14,219
Whipple's (H_W)	171	302	172	175	163	151	170
Dozen (H_D)	98	50	94	100	83	111	32

particularly remarkable is that all categories have lower numeracy than shown in the analysis of the Amsterdam pre-marriage registers of 1600 and 1650. Whereas parts of the Low Countries were leading in terms of human capital investment in the fifteenth, sixteenth, and seventeenth centuries, it seems that Belgium around 1800 had lost its initial advantage over the rest of western Europe in this regard.[69]

Lastly, we can for the end of the eighteenth century, also analyze regional differences in literacy and age heaping in the southern Netherlands. The degree of literacy in the south was still, in comparison with the rest of western Europe, rather high, although this applies more to Brabant than to Flanders.[70] The figures in table 3.10 indicate that also in this perspective, Belgium was no longer part of the advance guard. The regional pattern is, moreover, different from that of numeracy. Whereas the latter had a clear west–east gradient, the degree of literacy seems to be high in (Flemish) Brabant, whereas Flanders does not have particularly high levels of literacy (in particular, not for literacy of women). There does not appear to be a close link between literacy and age heaping, which suggests that when charting changes in age-heaping patterns, we are studying a different aspect of human capital than literacy.

Indications of Ages on Early Modern Portraits

Finally, we look at another way to reconstruct levels of numeracy, this time on the basis of a particular source: portraits. As we pointed out earlier, the inhabitants of the early modern Low Countries were increasingly "age aware." They made this

[69] Vandenbroeke 1981.

[70] Van der Woude 1980b, 262–264. Compare also with estimates of levels of literacy for a number of other European countries, in Allen 2003.

Table 3.10 **Estimates of the Degree of Age Heaping and Literacy of the Population of the Southern Netherlands, 1796 and 1778–1792**

Provinces	*Age Heaping (Whipple's Index)*			*Literacy (Percent of Population)*		
	M	*W*	*Total*	*M*	*W*	*Total*
West Flanders*	123	117	120	49	24	37
East Flanders*	165	156	161	49	23	36
Flemish Brabant**	160	146	154	62	39	50
Walloon Brabant**	220	193	206	53	40	46
Belgian Limburg**	195	176	185	48	28	38
Dutch Limburg***	192	200	196	66	42	54

Sources: Algoet and Vandenbroeke 1977; Ruwet and Wellemans 1978. Both show that the increase in literacy in the first half of the nineteenth century was very modest. The development of literacy in Belgium shows similar traits as that of England, the other early industrializing country that also faced a long stagnation of literacy during the industrialization process. Compare also with Stephens 1990, 72.

Data on literacy is as follows: *Data on ca. 1785 are taken from Algoet and Vandenbroeke 1977, 154–155.**Data on 1779 are taken from Ruwet and Wellemans 1978, 24–28.***Data on 1813–1819 are taken from van der Woude 1980b, 260.

visible in, among other things, the portraits of the well-to-do. Portrait painting became a major genre in the Low Countries during the fifteenth to seventeenth centuries. More than 50,000 portraits from this period that were painted in the former northern Netherlands have survived to today.[71] Art historians view the portrayal of individuals, sometimes in the company of family members, as a clear indication of the emergence of an individual identity. But what were the specific motivations for having one's portrait or that of a family member or friend painted? There are many answers to this question.

Very generally, portraits were painted to remember the person portrayed. Another obvious reason was prestige, which was true for the rising middle class, as well as the nobility. Noteworthy is that for the portraits of this latter group, there are often no references to age. Our analysis does, indeed, show that the majority of indications of age are on paintings of burgers, immortalized in, what

[71] This is an estimate on the basis of contents of the images database of the *RKD-Nederlands Instituut voor Kunstgeschiedenis*. The chapter is based mainly on data from a selection of cases from those collected by the RKD and by the *Museum voor Schone Kunsten* (MSK) in Brussels. We would like to express our gratitude to Rudi Ekkart, Peter Voorloop, Sabine Craft-Giepmans of the RKD, and Sabine van Sprang of the MSK.

Figure 3.3 Portrait of Elisabeth van Culemborg. Source: Photo by René Gerritsen-Kunst en Onderzoeksfotografie. Collection Elisabeth Weeshuis Museum.

are called, regent portraits.[72] Portraits were made as a way to commemorate the sitter, often pictured in his or her family context. In a substantial number of cases, this commemoration should be considered a token of gratitude for the generosity of the sitter, as in the portrait of Elisabeth van Culemborg, accompanied by both her (deceased) husbands, all of them painted as if they were age 30 at the time (*etatis cuiuslibet eoru(m) circa an xxxi*) (see figure 3.3.).[73]

For many such early modern paintings and engravings, studies of numeracy can be based on an inscription indicating the age of the sitter; in some cases, the information is recorded on the back of the portrait.[74] In the Low Countries,

[72] Adams 1997.

[73] As explained later, for a number of reasons we have not included this portrait in our database.

[74] For our analysis, we have also considered such information when written on the backs of paintings, assuming that this would have the same informative value as if it had been on the front,

Figure 3.4 Close-up of the *aetatis* reference "*aetatis* 34 1622" on the painting of Grietje Adriaendr Groote, probably painted by Jacob Waben (1622). Source: Collection Westfries Museum inv. No. 00238.

these inscriptions were usually accompanied by the term *aetatis* or *aetatis suae*, meaning "at the age of," and the age was often given in Roman numerals; sometimes the sitter's name and the year was also included (see figure 3.4). (The term *aetatis suae* is not only frequently indicated on portraits of the period but is also a standard term on gravestones, although these are not included in our study.[75]) Usually, the reference to the age of the sitter is in Latin, but there are some cases in which it was indicated in German or Dutch, as in the painting of Jost Amman[76] and in a number of Dutch paintings; for the latter, instead of *aetatis suae*, the age was preceded by *out* (equivalent to the English "old").[77] For our study, we used

although indeed there is no absolute certainty as to when this information was added (but this goes, of course, also for inscriptions on the front).

[75] Van Belle 2006. We have not included any of these in our analysis: as the person the age refers to would have been dead when the tombstone was engraved, it is not likely that this person had reported his or her age directly to the engraver.

[76] De Jongh 1986, 20.

[77] See, for example, the painting by Zierick Florisz, or the painting of a child by Peter van Lint, painted in 1645 (currently in the Royal Museum of Fine Arts in Antwerp), which has the notation "OUT 5 M. Den 16 MAERT A°1645," meaning "age 5 months on March 16, 1645" (Service de la

Figure 3.5 Portrait of Meynerts dr. Semeyns, in honor of her marriage to Jan Huygen van Linschoten (April 2, 1595) at the age of 31. Portrait by Jan Claesz. Source: Collection Stichting Portret van Enkhuizen

the data derived from portraits of partners so as to study the difference in numeracy between men and women.

These *aetatis suae* inscriptions on portraits are a typical northwestern European—and in particular, Dutch, Flemish and English—custom that began in the fifteenth century. They are often associated with the historic emergence of the individual and the modern family, as recognition of an individual's age was an important factor in that individual's position in society (see figure 3.5).[78] By the middle of the seventeenth century, this custom of inscribing ages on portraits had dwindled substantially, but in later periods the inscriptions can still be found occasionally. For example, paintings by an early American (eighteenth-century)

Propagande Artistique 1952, 40); see also the painting of an unidentified mother and daughter by Jacob Adriaensz Backer, which carries the inscription "O]VT.80 JAREN/NO.1639" and "OYT [OUT].6.JA" (Craft-Giepmans and de Vries 2012).

[78] Ariès 1962, 15–18; Wrightson 1982, chaps. 3–4.

painter often referred to as the "*Aetatis suae* Limner [of Albany]," contain the expression as a way for the artist to invoke an old European tradition that by that time had long ended.[79]

As with all age-heaping studies, we need to be careful which sources we use and which are not suitable. De Moor and Zuijderduijn developed a list of criteria in order to exclude as many "problematic" mentions of ages as possible.[80] Based on those criteria, a dataset of 1,807 portraits, of which 648 were of women and 1,159 were of men, all indicated within the range of 23 to 62 years of age, was developed. The age distribution (according to the reported age) in the dataset was fairly uniform over the various age categories, but there was a majority for the age category 23–30 for women and 31–40 for men. This is as expected, as weddings were particularly important occasions for (pairs of) portraits. These are also the respective age categories in which most portraits that were part of a pair could be found.[81] The dataset thus consists of data for the period 1439 to 1799, of which very few actually date from the fifteenth century.

The levels of age heaping in this dataset were very low compared to other areas, such as southern Europe, with a Whipple's index of 117.3 (see table 3.11). This indicates that the collection of sitters in this group was extremely numerate. The dataset is divided into subperiods of 50 years each, which enables us to see an evolution in the level of age heaping from 112 for the second half of the sixteenth century to 122 in the first half and 117 in the second half of the seventeenth century (see figure 3.6). Subsequently, there is a drop in the eighteenth century to a score below 100 in the first half of the century (which means that ages ending with 5 and 0 are underrepresented, which must be the statistical anomaly).[82] For the seventeenth century, this finding is in line with those for Amsterdam (see earlier in this chapter), although the level of age heaping does not increase in the eighteenth century.

[79] Cf. Blackburn 2003; Piwonka 1991; Quimby 1971. For the record, these paintings have not been added to the sample we used for this chapter. Even in the twentieth century, dating was used on some occasions, as in the portrait by Gabriel Ferrier done to commemorate the art collector Harry Elkins Widener (1885–1912), who died when the *Titanic* sunk, *aetatis suae* 27. But clearly, including inscriptions was most popular during the Dutch Golden Age.

[80] Portraits that met one or more of the following criteria were not included in the portraits database that appears in De Moor and Zuijderduijn (2013): portraits that were made after the death of the sitter; portraits with more than one sitter; copies of older portraits; portraits that included deceased sitters; portraits that were of a clear mythological nature; portraits in which the sex of the sitter could not be identified; and portraits with sitters younger than 23 or older than 62.

[81] Eighty-five of 249 such cases for women were found in the age category 23–30, and 138 of 448 such cases were found in the age category 31–40 for men.

[82] We have excluded any cases before 1600 and after 1800, as the total number was too small; because of this, the total Whipple's index for the period shown in figure 3.6 is slightly different compared to the total Whipple's index for the whole dataset.

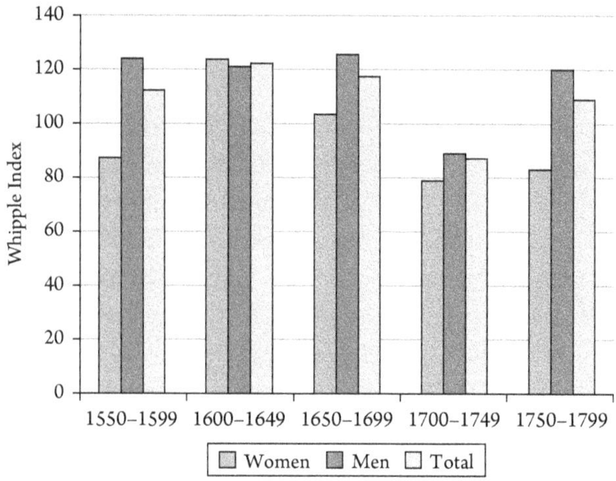

Figure 3.6 Whipple's index per half century, per sex and total
Whipple's indices per half century, per sex

	1550–1599	***1600–1649***	***1650–1699***	***1700–1749***	***1750–1799***
Women	87.63	124.33	103.60	78.95	83
Men	124.39	121.42	125.65	89.55	120.25

Note: In some cases, in particular the beginning and end of the studied period, the Whipple's index drops below 100. This is most likely because our sample sizes are small for these periods, as some random individuals preferring non-round-off ages might therefore weigh heavily in these calculations.

Source: Portrait database. Previously published in De Moor and Zuijderduijn 2013, 41–56.

For the upper classes, this should not be surprising: their level of education would probably be less affected by economic downturns than would that of the population in general, or women are at least as good in counting and calculating as men (a total Whipple's index of 113 for women versus 119 for men). Looking at the distribution of the data over the ages, it immediately becomes clear that most of the differences in age heaping are probably due to the much higher age heaping among men of 50 years and older. This is truer for men than for women over 50, compared to younger men and women. Remarkably enough, there is no age heaping at all at the age of 30 for men, which could have been expected in light of the symbolic value of these ages.

Although these results suggests that women's numeracy may be slightly overestimated when married women are included, the overall picture of numeracy levels for women remains remarkable: women scored the same as men, and both sexes did particularly well. Whereas for lower-class women, their activities in local trade may have contributed to lower age-heaping levels compared

Table 3.11 **Whipple's Indices for Women and Men in Stand-Alone Portraits and on Pendants**

	Pendant Women	*Single Women*	*Total Women*	*Pendant Men*	*Single Men*	*Total Men*	*Total*
N	249	399	648	448	711	1159	1807
H_w	110	115	113	126	115	119	117

Source: De Moor and Zuijderduijn 2013, 41–56.

to those of men (especially in the more commercial areas, such as the coastal region of the Low Countries), middle- and upper-class women are unlikely to have been involved in selling at all. The only explanation that can be given for women's excellent performance in numeracy among the "portrait classes" would be that they had better education in arithmetic.

How Numerate Were the Inhabitants of the Low Countries?

Historical research about numeracy on the basis of age heaping is still in its infancy, but in this chapter we were able to show that for the preindustrial period, there are quite a few possibilities to demonstrate numeracy—and undeniably, also various problems. It is clear that with this method we are measuring something else than literacy, although it is likely that in the long run there is a relationship here with this more traditional measure of human capital. In terms of degree of literacy, it has been suggested that from the late Middle ages onward, the Low Countries were running ahead of the rest of western Europe, though there is still insufficient quantitative proof for this.[83] Elsewhere, we have claimed that other indicators of human capital formation, such as the skill premium and book consumption, point in the same direction, toward a vanguard role for the Low Countries.[84]

The age-heaping material, even with all its flaws, contributes to this image: in (the surroundings of) Bruges and in Holland/Zeeland, we find as early as 1500 that levels of numeracy are unique for western Europe in the late Middle Ages. Whereas elsewhere in western Europe, 35 to 45% of the population reported a wrong age, this percentage was only around 15 to 20 in the Low Countries of 1500. Thereafter, in the sixteenth century it dropped to 5% or less. This means

[83] See, among others, Derville 1984, Kuijpers 1997, and van der Woude 1980b.
[84] Buringh 2014.

that the numeracy revolution that took place elsewhere between 1600 and 1900 was completed in (parts of) the Low Countries by 1600.

Our hypothesis about the advantage of the Low Countries is hereby confirmed, including the related hypothesis that differences between town and country were small. We also found that this revolution affected both men and women. The strong position of women in the world of numeracy is probably the most surprising outcome of our research; in this respect, the Low Countries as early as the late Middle Ages appear to have been very different from other parts of western Europe. Flemish and Dutch women were able to count and calculate as well as men, and were—following Max Weber—therefore perhaps as representative of the capitalist spirit as their male compatriots.

The late eighteenth-century data also suggest that this revolution took place in a rather limited area, along the North Sea coast. Further inland, the level of age heaping in 1800 was not very different from that of the rest of Europe. The situation of these regions around 1500 has not been reconstructed, which makes it hard to conclude whether there was a backlash at some point (as suggested for the eighteenth century by Algoet and Vandenbroeke),[85] or whether these regions were constantly lagging behind the North Sea area with its medieval "girl power."

[85] Algoet and Vandenbroeke 1977, 42–178.

4

The Effects on Capital Market Development

The Importance of Capital Markets for Economic Development

Capital markets enter the story of the European Marriage Pattern (EMP) in a number of ways. First and foremost, the new marriage system with its focus on neolocality required people to save money in secure ways. Savings were necessary for setting up a new household upon marriage, in contrast to a patrilocal system, in which the married couple moved into an existing household—that of the father of the groom. And savings were necessary as a buffer against the loss of earning power that would be incurred in old age, again in contrast to a patrilocal system in which the aged were taken care of by their married children. Of course, such savings could take many forms, particularly commodities. The to-be-married couple typically collected clothes, linen, utensils, and perhaps furniture in preparation for establishing the new household, and these items formed the beginnings of their assets, or savings. Or, they may simple have stored extra money in a safe place to use when required. But the most flexible way of saving was to make use of an efficient capital market that offered income-earning assets (annuities, bonds) or to invest in real assets themselves (land, shares in companies, etc.). In this chapter, we explore whether the capital markets in late medieval Holland offered this kind of service to the men and women living there.

There are additional reasons why the study of the Holland capital markets during this period can shed some light on the issues analyzed in this book. The degree to which women had access to the capital markets can be seen as an important proxy for their societal status and economic position. Moreover, as acknowledged by the recent microcredit/microfinance movement, facilitating women's access to capital markets at that time could enhance overall economic development, as this would encourage relatively poor men and women to develop their entrepreneurial capabilities.[1] This research may also lead to a new examination of the sources of economic growth in western Europe: What role did capital markets play in the area's economic development, and when did (more or less) "modern" capital market institutions originate?

There is a large literature on the "financial revolution" that took place in different parts of western Europe, and it partially addresses this question.[2] For example, various authors have identified "financial revolutions" in the fifteenth century, but these revolutions were about the (increased) capacity of states to borrow money.[3] Thus, it is not always clear how the private sector was affected by these developments. In fact, Clark and Epstein have argued that, in regard to England, there were important developments in the private capital markets that preceded this public "financial revolution" by as much as three centuries.[4] Though states have left many detailed accounts of their activities, the private sector often has no such records, and therefore it is much more difficult to reconstruct how these private capital markets functioned during this time. Who had access to credit? Who invested savings in which securities? How flexible or rigid were these markets? And how high were the interest rates on small and large loans?

New Institutional Economics (NIE) is a major source of inspiration for analyzing the problems and possibilities of today's microcredit movement and might also apply to this earlier era. The typical problem that the microfinance movement seeks to address is that, in many places in the developing world, transaction costs for small loans, typically granted to "small" female and male entrepreneurs, are very high, resulting in extremely high interest rates. This severely limits the number of projects that can be funded, and results in a lack of access to credit for both men and women. Our analysis considers whether this was the situation during the fifteenth and sixteenth centuries in Holland as well.

The accessibility of capital markets has an obvious gender dimension. In the literature on contemporary microcredit the vital position of women is stressed. The true test of the efficient functioning of a capital market is its accessibility to women as well as men: whether women can access its services, whether they can borrow money on reasonable terms, and whether their savings will increase in value. This is directly related to the matter of whether women in these societies can own property and can have a legal identity of their own (or alternatively, whether they always have to be accompanied by men to carry out

[1] Yunus 2008.

[2] Cf. the importance of "financial revolutions" for economic development, Sylla 2002.

[3] Northern Italy: Fratianni and Spinelli 2006; sixteenth-century Holland: Tracy 1985; late seventeenth-century England: Dickson 1967.

[4] Clark 2005, Epstein 2000.

certain transactions). But women's participation in capital markets is also rooted in their economic position in general: Do they earn their own income (in the labor market)? Do they share in inheritances? Can they have their own savings? Can they have their own debts? Obviously, this also works in the opposite direction: the more accessible the capital markets are for women, the stronger their bargaining position in the household will be.[5] Indeed, a study of women's participation in the capital markets of this earlier era can tell us a lot about their autonomy in the domestic sphere. Thus, this chapter focuses on these issues: the participation of women in the capital markets of the time, seen as a test of their economic dependence and their agency, and more broadly, of the efficiency of the institutional framework of the period and region we are concerned with here.

Clearly, the efficiency of capital markets is highly dependent on the broader institutional context in which they are embedded. The first, and perhaps most fundamental problem—what we call the "De Soto problem"[6] —is that potential entrepreneurs own certain assets that might be used as collateral, but owing to imperfect property rights, they cannot be used as such. This may result from an absence of clear titles to land and real estate; from an insecurity of property rights in general, owing to corruption and bad governance; from an absence of rules about bankruptcy and/or the liquidation of collateral; and similar institutional problems. In this case, the assets cannot be used as collateral for loans—or only for loans granted at very high interest rates, because it is unclear whether and how the asset can be liquidated in the event the debtor defaults on the loan. When capital markets are embedded in very unequal sociopolitical structures, it is difficult for them to develop the kind of transparent property rights that are necessary for them to function efficiently.

The second institutional problem is that of information asymmetries at work in capital markets that raise transaction costs. When no collateral is available, or if when it is available, there are large costs involved in the liquidation of such collateral then, there is an *ex ante* information problem: the bank or lending agency has to assess the viability of the project for which the loan is to be granted— but how can the lending agency select the most promising projects?[7] And there is an *ex post* information problem: the lending agency will have to know the borrower's capacity to pay back the loan and will have to monitor the payments; but if the debtor does not pay the loan back, is this because of *force majeure* (circumstances beyond the control of the debtor), or is the debtor simply being opportunistic? Answering these questions raises transaction costs.

[5] Pitt, Khandker, and Cartwright 2003.

[6] This argument goes back to De Soto 2001.

[7] Hoffman, Postel-Vinay, and Rosenthal 2000, 62–68.

Third, transaction costs can be high because of the size or volume ("thickness") of the loan market. A lending agency incurs operating costs, such as overhead, that become part of the transaction costs (ultimately, covered by interest on the loan). It can be argued that the thinner the capital markets (having a lower number of debtors), the more these overhead costs will contribute to total transaction costs. Smaller loans, moreover, have greater fixed—per loan—costs than do larger loans, thereby "punishing" small entrepreneurs. Once a thicker loan market develops, the transaction costs on small loans should go down proportionally more than those on larger loans.

The efficiency of both contemporary and historical capital markets can be analyzed from this perspective. In our case study of fifteenth- and sixteenth-century Holland, we explore to what extent inefficiencies in the institutional structure limited access to credit by small female and male entrepreneurs. The criteria we put forward for assessing the efficiency of this specific capital market are:

1. The degree to which entrepreneurs could use their assets as collateral (and in general, the extent to which property rights were protected).
2. The interest rates at which entrepreneurs could borrow money, and how this rate compared with yields on risk-free investments (so as to assess the relative costs/risks of lending to entrepreneurs).
3. The relationship between the size of loans and corresponding interest rates, or the extent to which interest rates on small loans were higher owing to large fixed costs.
4. The degree to which both men and women could access the capital market—if the capital market was accessible and well organized, could women then benefit from this? And if so, does their participation in the capital market differ from that of men?

As a case study, we focus on the capital markets in the small town of Edam and its surrounding area, De Zeevang, in the northern part of Holland in the late medieval period (1460–1560). This was a region that, from the fourteenth century onward, had experienced economic growth and structural transformation, eventually resulting in the famous Dutch Golden Age of the seventeenth century. We want to understand why this process of growth began so early in this region, and in particular what role the capital markets played in the process.

If NIE is correct, then this precocious growth must have had its birth in efficient institutions that were directly related to the capital market, which would have allowed interest rates on loans to be set at relatively low levels. This would imply that large groups of households—not only the rich but also the middle class and perhaps even those in lower classes—participated in the capital markets, both as lenders and as borrowers, and that this applied not only to households headed by men but also those headed by women.

The outline of this chapter is as follows. First, we briefly introduce the region studied and the main institutions governing the capital markets in the area. This results in a (necessarily) brief answer to the first "De Soto" question: How well were property rights developed and did this allow households—headed by men and women—to use their assets as collateral? Next, thanks to a very rich source covering the capital market of Edam and Zeevang in the period 1462 to 1563, we analyzed the participation of men and women in capital markets. Finally, we established a link between the size of loans granted and the interest rate—or perhaps the absence of such a link, which is also significant.

The Importance of Savings for EMP Functioning

Test Case: Edam and De Zeevang

The small town of Edam lies about twenty kilometers to the northeast of Amsterdam, at the border of what was then and still is known as the Zuiderzee. Recent calculations of population figures suggest there were 2,398 inhabitants in 1462; 2,337 in 1514; and 3,752 in 1563. Together with the surrounding countryside—called "De Zeevang"—it was a region typical of Holland at the time. De Zeevang was inhabited by 3,363 people in 1462; 3,655 in 1514; and in 5,765 in 1563.[8] The entire region was highly urbanized (in 1462, more than 40% of its population lived in Edam), and the population was dependent on a mix of activities: agriculture was still important, but a rapidly growing part of the workforce was active in fisheries, industries, and trade.[9] The economy was characterized by small holdings, another typical feature of the Holland economy. Most (rural) households owned small plots of land they often used to herd cattle. They sold cattle and dairy products on the market.[10]

The sources we used to analyze the Edam and De Zeevang capital market—the *schotkohieren* and *verpachtingskohieren*—are registers used by the Edam and De Zeevang government to levy taxes on its population.[11] The *verpachtingskohieren*

[8] Cf. population figures: Boschma-Aarnoudse 2003, 421–426.

[9] Cf. economic development: Boschma-Aarnoudse 2003, 367–375 and passim.

[10] Cf. the economic history of this region: Van der Woude 1972a, 362–363, 457–458, 511–513. On the development of the Holland economy in this period, see van Zanden 2002a; Hoppenbrouwers 2001, 49–50; De Vries and van der Woude 1995, 236–238.

[11] The sources we used for Edam and Zeevang can be compared to the northwest European *Schöffenbücher*; Zuijderduijn 2009b, chap. 6.2.

are estimates of household wealth, which were used for taxation purposes, drawn up in the *schotkohieren.*—which assessed the amount of capital tax to be paid We know little about the incentives the government of Edam had to create the *verpachtingskohieren.*[12] Clearly, it was necessary to apportion the taxes that rulers levied on the city of Edam and villages of De Zeevang. The local government apportioned payment for every household according to the *schot,* a division of taxes based on estimates of wealth. Usually, local authorities based such assessments on land ownership or rough estimates, but in 1462, the Edam government decided to take a large number of assets into consideration when it assessed the *schot,* listed as:

> goeden, huijsen, erven, landen, ewelicke renten, losrenten, lijffrenten, gelt, schult, schepen, waeren, comanscappen, beesten, bedden, ende alle andere goeden[13] [goods, houses, property, land, hereditary tenure, *losrenten, lijffrenten (annuities),* money, debts, ships, merchandise, merchants's capital, animals, beds, and all other goods]

Inhabitants were supposed to have their assets registered when the *verpachtingskohieren* were drawn up, every seven or eight years. The earliest *verpachtingskohier,* from 1462, was probably drawn up to assess the taxes the Edam and De Zeevang inhabitants had to contribute to the ten-year subsidy (*bede*) that the Holland Estates (*Staten van Holland*) agreed to in 1462.[14] An assessor walked through the city and villages, and stopped by the houses to question the inhabitants. He recorded hundreds of statements, such as the following:

> *Item lijsbeth jan woutersdr. tverndeel van jan woutersz. huus, II deymt in die langweren after an vegers langweren, I Rijnsgulden ter los, XV Rijnsgulden an gelt, een bed*[15] [Lijsbeth, Jan Wouters' daughter: a quarter of Jan Woutersz's house, 2 *deimt* in the *langweren* behind Veger's *langweren,* 1 *Rijnsgulden* redeemable, 15 *Rijnsgulden* in cash, one bed]

That is, Lijsbeth, the daughter of Jan Woutersz, owned a quarter of her father's house, some land (2 *deimt,* a square measure), and a bed. She either received or owed a *losrente* of 1 *Rijnsgulden* (Rg.) and held 15 Rg. in cash. The source

[12] It is likely the incentives were much like those of the Florentine government, which drew up a similar register in 1427, the famous *Catasto.* According to Anthony Molho (1995), the Florentines did this because they wanted "a more scientific and rational system of taxation" (79)

[13] Boschma-Aarnoudse 2003, 405.

[14] Boschma-Aarnoudse 2003, 403.

[15] Waterlands Archief (WA), *Stad Edam* (SE), inv. no. 237 f. 1v.

provides a very detailed report for every household in Edam and the surrounding area of De Zeevang.

Mentions of annuities (*lijf-* and *losrenten*) play a large role in these two sources, so a few words are in order to explain these financial instruments. Since the second half of the fourteenth century, public bodies and individuals traded *renten*: annual pensions that were in fact cleverly concealed usurious loans.[16] *Lijfrenten* were paid until the buyer (*rentenier*) (or the person on whose life the annuity was vested) died, and *losrenten* until the loan was redeemed. Both were long-term loans, often running for several decades. By selling a *rente*, the *rente* payer attracted funds, or investments, whereas the *rentenier* bought an annual pension. The capital market facilitated trade in *renten* and thus helped the redistribution of savings. *Los-* and *lijfrenten* were initially used to finance the long-term debts of cities and other public institutions—including, increasingly, states such as the province of Holland. But the system became so popular that it trickled down rapidly: in the fifteenth and sixteenth centuries, it was also used for financing people's retirement and for arranging income flows between generations. For example, when the son (or daughter) took over the family properties (the farm or workshop), a *lijfrente* could be vested in the father and/or mother who retired, with the properties of the family used as collateral to ensure the parent a permanent income for the rest of his or her life. Similarly, if, for example, a daughter decided to remain single and join a *begijnhof* (beguinage), her share in the family property could be converted to a *lijfrente* for the same purpose.[17]

The historian Sparreboom was the first to call attention to these unique sources.[18] In the introduction to her dissertation, Boschma-Arnoudse elaborated on the *schotkohieren* and *verpachtingskohieren*, and based part of her dissertation on the economic development of Edam and De Zeevang as illustrated in these sources; however, she left out *renten*, obligations, and cash, which are the most interesting aspects for our work.[19] It is unfortunate she did not deal with these, as they allow for a unique view of the distribution of financial assets in late medieval Holland, as well as the depth of the market for *renten*. The source lists hundreds of heads of households owing *lijfrenten* (life annuities) and *losrenten*, and hundreds receiving an annual *rente*, or interest payment. Thus, it allows us to examine the socioeconomic position of both creditors and debtors.

[16] Zuijderduijn 2009b, 20–21, 48–50; Munro 2003.

[17] Beguines often brought considerable amounts of capital with them. For a tentative analysis of the relationship between the EMP, the development of capital markets, and the emergence of beguinages, see De Moor and van Zanden 2006, and chapter 7, this volume.

[18] Sparreboom 1981.

[19] Boschma-Aarnoudse 2003.

There are a few problems with these sources, however. First, tax registers based on interviews are likely to yield a biased picture because the taxable community would have done everything possible to appear impoverished so as to escape high taxation. On the other hand, these were small communities in which everybody knew a great deal about everyone else, and citizenship was considered a virtue, which may have enhanced willingness to pay for community services.[20]

The *verpachtingskohieren* provide detailed overviews of the assets and debts of the households in Edam and De Zeevang for three years (1462, 1514, and 1563). The problem with this source is, as the example of Liesbeth Wouters shows, the values of property—particularly real estate—are not given in any systematic way: they indicate how many pieces of land or how many beds in how many houses a household may possess, but not their value, or at least not in a way that allows for easy comparison. Only for different kinds of debts and securities (*losrenten*, for example) and, of course for cash, can we establish the value, although in the case of *los-* and *lijfrenten* (see again the example of Liesbeth Wouters), we often know only the value of the annual sum paid to the household, and therefore have to estimate the value of the principal.[21]

The other source are the *schotkohieren*, which give, for the same households in the same years, the amount of capital tax (the *schot*; often today called a tangible personal property tax), which was based on an assessment of the net value of the assets of the household, as registered in the *verpachtingskohieren*. For 1514 and 1563, it is possible to link the two sources for many of the households. For 1514, 74%, or 821 out of 1,110 households listed in the *verpachtingskohieren* can be linked to the information in the *schotkohier* of that same year. For 1563, for example, we can link nine out of ten of the households mentioned in the *verpachtingskohier* (1,559 out of 1,665, or 93.6%). Because the data were collected in a less systematic way and there was less detail in the notation of names in both sources for 1462, so far we were unable to link more than 34% (35 out of 1,025) persons in the *verpachtingskohieren* to the data in the *schotkohieren*, which is insufficient for further analysis.

Another problem in analyzing the data was the difficulty in classifying a head of household as a debtor or a creditor of an annuity. In the *verpachtingskohieren*, it is not always clearly indicated whether households received or paid a *rente*. We encounter references such as "25 guilders annual *losrenten*," without any further information; the 1563 register has a particularly large number of these records. We have reason to believe that these must have been *renten* that the household received. Often, such unclear references to *renten* are found in the middle

[20] Cf. Van Zanden and Prak 2006, 111–145.

[21] For a more detailed discussion of these sources, see Zuijderduijn 2009a; Boschma-Aarnoudse 2003.

of a long list of household possessions—for example, Reijner Jan Coppertsz, who declared he owned "half a share in Pieter Jaep Claesz's [ship], half a share in Jan Geert Rengertsz's [ship], another 54 guilders annual *losrenten*, furthermore in his business, cash and merchandise worth 2300 guilders."[22] Although the source does not explicitly state whether this Reijner received or paid the *losrenten*, the way in which the record is structured suggests that it must have been a possession, like the shares in ships that precede the *losrenten* and the cash and merchandize that follow in the list. Thus, Reijner received this *losrenten*, and has thus been considered a creditor in our dataset.

Another important problem regarding these sources is related to the identity of the people mentioned in both. Some names could refer to either men or women, and in some cases it was difficult to distinguish surnames from occupations (which will not be further discussed in this chapter, but did help us to identify the person). Here, linking both sources helped a great deal (at least for the years 1514 and 1563); often, identifying the same person in the two different sources confirmed our earlier assumptions about the sex, marital status, or occupation that had been made on the basis of the each source individually. Thus, the information used here was based on a combination of the sources.

We also needed to determine how representative these entries were and the position of the persons in the *verpachtingskohieren* in terms of wealth distribution by means of the taxes they paid (using the *schotkohieren*).[23] Tables 4.1 and 4.2 show that at least for 1514 and 1563, we have a representative sample of the total population for tax assessment. For 1462, the selection that could be linked is very small and clearly skewed toward higher tax groups, and hence was less suitable for analysis. Therefore, for 1462, only the data from the *verpachtingskohieren* were used, and not those linked to the *schotkohieren*.

On the basis of tables 4.1 and 4.2, then, it becomes clear that the tax assessments hardly changed in the course of a century: three-quarters of the population remained in the lowest segment, paying less than 1 guilder (the distribution within the group that paid 0–0.99 guilders also hardly changed during the century).

It was also important to know to what extent our sample of the *verpachtingskohieren* correctly represented the human sex balance within the area and during the years covered in the *schotkohieren*. Here again, we see no reason to doubt that the population in the *verpachtingskohieren* correctly represents the distribution of sexes for all years, although there are more women in the *verpachtingskohieren* sample (tables 4.3 and 4.4).

[22] WA SE inv. no. 238 f. 25v.

[23] Therefore we used those heads of household of the *verpachtingskohieren* whose names could be linked to the *schotkohieren*.

Table 4.1 **Percentage/Number of Households in *Schotkohieren* per Tax Group; 1462, 1514, and 1563**

Year/Guilders	*0–0.99**	*1–1.99*	*2–2.99*	*3+*	*Total*	*0–0.99*	*1–1.99*	*2–2.99*	*3+*	*Total*
1462	63.50%	22.65%	5.95%	7.90%	100%	715	255	67	89	1,126
1514	75.85%	16.05%	4.33%	3.76%	100%	1,068	226	61	53	1,408
1563	73.70%	15.76%	4.83%	5.71%	100%	1,342	287	88	104	1,821
Total	71.76%	17.63%	4.96%	5.65%	100%	3,125	768	216	246	4,355

Note: *We have included people mentioned in the *schotkohieren* but for whom no *schot* was registered; these amount to only a very small percentage of the population ($N = 56$ for the three years).

Source: *Schotkohieren* of 1462, 1514, and 1563

Table 4.2 **Percentage/Number of Households in *Verpachtingskohieren* Linked to the *Schotkohieren* (per tax group)**

Year	*0–0.99**	*1–1.99*	*2–2.99*	3+	*Total*	*0–0.99*	*1–1.99*	*2–2.99*	3+	*Total*
1462	48.57%	8.57%	14.29%	28.57%	100%	17	3	5	10	35
1514	70.40%	20.22%	5.60%	3.78%	100%	578	166	46	31	821
1563	72.35%	16.36%	5.20%	6.09%	100%	1,128	255	81	95	1,559
Total	71.35%	17.56%	5.47%	5.63%	100%	1,723	424	132	136	2,415

Note: *We have included people mentioned in the *schotkohieren* but for whom no *schot* was registered; these amount to only a very small percentage of the population ($N = 56$ for the three years).

Source: *Schotkohieren* and *verpachtingskohieren* of 1462, 1514, and 1563

Table 4.3 **Percentage of Men and Women in the *Schotkohieren* (per year), 1462, 1514, and 1463**

Year	*Male Households**	*Female Households**	*Male Households**	*Female Households**	*Total*
1462	84.01%	15.99%	946	180	1,126
1514	74.57%	25.43%	1,050	358	1,408
1563	73.82%	26.18%	1,345	477	1,822
Total	76.70%	23.30%	3,341	1,015	4,356

*Note:**References to (fe)male households in the tables of this chapter refer to households headed by a (fe)male.

Source: Schotkohieren of 1462, 1514, and 1563

Table 4.4 **Percentage of Men and Women in the *Verpachtingskohieren* Linked to the *Schotkohieren* (per year), 1462, 1514, and 1463**

Year	*Male Households*	*Female Households*	*Male Households*	*Female Households*	*Total*
1462	80.00%	20.00%	28	7	35
1514	71.38%	28.62%	586	235	821
1563	72.35%	27.65%	1,128	431	1,559
Total	72.13%	27.87%	1,742	673	2,415

Source: Schotkohieren and *verpachtingskohieren* of 1462, 1514, and 1563

So, 1462 is again (slightly) less accurate.[24] Noteworthy here is that women were mentioned in a fourth of all cases as head of household. Further analysis shows that the *verpachtingskohieren* as a whole had a very similar sex distribution as the *schotkohieren*. This is in itself not really surprising, as the documents included most of the population; on the other hand, together with table 4.1, it does provide the very first indication that households headed by women must have had a fairly strong position within society.[25]

[24] To determine whether the person mentioned was a woman or man, we brought together indications in both datasets. In some cases, the sex became clear on the basis of the *schotkohieren*; in other cases, the *verpachtingskohieren* were helpful. Often one source confirmed the other. Where there was serious doubt, we chose to consider the person as a man. The same procedure was followed to determine marital status, although we could only distinguish whether a woman—not a man—was a widow or not.

[25] In this respect, it may be worthwhile to compare the percentage of female households in the area of our study with those in Tuscany in the 1427 *Catasto*: here, the proportion of women

Protection of Property Rights

There is a substantial body of evidence that shows property rights in Holland were adequately defined so as to allow for the emergence of capital markets, at least since the fourteenth century.[26] The origins of this situation are to be found earlier, during the large-scale reclamations of peatlands in the high Middle Ages. To attract colonists willing to reclaim the area, territorial lords offered peasants their freedom and near-absolute property rights; as a result, even centuries later, peasants still held about two-thirds to three-quarters of the land.[27]

Titles to land were protected through a property rights system based on ratification by local authorities in the towns and villages. So, transfers of land within Edam were valid only when contracted in the authorities' presence; transferring land in any other way did not invest buyers with property rights. Since conveyance was also required to validate mortgages, there was only one place where such property rights for land in Edam could be obtained, checked, and disputed: the court of Edam.[28]

Local conveyance of property rights was already practiced in the thirteenth century. At first, judges or aldermen merely witnessed the transactions and had to rely on memory in the event they were later consulted about the ownership. Over time, they began to issue written contracts, presumably because the growing number of transfers required this and because the increase in literacy allowed it. This development is evident in the fifteenth century, from which period a number of contracts issued by the court of Edam are available, but the practice probably started at least a century earlier.[29] The next step in the evolution of conveyance was the recording of the ratified contracts in registers of the minutes. In Edam, the oldest available register dates from 1564,[30] but there is ample evidence that this practice may have started much earlier.[31]

This property rights system, in which there was only one institution capable of investing property rights, resolved much of the "De Soto problem" mentioned earlier. The situation in 1564, for which we are sure that Edam kept a register of

household heads ranged from 15 to 17% in the large towns, and 13% in smaller towns, to 9% in the countryside; Herlihy 1977, 145; cf. similar findings Herlihy 1973, 109; Herlihy and Klapisch-Zuber 1978, 273.

[26] Zuijderduijn 2009b.

[27] Cf. the property rights colonists received: van Bavel 2010, 83–86.

[28] Zuijderduijn 2009b, 184–190.

[29] Waterlands Archief (WA), Stad Edam (SE), inv. nr. 448 (1451), 452 (1490). Cf. contracts in writing in the north of Holland in the fourteenth century; Vangassen 1964.

[30] WA SE, inv. nr. 3813.

[31] cf. Zuijderduijn 2009b, 202–203.

property rights, even resembles the land registries of today.[32] To be sure, elsewhere in the Low Countries property rights were often less clear—for instance, in regions where property rights were invested by the courts of capital cities, as well as those of small towns and villages.[33]

Of course, this property rights system also had to function. To what degree did creditors risk bad governance? Medieval governments often involved nepotism and corruption; any officials leased offices, and so had to look for ways to make good on their investments.[34] Others, such as aldermen, were volunteers recruited from local elites; they were more or less expected to make up for the time they spent in public service in more "informal" ways.

There were a few checks on corruption, though. From early on, territorial lords took great care to prevent abuses of power. They installed regional, high courts, and supreme courts to which plaintiffs could appeal.[35] The officials in charge of regional courts also had the task of monitoring the functioning of local authorities. They kept a particular eye on sheriffs and government agents who presided over local courts, and fined or removed them from office if they engaged in corruption and abused their power.[36]

What happened when mortgagors reneged? Creditors in possession of a ratified contract could immediately ask the sheriff of Edam to seize the property, without having to go to court. Debtors could appeal a seizure, but they risked a fine of 6 stuivers if their appeal was not upheld, which reduced the possibility of stalling the legal proceedings.[37] The debtor was allowed some time to offer a solution—for instance, payment in installments—but if he failed to do so, the sheriff would grant the creditor the property rights. When there was more than one plaintiff, those with the oldest titles were preferred.

How would this system relate to some of the other problems we have identified, such as information asymmetries? Investors looking for ways to assess the payback capacity of potential debtors had only one place they could go: the court of Edam, where they could get a credit rating for the prospective recipient

[32] Cf. De Soto 2001, 52, who acknowledges the early emergence of formal property registries in the Middle Ages, but also stresses the importance of national registries. The evidence presented here would suggest that local registries could also contribute to efficient capital markets.

[33] For instance, in the surroundings of Bois-le-Duc, property rights could be invested by this town and village authorities. This unclear situation caused many disputes; van der Ree-Scholtens 1993, 90–98.

[34] Blockmans 1985.

[35] The Supreme Court was operational since 1446, and after some changes in the first decades of its existence, it was permanently established in Malines in 1503.

[36] Zuijderduijn 2009b, 46–52.

[37] Bezemer 1894, 152.

of the mortgage they were considering granting. We also know that elsewhere in Holland, local courts actively tried to prevent fraud before it occurred, and aldermen took great care to investigate whether or not properties put up as collateral were already mortgaged.[38]

This all suggests that property rights were rather well protected. This was in part because it was a rather egalitarian society, with only a small "feudal" elite, the nobility. This nobility dominated "high politics" in Brussels, but its influence was counterbalanced by the growing power of urban merchants, who were increasingly important in the political process. Many farmers owned their land, although the share of urban citizens and institutions also owning land increased rapidly in these years. One gets the impression that people had substantial trust in markets: a large share of the population (30 to 50%, according to different estimates) was (partly) dependent on wage labor.[39] The staple foods—rye and wheat—were imported from the Baltic and sold on local markets; most farmers specialized in livestock products, such as butter, cheese, and meat. De Vries and van der Woude have described this economy as the first "modern" market economy—they clearly have a point.[40]

The Efficiency of the Credit Markets

What is striking about the sources for Edam and De Zeevang is the high level of differentiation and specialization of assets, portraying a very flexible capital market. All kinds of properties were being traded and used as collateral; for example, households did not simply own houses but also shares in houses (for example, in 1514, Baernt Jansz owned the house in which he lived, as well as two rooms elsewhere in Edam, one of which was rented to Pieter Pelser).[41] This led to a very active market in real estate, in which some people owned shares in many houses. The division of a property into shares was a general phenomenon, applied to land, wharves, mills, fishing nets, and ships. Most famous is perhaps the system of issuing shares in ships (*scheepsparten*) that emerged in the fifteenth century, as a way to finance (and profit from) the rapidly growing shipping industry. People could easily buy such shares, which sometimes were as small as 1/256th part of a ship. According to Boschma-Aarnoudse,[42] about 15% of the households of Edam owned such a share in a ship.

[38] Zuijderduijn 2009b, 193–197.
[39] Van Bavel 2006.
[40] De Vries and van der Woude 1997.
[41] WA SA inv. nr. 237 f. 228v.
[42] Boschma-Aarnouse 2003, 156–157.

Shares in real estate could be financed through various kinds of loans. Loans contracted for a few years—called *custingen*—were widely used to finance the purchase of real estate, as well as other goods.[43] We frequently encountered records of *custingen* in Edam, where they were secured on real estate and ships, and had terms from two to twelve years.[44]

Jaime Reis has suggested a way to assess the efficiency of local capital markets, which he applies to the Portuguese rural capital markets during the second half of the nineteenth century.[45] This method measures the difference in interest rates between low-risk offerings such as government loans and those usual for mortgages in the countryside; this difference, he explains, is a measure of the risk premium for lending to farmers and other rural inhabitants, and therefore is an indicator of the degree to which rural capital markets worked well and were able to protect the property rights of creditors. The difference he found for Portugal was significant; from 1870 to 1910, there was a difference of 3 to 4% between interest on risk-free loans at 4 to 6% and the 7 to 10% interest that farmers paid. He also found evidence that this was fairly usual for the region; in Spain, the risk premium was of a similar level).

Applying this idea to Holland in the fifteenth and sixteenth centuries was relatively straightforward. Several studies showed that interest paid on government annuities (*losrenten*) was between 5 and 6.25% in this period;[46] similarly, the town of Edam in 1550 paid 5 to 5.6% on a number of *losrenten*. The sources analyzed here also mention a number of interest rates on different loans to or by citizens of Edam and Zeevang; we present this information in table 4.5. For this area, it appears that there was in fact no appreciable difference between interest paid on (almost) risk-free government *losrenten* and that paid on the mostly private *losrenten*. The spread around the mean was also fairly small (in 1514, 61% of the *losrenten* had an average interest rate of 5.6%—or 18 penning—and this share was 81% in 1563).[47] This points to an extremely efficient capital market in which rural households—both men and women—could borrow at very low interest rates and were considered (almost) as reliable as the state.

Another way to get an impression of the default risk premium is to compare interest rates to rental values. Data from 1514 shows that annual rental values

[43] Zuijderduijn 2008, 7.

[44] Especially for 1563. We consider these *custingen* (referred to in the source as *custingbrieven*) as a particular type of debt. Cf. *custingen* on real estate: WA SE inv. nr. 237 f. 16, 187, 221v.; on ships: WA SE inv. nr. 237 f. 202, 204, 274v; WA SE inv. nr. 238 f. 1v; the time span: WA SE inv. nr. 238 f. 8, 34v, 35.

[45] Reis 2007.

[46] Zuijderduijn 2009b, 175–179; Hanus 2007, 38; Van der Heijden 2006; Tracy 1985, 204–214.

[47] The coefficient of variation is also very small, declining from 0.11 in 1462 to 0.09 in 1514 to 0.07 in 1563; by contrast, Reis found coefficients of variation from 0.16 to 0.31

Table 4.5 **Average Interest Rates (%) on *Losrenten* for Edam and De Zeevang**

	1462	*1514*	*1563*
Edam	6.1 (9)	5.7 (103)	5.6 (109)
Zeevang	–	5.3 (11)	5.8 (3)
All	6.1 (9)	5.7 (114)	5.6 (112)

Source: Zuijderduijn 2009b, 177, and a few additions based on a more detailed analysis of the source

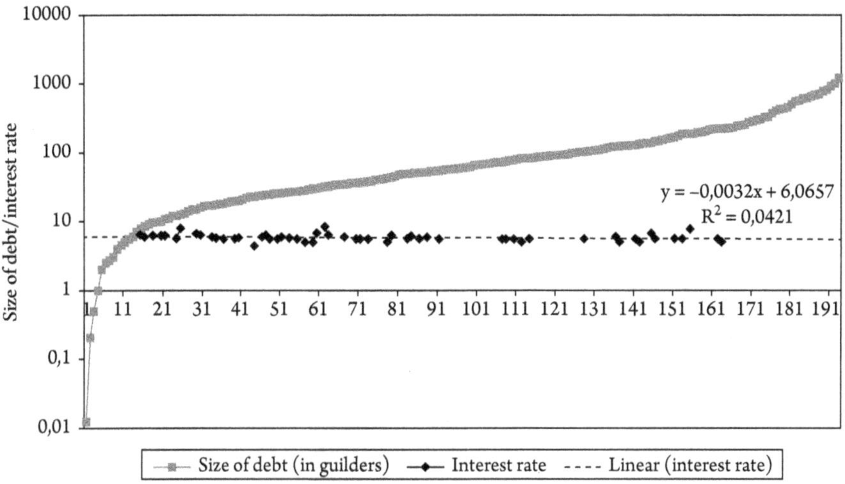

Figure 4.1 Relationship between size of debt (in guilders) and interest rate listed in the verpachtingskohieren for Edam and De Zeevang, 1514. Source: Zuijderduijn 2009b, 177, and a few additions based on a more detailed analysis of the source.

in Holland were about 5% of the value of the land,[48] whereas interest rates in Edam were about 5.7%. When we assume that leasing out the land was relatively risk-free and involved more or less the same transaction costs, it seems that a premium of 0.7% sufficed to convince people to invest their money in private capital markets rather than in land.

We also studied the relationship between the size of debts and their interest rates. Figure 4.1 gives data on both. The horizontal axis in the figure presents all debts in ascending order; the smallest (no. 1) is less than 0.1 guilders (or less than the daily wage of an unskilled laborer), and the largest (no. 194) is 1,200 guilders.

[48] Zuijderduijn and De Moor 2010: the average rate of return to land was calculated using data from 24 villages in the north of Holland.

The figure also presents interest rates on the same debts for those annuities for which we have this information. Two things stand out: there is, as we expected, a (slightly) declining trend: interest rates on large loans were somewhat lower than those on small ones, but the variation is very small—from about 6% on the smallest to 5.5% on the largest. In other years (1462 and 1563) for which we have similar data, we found a similar small decline (in 1462) or no relationship at all (in 1563). The figure also shows the range of debts involved: there are a few that were very small and a few that were very large, but most were in the intermediate range between 10 and 100 guilders. The median loan was 58 guilders, which is quite a large sum—about double the income per capita of Holland in the same year (or representing almost 390 daily wages of an unskilled laborer).[49] In other years, distributions were very similar to that observed for 1514 (the median in 1462 was 56 guilders; in 1562, when prices had doubled, it was 144 guilders).

Access to Credit for Men and Women

The description above indicates that in late medieval western Europe, the performance of capital markets had already greatly improved, which led to a decline in interest rates to levels that are still considered quite low. Although we now know a great deal about the efficiency of the capital market, we still know fairly little about its function at the micro level. Did households, as a result of the rapid expansion of the capital market, obtain better access to capital, and if they did, at what cost? What was the premium paid by middle-class or lower-class households on their debts, compared to the interest paid on more or less secure securities such as government bonds? Was this capital market able to supply low cost microcredit to such households? Were households able to use the capital market to invest their savings? Or was this late medieval capital market restricted to the happy few among the urban and rural elites?

These are the questions we address in this chapter. In chapter 1, we hypothesized that there was a link between the emergence of the European Marriage Pattern in northwestern Europe and the development of capital markets (and other factor markets). As mentioned, one of the features of this marriage pattern was neolocality: sons and daughters left their parents' household when they married, and set up a household of their own. They could only do so after accumulating savings; moreover, parents in the EMP were no longer guaranteed that their children would take care of them in their old age and therefore needed to save. Thus, intergenerational transfers became less important,

[49] Van Zanden 2002a.

and were to some extent replaced by intragenerational transfers, made possible by a well-functioning capital market. This situation also helps to explain the popularity of *renten,* as these were typically financial instruments to facilitate saving for old age.

But could households in this period use the capital markets for these purposes? Another element of the EMP is the strong domestic position of married women—and linked to that, their position in the labor market. Again, the question may be asked if this strong position applied to capital markets as well. To what extent did women have access to microcredit under reasonable lending conditions? Was the capital market able to supply small-scale credit to households and also offer small-scale savings plans for these households? Did women (as heads of households) have equal access to the capital market under similar conditions as men (who may have been more prosperous)? And, alternatively, when they entered this capital market, did female heads of household follow similar savings and investment strategies?

Studying the depth of the capital markets in the late medieval period may help explain the level of efficiency of those markets. When the markets are "thin" and transactions occur only occasionally, the transaction costs are probably high, as the capital market is largely based on information acquired on the basis of past performance. Growth in the volume of transactions may lead to significant learning and scale effects, which lower transaction costs, as well as thresholds for either credit or debt transactions. There may be multiple equilibria; a situation of high transaction costs, high interest rates, and low turnover may be as stable a market as one with high volumes and low interest rates.[50] Analyzing the depth of the capital market can therefore help explain why capital markets are (in)efficient.

What is striking about the sources we have used here is the extreme flexibility that is portrayed. To begin with, all kinds of properties were being traded and used as collateral; for example, households did not simply own houses but also shares in houses (which the example of Liesbeth Wouters demonstrates, who owned a quarter of her father's house); this may be related to the fact that family properties were divided up among children (as was probably the case with Liesbeth). This led to a very mobile market in real estate in which some people, men and women, owned shares in many houses, as sketched earlier.

In table 4.4 we saw that about a quarter of households was headed by women. This large number of female heads of household cannot be attributed to the

[50] Western Europe seems to have been on a trajectory of high savings, well-developed capital markets, and low interest rates from the late medieval period onward. Other parts of the world, such as Southeast Asia, have an equally long history, in contrast, of low savings, poor capital market institutions, and high interest rates. Cf. van Zanden 2008.

Table 4.6 **Number of Beds (on average) per Female and Male Household, 1462, 1514, and 1563**

Year	*Beds per Female Household*	*Beds per Male Household*	*Total*
1462	2.33	2.43	2.42
1514	2.02	2.30	2.22
1563	2.05	2.23	2.18
Total	2.08	2.30	2.25

Source: Verpachtingskohieren 1462, 1514, and 1563

season in which the tax registers were made because, as far as we know, this recordkeeping was done in winter, when the fishing and shipping seasons were over and the men would be at home.[51] The high proportion of women heading households appears to have been a general feature of Holland society in the late medieval and early modern periods. We encountered an equally high proportion of female households in the town of Hoorn: in 1478, there were 112 widows and 63 unmarried women among the 618 heads of households listed in a tax assessment record; this is 18.1% and 10.2%, respectively, of all households.[52] Van der Woude found a similarly high percentage of women heads of household for the Noorderkwartier in the seventeeth and eighteenth centuries: 21% of the households were headed by single people, and the very high percentage—three times higher than in England in that period—is striking.[53]

In table 4.6 we can see that female headed households, judged by the number of beds, tend to be slightly smaller/less affluent than their male counterparts but this difference is marginal and the development over time for the sexes is similar. Both experience a drop, although the measure for women drops slightly more than that for men. The evolving position of women in the society of Edam and Zeevang, judged from the tax categories to which they belonged, shows that in 1462, a large proportion of female-headed households (over three-quarters) paid less than 1 guilder in tax (see table 4.7). This proportion remained the

[51] Especially the dates that could be retrieved for the *verpachtingskohieren* were in the middle of the winter season, as on January 22, 1563. For the *schotboek* of 1462, we were able to determine that the information was collected on January 7, and for the *schotboek* of 1514, on March 28 (WA SE inv. no. 237 f. 164; WA SE inv. no. 238 f. 1; WA SE inv. no. 239 [1462] f. 1; WA SE inv. no. 239 [1514] f. 1.

[52] Also the province of North Holland, located on the Ijsselmeer, north of Edam; Koster 1929, 92. For 1483, we found 915 heads of households, 115 headed by widows, and 33 by single women; Koster 1929, 95.

[53] Van der Woude 1970, 202–241, 227–228.

Table 4.7 **Percentage of Female and Male Households in Different Tax Categories According to the *Schotkohieren*, 1462, 1514, and 1463**

Female Households	*0–0.99*	*1–1.99*	*2–2.99*	3+	*Total*
Year					
1462	77.78%	15.00%	2.78%	4.44%	100%
1514	77.93%	15.92%	3.91%	2.23%	100%
1563	73.17%	16.14%	5.45%	5.24%	100%
Total	75.67%	15.86%	4.43%	4.04%	100%
Male Households	***0–0.99***	***1–1.99***	***2–2.99***	**3+**	***Total***
Year					
1462	60.78%	24.10%	6.55%	8.56%	100%
1514	75.14%	16.10%	4.48%	4.29%	100%
1563	73.88%	15.63%	4.61%	5.88%	100%
Total	70.57%	18.17%	5.12%	6.14%	100%

Source: Schotkohieren of 1462, 1514, and 1563

same in the second and third quarters of the sixteenth century, when the proportion of male-headed households in that tax category rose to the same level. By 1563, they were on a par. Around 1462, men figured more in the higher tax categories, but they seem to have had difficulties maintaining their position. By 1563, the distribution of households across tax categories is nearly identical, men and women seeming to have become equal in this respect, which is remarkable.

To what extent did these men and women have access to the capital market, and how did they invest their savings? First, it is important to explain how female households acquired capital assets. Holland women were relatively independent in judicial and financial matters, thus allowing them to be active on the capital market. Most were under the custody of their fathers or husbands, but widows, wives of men who were abroad, and women having express or tacit power of attorney could engage in judicial actions aimed at the acquisition of property.[54] We know from a number of studies that women in Holland and elsewhere in the

[54] Van der Heijden 2006, 161–162; Niessen 2005, 52–53.

Low Countries participated in the capital market, and that they had ample opportunity to decide how to manage their savings.[55]

Tables 4.8 and 4.9 demonstrate, first, that there was a tendency to change from saving cash to acquiring financial assets over time: the number of households that invested in *los- or lijfrenten*, or in other forms of debt, increased with time (from only 4–5 percent in 1462 to about 20% in 1563), which is a sign of the growing efficiency of the capital market.[56] The amounts invested also increased much more than did the sums held as cash, especially *losrenten* and other forms of debt (including *custingbrieven*, which started to appear in 1563), were increasingly popular as a means to invest savings. These trends are clearly apparent among both men and women; additionally the differences in investment strategy between men and women are very small and quite insignificant. Men tended to stick with cash savings slightly more than did women (in 1462 and 1514); moreover, there was no strong preference for conservative investments, such as the *lijfrenten*, among women from Edam and Zeevang, a feature of women's saving behavior which has been shown in other studies.

A similar story unfolds with respect to people's access to credit. How many households (men/women) owed money at this time? The capital market was highly developed by 1462, when 28% of women and 32% of men had some kind of financial debt. *Losrenten* were clearly the most popular form of debt. As explained earlier, *losrenten* were collateralized with certain capital goods, such as houses, land, shares in a ship, and so on. Women became somewhat less dependent on borrowing money (in 1563, only 18% of women had a *losrente* or another kind of debt vested on them or their properties), whereas the indebtedness of men had increased (to 38% in 1563), a divergence we find difficult to interpret. Were women becoming more cautious? Was their access to credit restricted? Or were they just doing better economically than men, and therefore able to repay their debts? The fact that, on average, in 1563 for the first time, women's cash holdings were larger than those of men means that a pessimistic interpretation is unlikely.

[55] Hanus 2006, 18–20; van der Heijden 2006, 161–165; Tracy 1985, 144–145.

[56] In order to compare all capital assets and debts, for the *renten* we used the principal sum. In many cases, the principal (*hoofdsom*) was given, but for the most part, we knew only the *rentesom*. On the basis of studies by Jaco Zuijderduijn (2008, 2009a or 2009b) about the interest rates in these periods and a sporadic mention of interest rates in these sources, we were able to convert all *rentesommen* into main sums and used these for the further calculations. Unless there were indications in the source to use other interest rates, we used the following rates for the three different years

1462: *Losrenten*: 6%; *Lijfrenten*: 10%

1514: *Losrenten*: 5.6%; *Lijfrenten*: 10%

1563: *Losrenten*: 5.6%; *Lijfrenten*: 10%

Table 4.8 **Position of Women as Creditors and Debtors for Different Categories of Capital, 1462, 1514, and 1563**

Female Households		*Cash*	Lijfrenten		Losrenten		*Debt*		Custingbrieven	
Year		*Creditor*	*Creditor*	*Debtor*	*Creditor*	*Debtor*	*Creditor*	*Debtor*	*Creditor*	*Debtor*
1462	Total value in guilders	3,367	77	325	371	1178	4	290		
	N	59	1	5	6	23	1	17		
	Average guilders	57	77	65	62	51	4	17		
(*N* = 160)	% of total no. of women	37%	1%	3%	4%	14%	1%	11%	0%	0%
1514	Total value in guilders	4,815	447	179	3.573	833	621	705		
	N	63	5	6	54	20	10	21		
	Average guilders	76	89	30	66	42	62	34		
(*N* = 324)	% of total no. of women	19%	2%	2%	17%	6%	3%	6%	0%	0%
1563	Total value in guilders	15,602	1590	840	29,808	5,029	2,370	3,676	1,549	533
	N	41	13	10	67	42	15	28	10	3
	Average guilders	381	122	84	445	120	158	131	155	178
(*N* = 460)	% of total no. of women	9%	3%	2%	15%	9%	3%	6%	2%	1%
Total		23,784	2,114	1,343	33,751	7,040	2,994	4,671	1,549	533

Source: *Verpachtingskohieren* of 1462, 1514, and 1563

Table 4.9 **Position of Men as Creditors and Debtors for Different Categories of Capital, 1462, 1514, and 1563**

Male Households		*Cash*	Lijfrenten		Losrenten		*Debt*		Custingbrieven	
Year		*Creditor*	*Creditor*	*Debtor*	*Creditor*	*Debtor*	*Creditor*	*Debtor*	*Creditor*	*Debtor*
1462	Total value in guilders	31,639	375	747	2,845	2,792	590	3,132		
	N	348	5	25	25	128	9	124		
	Average guilders	91	75	30	114	22	66	25		
(*N* = 865)	% of total nr. of men	40%	1%	3%	3%	15%	1%	14%	0%	0%
1514	Total value in guilders	26,181	1,666	642	4,046	3,309	2,608	5,049		
	N	185	15	66	67	60	33	127		
	Average guilders	142	111	10	60	55	79	40		
(*N* = 786)	% of total no. of men	24%	2%	8%	9%	8%	4%	16%	0%	0%
1563	Total value in guilders	46,455	1,140	4,180	38,214	14,328	7,485	28,752	13,129	983
	N	131	9	128	127	151	48	160	49	7
	Average guilders	355	127	33	301	95	156	180	268	140
(*N* = 1205)	% of total no. of men	11%	1%	11%	11%	13%	4%	13%	4%	1%
Total		104,275	3,181	5,569	45,105	20,429	10,683	36,932	13,129	983

Source: *Verpachtingskohieren* of 1462, 1514, and 1563

In a similar comparative vein, did men and women in different wealthclasses have different investment strategies? By combining evidence from the two sources studied here, we tried to answer this question for the years 1514 and 1563 (see table 4.10). It appears that in 1563, the differences were minor; in fact, it is striking how similar the investment strategies of different classes were: men and women in different wealth groups invested almost the same amount of money in cash, *lijf-* and *losrenten*, and different kinds of debt, and there is nothing to indicate a more pronounced risk-averse investment strategy for women than for men. The only really significant difference between the classes related to holding cash in 1514: men in the higher wealth classes held much larger amounts of cash, which may indicate that they were relatively conservative financially, as the alternative at the time was to invest in income-yielding assets. In all other aspects, there was a high degree of similarity in the investment profiles among the wealth groups.

A last analysis, presented in table 4.11, reveals additional information about the position of urban and rural women and men. To what extent did women follow the same investment trends as men (cash and *losrenten*) depending on whether they were in a rural or urban setting? The first surprise was for women in the countryside: they held roughly equal amounts of cash, on average, for all three years of the study. The average amounts held increased over the years, but definitely not as sharply as cash averages in the city. This is clearly a consequence of greater economic development in the city. In the town of Edam, female households lagged behind male households in the first two years, but overtook men's holdings in our last benchmark year. The same happened with respect to the average amount invested in *losrenten*, by both city and country dweller. This is remarkable, to say the least.

To put these findings into a broader perspective, we compare them with data for Tuscany. We acknowledge the political and socioeconomic differences between Tuscany and Holland, as well as problems related to scale; for instance, Edam is perhaps more comparable with small Tuscan towns such as Volterra, Arezzo, or Cortona.[57] However, since there is not a great deal of literature on women's access to credit in such small towns or the Tuscan countryside, our comparison can only be tentative.

Judging from the 1427 *Catasto*, people in Tuscany probably had a number of ways they could borrow money. Herlihy and Klapisch-Zuber discovered that indebtedness was common, even among the lower classes.[58] But the conditions for such loans may not always have been favorable; for instance, professional

[57] Della Pina 1982, 51–52.

[58] Herlihy and Klapisch-Zuber 1978, 258–259. Cf. various types of credit the articles in Menant and Redon 2004.

Table 4.10 **Average Investment per Creditor in Different Income Classes, 1514 and 1563 (in guilders)**

Type of Investment		*Tax Category (in guilders)*				*Total*
		0–0.99	*1–1.99*	*2–2.99*	3+	
1514						
Cash	Women	44	50	85	53	53
	Men	55	131	155	463	135
	All	**53**	**104**	**131**	**402**	**112**
Lijfrente	Women	58				58
	Men	126	20	18		76
	All	**92**	**20**	**18**		**69**
Losrente	Women	40	53	54	23	42
	Men	30	37	37	27	32
	All	**35**	**42**	**42**	**26**	**36**
Debt	Women	23	115			75
	Men	39	56	41	52	44
	All	**37**	**73**	**41**	**52**	**48**
1563						
Cash	Women	135	333	448	685	386
	Men	142	289	568	889	318
	All	**141**	**301**	**531**	**806**	**334**
Lijfrente	Women	147	260		120	174
	Men	147	353	145	87	174
	All	**147**	**294**	**145**	**95**	**174**
Losrente	Women	162	414	583	659	311
	Men	178	227	290	490	245
	All	**172**	**277**	**397**	**538**	**267**
Debt	Women	139	78	65	24	112
	Men	110	177	214	198	143
	All	**118**	**160**	**150**	**163**	**136**
Custingbrief	Women	134	189		149	153
	Men	130	295	548	530	222
	All	**131**	**279**	**548**	**421**	**213**

Source: *Verpachtingskohieren* and *schotkohieren* of 1514 and 1563

Table 4.11 **Average Amount of Guilders, in Cash and *Losrenten* (creditors only), Among Female and Male Households in Edam and De Zeevang, 1462, 1514, and 1563**

CASH	Female Households						Male Households					
Year	EDAM			DE ZEEVANG			EDAM			DE ZEEVANG		
	Total amount in guilders.	*N* with cash	Average in guilders	Total amount in guilders	*N* with cash	Average in guilders	Total amount in guilders	*N* with cash	Average in guilders	Total amount in guilders	*N* with cash	Average in glds
1462	2,607	45	58	760	14	54	27,017	267	101	4,622	85	54
1514	3,877	43	90	939	20	46	23,433	140	167	2,723	44	61.88
1563	14,698	31	474	904	10	90	44,984	111	405	1,472	20	73.58
Average/ total	21182	119	178	2,602	44	59	95,434	518	184	8,816	149	59,17

(continued)

Table 4.11 **Continued**

LOS RENTEN	*Female Households*						*Male Households*					
Year	*EDAM*			*DE ZEEVANG*			*EDAM*			*DE ZEEVANG*		
	Total amount in glds.	*N* with *losrente*	Average in guilders	Total amount in guilders	*N* with *losrente*	Average in guilders	Total amount in guilders	*N* with *losrente*	Average in guilders	Total amount in guilders	*N* with *losrente*	Average in glds
1462	330	7	47	98	1	98	3,131	31	101	118	4	29
1514	4,478	66	68	942	12	78	6,522	89	73	497	21	23
1563	44,214	128	345	3,419	21	162	76,500	258	297	4,546	39	116
Average/Total	4,022	201	244	4,459	34	131	86,152	378	228	5,160	64	80

moneylenders offering short-term credit at high interest rates were still quite prominent in fifteenth-century Tuscany.

In the fifteenth century the *Monte di Pietà* was created in Tuscan towns, which offered small loans, free of interest.[59] Women living in large towns may have borrowed there, but whether this institution did more than help people who were on the brink of starvation is doubtful. According to Pullan, the *Monte di Pietà* "did not . . . lend to small artisans or shopkeepers to help them start up in business."[60] Borrowing from the *Monte di Pietà* also required that women provided collateral in the form of pawned objects. This means that they may have received money but lost capital goods; in contrast, the capital market of Edam and De Zeevang allowed women to use mortgages to secure loans and to borrow considerable amounts for longer periods of time.

In the countryside of Tuscany, there were few possibilities to borrow money under reasonable conditions. Hopcroft and Emigh believe that Tuscan peasants could borrow from pawnshops in Florence, rural and local moneylenders, Jews, and notaries, who often charged 20% interest or more.[61] According to Botticini, "Tuscan credit markets were local and isolated, especially for peasant households . . . peasants lacked access to a regional or larger credit market."[62] As a result, peasants often had to go into debt to their landlords, increasing their personal bonds and risking expropriation. According to Emigh, "the usual practice . . . was for landlords to provide either loans, or livestock, or both."[63] As elsewhere in southern Europe, Tuscany's problem of peasant indebtedness was acute. In this respect, Ackerberg and Botticini point out that a lack of access to credit contributed to the rise of sharecropping.[64] Therefore, while men and women in Tuscany may have been able to borrow, they often did so under unfavorable conditions—for a short time, at high interest rates, pawning valuables to provide collateral—and thus they were at risk of expropriation.

Looking more closely at women who were creditors, we see that important types of investment, such as the forced loans by the Florentine *Monte* commune, were generally restricted to the Florentine elite, meaning that few women had an opportunity to invest.[65] In this respect, it is also important to note that several studies indicate that these forced loans were not real investment opportunities

[59] Menning 1993, 6:13–15, 28, 77–78; Pullan 1971, 470.

[60] Pullan 1971, 471.

[61] Hopcroft and Emigh 2000, 15–16.

[62] Botticini 2000, 170.

[63] Emigh 1996, 714.

[64] Ackerberg and Botticini 2000, 242; Herlihy and Klapisch-Zuber 1978, 261, 277–279.

[65] Herlihy and Klapisch-Zuber 1978, 251–254. It seems that Siena imposed forced loans in the countryside more often; Caferro 1994, 93–94.

for the lenders; towns such as Siena often managed to renege on interest payments owed to the lenders.[66]

Other financial institutions, such as the *Monte* commune, founded around 1340, did offer women the possibility to deposit money at an annual interest rate of 5%.[67] The *Monte di Pietà* of Florence (founded in 1496) allowed women to deposit savings as well; after 1530, they earned 5% interest on their investments. Among these investing women were rich and "middle-class" widows.[68] Perhaps such financial institutions allowed women to save for old age, as well. It is doubtful, however, that many Tuscan women had opportunities to invest their savings. Urban financial institutions may have allowed some to do so, but the situation in small towns and in the countryside seems to have been less favorable for doing so. Participation in the capital markets, both as creditors and as debtors, was easier in Holland, at least for the women of Edam and De Zeevang.

Capitalist Women?

We have demonstrated that the capital market institutions in Holland were already fairly efficient in the fifteenth century, offering loans at (very) low interest rates, as well as forms of microcredit at low cost to both men and women. In 1514, for example, the interest rates on loans were between 6.1% (for small loans) and 5.5% (for large ones); in 1563, though, we no longer find a relationship between interest rates and size of loan.

As for investment, we found that households headed by both men and women participated in capital markets and, as the register of 1564 demonstrates, there was lively trade in assets of all kinds. Also, we found that women were quite active in these markets (about a third of all transactions). The explanation for the high level of efficiency of this late medieval capital market is that transaction costs must have been extremely low; this is evident from the low interest rates, the very small spread of interest rates between small and large loans, and the high level of participation by inhabitants of Edam and De Zeevang in the capital market.

Additionally, property rights were well protected right from the start, due to the official registration of transactions and a transparent legal and sociopolitical system, which put severe constraints on the power of the mighty. Note that when, in 1555, Spanish King Philip II tried to introduce an authoritarian style of government in the Low Country, it led to open revolt beginning in 1566, and

[66] Caferro 1994, 95.

[67] Heers 2003,; Molho 1971, 64.

[68] Menning 1993, xi, 13–15, 28, 77–78.

eventually to the establishment of the "free" Dutch Republic. Well-protected property rights were clearly an important part of the story, but capital markets in general functioned relatively efficiently and transaction costs were fairly limited.

The importance of the EMP is apparent when we look at the effective organization of the capital market. This market was necessary to support the new forms of household organization, in which parents needed to set aside capital to support themselves in their old age and prospective couples had to begin acquiring assets to establish their new households. New financial instruments such as the *los-* and *lijfrenten* granted people flexibility in meeting their capital needs, independent of the vested forms of intergenerational transfers and instead increasingly focused on an intragenerational exchange of capital.

Their position on the capital market was one of the key elements allowing women to survive in the early modern society. It is clear from the *verpachtingskohieren* and *schotkohieren* for the town of Edam and the Zeevang that women held positions equal to men with respect to capital assets. As a group, they participated less in the capital market in regard to the total amount of capital they owned, but at the household level, they were not only in charge of similar budgets but also did not shun risk. In fact, contrary to our expectations, we found that the wealthier the men, the more conservatively they behaved with respect to their capital investments. Also, over the course of the century studied, from 1462 to 1563, women's per capita (household) capital investments grew, becoming ever more similar to those of men.

In sum, the economy of Holland at a very early stage—from the fifteenth century onward—had already "solved" the microfinance challenge, and was able to give its female and male entrepreneurs access to the capital they needed to develop their projects. It is therefore perhaps not a surprise that this economy was able to generate economic growth that resulted in an almost continuous increase in GDP per capita from the fifteenth century onward.[69] This resulted, in the century after 1563, in the Dutch Golden Age, when Dutch merchants dominated international trade. We believe that this long period of prosperity had a solid foundation of well-functioning microcredit, inherited from the late medieval period.

[69] Van Zanden and van Leeuwen 2010.

5

The Effects on the Labor Market

Women's Wages, Human Capital Formation, and Fertility

Between the Labor Market and the Household

One of the reasons economists and economic historians are interested in demographic changes is that these changes play a large role in the transition from a Malthusian economy with high levels of fertility to a "modern" demographic system with much lower levels of fertility and higher human capital formation. In this chapter, we argue basically that this demographic transition occurred in stages, and that the rise of the European Marriage Pattern (EMP) was the first step in that direction. There are two happy stories about this demographic transition—and there is a problem in between. The first happy story is the genesis of the EMP in the late medieval period. As we argued in chapter 2, this is a story of women's empowerment, as a result of the emergence of a marriage pattern based on consensus, which was then linked to high levels of participation in the labor market and which widened the scope for greater formation of human capital, for both women and men. This was, in our view, the first step in a switch from quantity to quality of offspring in western Europe's long developmental trajectory, and laid the basis for (among other things) the gradual build-up of human capital that was so fundamental to the economic success of the region.

The second happy story is the demographic transition that occurred in western Europe in the post-1850 (or post-1870) period, owing to a decline in mortality, which was followed, after a certain time lag, by a similar decline in fertility. This latter story has often been seen as the crucial switch toward "quality," in which the increased human capital of women may have played a role, but there is still considerable debate about the forces that drove the decline in fertility (see, for example, the discussion in Janssens).[1]

[1] Janssens 2007.

In between these two happy stories, however, is the rather grim eighteenth century—or, by extension, the "very long" eighteenth century that actually may have started in the seventeenth century and ended in about 1850 (as "long centuries" are supposed to do). This was, even in the most prosperous part of Europe—England—the world of Robert Malthus, where population growth had accelerated, real wages were depressed (in spite of the fact that per capita GDP was rising in the long run), and levels of literacy stagnated. The combination of a "baby boom" and stagnating human capital formation during this "long" eighteenth century has led economic historians such as Mokyr and Allen to doubt, for example, the importance of human capital in explaining the Industrial Revolution that marked this period.[2] Other economic historians have characterized the British economy of that time as Malthusian, dominated by a growing tension between the needs of a growing population and an inelastic supply of foodstuffs.[3]

The question therefore is how to explain the "great conundrum" of this long eighteenth century.[4] Why did the first stage in the switch from "quantity" to "quality"—the rise of the EMP—not lead to the kind of accelerated economic growth and related decelerated population growth as is expected in economic theories modeling these processes? Why did this Malthusian intermezzo suffer such long-term stagnation in human capital formation? This stagnation was, admittedly by international standards, at a relatively high level, but that is also exactly the problem: Why did the movement toward more investment in human skills and education, that had started in the late Middle Ages, stop suddenly in this period of, by all other measures, gradually accelerating economic growth? That is, why did it take so long for the second phase of the switch from "quantity" to "quality" to occur?

To find out what went wrong, we start this chapter in the late medieval period and analyze how the position of women in the labor market changed during this time. Indeed, we show that this is the most logical starting point for a reconstruction of this story. Here again, we need to go back to chapter 2's discussion of the EMP where we tried to show that, in the century and a half after the Black Death, female wages were often comparable to those of unskilled male laborers and employment was booming, thanks to a general scarcity of labor. There are signs, however, that things began to change during the sixteenth century, and that women's economic position came under increased pressure in the two centuries before the Industrial Revolution.

[2] Mokyr 2002, Allen 2003.

[3] Clark 2007b.

[4] Mokyr 1990.

There are reasons to believe that this was especially the case in England, which is the focus of this chapter. There, structural changes in the agricultural sector led to a long-term decline in the demand for female labor, which in combination with the continuing growth of the population, meant that a labor scarcity turned into a labor surplus, which consequently resulted in a strong decline in the relative pay for women. Following the argument developed in the chapter 2, we show the links between the relative remuneration of women's work, their demographic behavior (for example, age at marriage), and investment in human capital (of themselves and of their children).

During the two periods of demographic transition—the late Middle Ages and the post-1850 period—these links resulted in a move toward "quality" of offspring. During the eighteenth century, however, the movement was in the opposite direction. The age at marriage declined and population growth accelerated, so the switch away from "quality" and toward "quantity" of children resulted in a stagnated investment in human capital. This all helps to explain the Malthusian intermezzo.

Relative Wages of Women, 1500–1800

One of the factors behind the emergence of the EMP was high labor-market participation by women in the late Middle Ages, as well as the relatively high wages they earned. This situation most likely underwent significant changes in the early modern period, however. To establish what happened, we build on the work of a number of scholars, including Sandy Bardsley, John Langdon, and Joyce Burnette, who have put together a lot of data for various periods (the high Middle Ages and the eighteenth and early nineteenth centuries) that point to the same trends that we identify here.[5] Moreover, Humphries and Weisdorf have put together a large dataset of female wages in England between 1300 and 1800, documenting the same trends we show below.[6] They present two series of female wages, one of casual, unskilled laborers working on a daily basis, and one of servants who had long-term (usually annual) contracts. The first series shows the same development as the research we carried out for this chapter (originally published in 2011).[7]

[5] Bardsley 1999, Langdon 2010, Burnette 2008.

[6] Humphries and Weisdorf 2015.

[7] The series of wages earned by servants is strongly affected by the assumption that their board and lodging consisted of barebones offerings that are estimated by Allen and Weissdorf 2011, implying, for example, that these servants did not share in the general increase in real income following the Black Death; we therefore do not rely on this series here.

One way to reconstruct the development of female wages is to study wage setting by the courts. From the mid-fourteenth century onward, the government actively intervened in English labor markets by trying to set maximum wages for all kinds of jobs and activities. This had been introduced in the aftermath of the Black Death as an attempt to protect the interests of employers—in particular, those in agriculture. In the 1560s, the national system of wage regulation was reorganized into a regional one, where the courts of different counties were expected to draft wage assessments concerning maximum wages.[8] Assessments like these have their specific legal and sociopolitical backgrounds, and probably reflect market condition only rather indirectly, but they can be used to get an impression of what the justices of the courts in various parts of England considered to be a "normal" wages—or perhaps the wage norm. Moreover, the assessments are usually very detailed: they distinguish different groups of workers: artisans first class (masters), second class, and apprentices; and different wages for agricultural workers: time wages for mowers, reapers (women and men), haymakers (women and men), and laborers in husbandry, as well as piece wages, such as remuneration for mowing and reaping per acre and for threshing per quarter. The wages were also specified according to the season ("Hallowtide–Candlemas" and "Candlemas–Hallowtide"), and whether or not the employer supplied the food ("with food" or "finding self").[9]

Beveridge collected a large number of wage assessments from many different sources, but did not publish them. From his files at the London School of Economics, we studied this collection to see what happened to relative wages of women as set by these courts. According to these records, the total number of wage assessments was almost 100, but the assessments do not all give full details, and women's wages are missing from many of them. For 53 of the assessments we can estimate the relative wages of women in reaping, and for 26 in haymaking; these are spread rather well over the country (17 counties are represented). There is a peak in their numbers in the 1680s, but for the rest of the time, the wages are more or less equally spread across the 1560–1760 period (the rise and decline of this institution is discussed in Minchington).[10]

For a number of counties we could trace the relative wages of women over a long period. For instance, in Northampton, wages for female reapers in 1560 were set at 5 d per day,[11] men at 6 d, which gives a ratio of .83; this declined to .67 in 1673 (the next assessment in the collection), when a man earned 12 d and a woman 8 d. In Rutland, in 1563, a female haymaker was set at 5 d, and man at 6 d, also implying a .83 ratio; in 1610, this was 5 d and 8 d, respectively (or a ratio

[8] Woodward 1980, Minchington 1972.

[9] Minchington 1972.

[10] Minchington 1972.

[11] The "d" indicates pence, for *denarius*, the Roman penny; 12 d was equivalent to 1 shilling.

Table 5.1 **Ratio of Female to Male Wages in Reaping and Haymaking, According to Wage Assessments, 1560/1609–1730/1769**

	Reaping	*N* =	*Haymaking*	*N* =
1560–1609	0.76	8	0.79	2
1610–1649	0.67	14	0.69	4
1650–1689	0.65	19	0.68	13
1690–1729	0.58	6	0.55	4
1730–1769	0.54	6	0.49	3
Total		53		26

Source: Dataset of wage assessments from Beveridge Files, London School of Economics (no. F1)

of .63). In Sussex, in 1606, a female reaper was assessed at 8 d, men were set at 10 d (second sort) and 12 d (first sort). It is clear from the later assessment that all women reapers were considered to be "second sort," so this would set the ratio at .80. In 1742, a female reaper would be earning 10 d per day and a "second sort" man 18 d, a ratio of .56.

The averages that can be calculated from these sources are presented in table 5.1. The trends in reaping and haymaking wages are very consistent: whereas in the late sixteenth century a ratio of almost .80 was considered to be normal, this consistently declined to .50 to .55 in the middle decades of the eighteenth century. The first national wage regulation that set wages for women laborers, that of 1444, was even more favorable than the sixteenth-century wage assessment: the maximum wage of a women laborer "finding self" was set at 4.5 d, which was somewhat higher than the maximum wage of "every other labourer," set at 3.5 d (the same paradox appears in the category "with food": for a woman laborer, the maximum is then 2.5 d, and for every other laborer, 2 d). The explanation is probably that female laborers were mainly employed during harvest time, and that the comparable wage is therefore not that of "every other laborer" but, rather, that of the reaper (5 d) and mower (6 d), which still would imply a wage ratio of .90 or .75, respectively.

In 1495 and again in 1514, the same maximum wages were set, indicating that the 1444 rules were not an error. John Langdon, who studied women working on medieval building sites, finds a wage ratio between men and women ranging from .66 (1290s) to .75 (early fourteenth century), but also occasionally, to levels as high as .80 to 1.00.[12] His results confirm that in the late Middle Ages, the

[12] Langdon 2010, 74–75.

wage gap was much smaller than in the eighteenth century (see also Bardsley's estimate of a late medieval wage ratio of .71).[13] All medieval evidence therefore points to a much smaller difference in wage level between women and men than in the eighteenth and early nineteenth centuries.

It would, of course, be even better if we knew what wages were actually paid out to women and men. In one of his papers, Gregory Clark estimated the determinants of the long-term evolution of nominal wages in England.[14] He also measured the degree to which women's wages were lower than those of men, and came to the conclusion that the effect of the female dummy (a binary variable used to test the effect of something that is either present or not on your outcome of interest) before 1560 was much lower than after 1560, which points in the same direction (but unfortunately he did not test this in more detail). Similar evidence for the late eighteenth and early nineteenth centuries has been published by Joyce Burnette.[15] The agricultural wage data in particular point to a further decline in relative wages of women: for between 1760 and 1800, she estimated a wage ratio of about .48, declining to .42 between 1800 and 1840. In 1833, the ratio had fallen even more, to .37 in winter, .38 in summer, and .45 at harvest time, suggesting that women's wages declined the most during the slack season, when demand for labor was low.[16] Linked to the evidence presented in table 5.1, this would mean that the female-male wage ratio more than halved between the sixteenth century and the 1830s. A similar conclusion can be drawn from data on female servants' wages: they declined from 75 to 95% of male wages in the early seventeenth century to 50 to 60% in the late eighteenth century, but note that the number of observations is quite small here.[17]

Burnette's data also make clear that the low wage ratio found for eighteenth- and nineteenth-century agriculture is more or less representative of the economy as a whole. Her explanation of the high gender gap, which she sees as caused by the lesser physical strength of women, resulting in their lower productivity, can seriously be questioned on the basis of long-term evidence. This also applies to similar explanations of the large gender gap at the start of the Industrial Revolution given by Goldin (1990), who likewise points to physical strength as the main explanation. We therefore share the doubts, most clearly expressed by Ogilvie, about whether women's position in preindustrial societies

[13] Bardsley 1999.

[14] Clark 2004. Unfortunately, in the published version of the paper, this part of the analysis was not included; see Clark 2007a.

[15] Burnette 1997, 2008.

[16] Burnette 2008, 207.

[17] Burnette 1997, 270.

was mainly determined by their "physical endowments."[18] The justifications for these doubts are elaborated upon further in this chapter.

The Beveridge collection also contains detailed data on the development of the actual wages paid by Winchester College, a school founded in 1382 (in Winchester, Hampshire), from whose records Beveridge collected a large set of wage data. In the late fifteenth century, women who were hired occasionally for jobs such as cleaning and winnowing earned 2 d, which was the same as the unspecified, unskilled laborers (probably, given the low level of these wages, food was supplied by the school). In the second half of the sixteenth century, this situation began to change: wages of male laborers went up to 3 to 3.5 d, whereas female wages did not move at all (and occasionally were even lower than at the beginning of the century; see table 5.2). Between the 1550s and 1590s, a wage gap emerged that would increase during the middle decades of the next century, when female wages were less than 50% those of males (but the ratio bounced back a little after 1670). Typically, there are no female wages recorded after 1683.

The trend of a gradually increasing gender wage gap that can be derived from these data points is confirmed by Humphries and Weisdorf.[19] How exceptional was the long-term decline in the relative wages of women? To answer that question, we reconstructed the development of the gender wage gap for the Netherlands. In the late Middle Ages in that region, we find a similar situation: different sources report a wage gap that is very small. In Holland, in the years just before the Black Death, we find a wage gap of 3% for carrying peat and of 14% for working at the chalk ovens.[20] The next observations suggest even smaller differences: in Vollenhove in 1507, women and men received the same wage for carrying peat.[21] Boschma-Aarnouds reports the same absence of a gender wage gap for Edam in the 1540s.[22] Nederveen Meerkerk found for seventeenth-century Leiden that piece wages in spinning were the same for men as for women, and that the relative pay of female spinners (thanks to the fact that this was "booming business" during the 1580–1670 period) was almost equal to that of male craftsmen.[23] Wage parity certainly disappeared in the eighteenth century here as well: in Zeeland until about 1700, women received the same wages as men for weeding, but this situation changed in the eighteenth century, when the wages for men went up but those for women remained the same.[24] And

[18] Ogilvie 2003, 7–8.

[19] Humphries and Weisdorf 2015.

[20] Hamaker 1875–76, 2:432–434, 440–465.

[21] Heeringa 1926, 746.

[22] Boschma-Aarnoudse 2003, 344.

[23] Nederveen Meerkerk 2010.

[24] Priester 1998, 643.

Table 5.2 **Ratio of Female to Male Wages in Winchester College, 1500/1509–1680/1689**

	Unskilled Laborers		
	Men	*Women*	*Ratio*
1500/09	–	2.0	
1510/19	2.0	–	
1520/29	–	2.0	
1530/39	–	2.0	
1540/49	2.0	2.0	1.00
1550/59	2.8	–	–
1560/69	3.5	2.0	0.57
1570/79	3.3	2.1	0.64
1580/89	3.2	2.0	0.62
1590/99	3.1	1.4	0.45
1600/09	3.2	–	–
1610/19	6.6	3.8	0.59
1620/29	8.2	4.0	0.49
1630/39	9.0	4.0	0.44
1640/49	8.8	4.0	0.45
1650/59	10.8	4.0	0.37
1660/69	12.0	4.7	0.39
1670/79	12.0	6.0	0.50
1680/89	12.0	8.0	0.67

Source: Wage data from Winchester College, in Beveridge Collection, London School of Economics (no. F8)

at the beginning of the nineteenth century, relative wages for women in agriculture were 60% those of men.[25]

Thanks to recent research, we can put these trends into an international perspective. In Sweden, the wage ratio developed in a similar way as in the Netherlands: until about 1600, wages of unskilled female laborers were only marginally lower than those of men, but in the course of the seventeenth and

[25] The decline in the Netherlands did occur, but it was more modest than in England and may also have started later; van Zanden 1985, 78–79, 116.

eighteenth centuries, a substantial wage gap opened up.[26] This appears to have been the pattern along the coasts of the North Sea: a very small female wage gap in the late Middle Ages (reflecting the "golden age" of the female worker in this period), followed by a sharp increase in the wage gap in the period after 1600.

In southern Europe, relative wages for female labor were much lower (about 50%), and they did not decline in the early modern period, as a result of which they match the English level.[27] Other research not yet published by De Pleijt points in the same direction: there was no "golden age" of female wage workers in southern Europe; in Spain, for example, wages of unskilled female laborers were, before and after the Black Death, about 50% those of men.[28] The "golden age" of the female worker, therefore, was a specific northwestern European phenomenon, which was intimately linked to the emergence of the EMP in that period, as we explained in chapter 2.

Why Did the Relative Wages of Women Decline So Much?

The large changes in the gender wage gap make it possible to more or less ignore ideas about the "customary" nature of female wages—for example, that they are always fixed at a certain level compared to men.[29] It also demonstrates that the productivity of women compared to men is, at best, only one of the factors affecting this difference. It is, we think, highly unlikely that the relative physical strength or the relative ability to perform certain tasks actually changed so much over time. We can, however, not exclude the possibility that the physical strength of women changed somewhat. Nicholas and Oxley have documented that the average height of English females born in the period 1790 to 1820 declined, both in absolute terms and relative to those of men, which may have caused their work ability to decline as well, but the decline in height was not huge. This fall in female height was more rapid in the countryside than in the cities.[30] On the other hand, Koepke and Baten have shown that in their European dataset, the relative height of women peaked in the fifteenth century, suggesting that in the late medieval period they may have been relatively strong.[31] The explanation Nicholas and Oxley offer for the relative decline in female stature is the decline

[26] Gary 2017.

[27] De Pleijt and van Zanden 2017.

[28] Hamilton 1936.

[29] See the discussion in Burnette 2008, 125–135.

[30] Nicholas and Oxley 1993, 746.

[31] Koepke and Baten 2005.

in employment opportunities and their relative wages: they earned less, so their share of consumption of goods also fell, as households concentrated their limited budgets on meeting the needs of the adult men who were generating the largest share of family income.[32]

Changes in physical strength may have played a role, but probably only a limited one, considering the radical increase in the pay ratio and the very large differences in the female wage gap internationally, which were particularly pronounced during the late Middle Ages. What, then, did decrease the relative bargaining power of women in the labor markets in such a dramatic way? Two developments help to explain this. The first is that women were, in general, a relatively marginal group in the labor market, in the sense that all kinds of "core" activities were carried out by men, while women often had a "supplementary" role as unskilled helpers. The women were particularly in demand during seasonal peaks in the demand for labor—such as during the harvest—but they played a less important role during the rest of the year.

This marginal position is perhaps best expressed in one of the answers to the question about the employment of women and children, given by Selattyn in the Report on the Poor Laws from 1834: "Women and children are not now so much employed as formerly, because labouring men are so plentiful, and their labour so cheap."[33] Similarly, Mate argues that, for the Middle Ages, "it was perfectly natural for women to be recruited in the labour force when the need arose, but in many places they functioned as a reserve pool of labour, to be called upon in times of scarcity, and ignored when supplies of male labour were adequate."[34] In short, men tended to crowd out women in the labor market when supply was abundant, even in the 1830s, when the relative wages of women were at a historic low. The small gender gap that we find in the late medieval period should also be seen in light of the long period of labor scarcity that began after the Black Death, a period during which women's relative position in the market improved, in particular during seasonal peaks in the demand for labor.[35]

A second development that helps to explain the deteriorating bargaining power of women in particularly the agricultural labor market is that, as a result of changes in the structure of this sector, the demand for their labor fell considerably. This is clear from an analysis of the structure of the labor force in the nineteenth century, when only a tiny share—less than 4%—of women were employed in agriculture, whereas the share of men was still about 31% (see table 5.3). In other parts of Europe, women continued to be very active in the

[32] Nicholas and Oxley 1993, Johnson and Nicolas 1995.

[33] Cited in Cunningham 1990, 135.

[34] Mate 1999, 28; similar quotes in Langdon 2010, 68.

[35] De Moor and van Zanden 2010a.

Table 5.3 **Occupational Structure of Men and Women in 1841, Compared with Tentative Estimates for 1522**

		Primary	*Secondary*	*Tertiary*
1841	Men	30.6%	44.7%	24.7%
	Women	3.5%	24.0%	72.5%
	Total	23.4%	39.2%	37.4%
1522	Men	70.0%	21.0%	9.0%
	Total	70.0%	21.8%	8.2%

Source: Broadberry et al. 2010.

agricultural labor market. Even in the Netherlands, which had a highly productive agricultural sector, with a similar employment structure, the proportion of women engaged in agriculture was still 47% (and 36% for men).[36]

In England, a number of changes in the structure of agriculture led to a rapid decline in the demand for female labor. The enclosure movement and the consolidation of small farms into larger farms, was part of this story: the smaller common lands had been an important source of income and work for women and children.[37] This movement was part of a general tendency toward large, capital-intensive farms. The peasant farms that had dominated English agriculture in the late medieval period, and that had supplied a lot of work for women and children (as had the relatively small farms on the Continent), disappeared. As David Davies wrote in 1795, when men occupied or rented portions of land, "their wives and children too, could formerly, when they wanted work abroad, employ themselves profitably at home; whereas now, few of these are constantly employed, except in harvest."[38]

Robert Allen has estimated the degree to which the employment of men and women (and children) changed with the size of farms.[39] His results point in the same direction: when farm size increases—say, from 0 to 50 acres to 600 or 700 acres—the labor input of men (per acre) declines by about 40%, whereas that of women fell by almost 90% and that of boys by about 80%. So, while the demand for labor from men and women on small farms was about equal, the labor demand for female labor on really large farms was only 20 to 30% of that for male labor.[40] On arable farms, these patterns were striking enough, but they also

36 Data for 1849 from Smits, Horlings, and van Zanden 2000, 112.

37 Humphries 1990, 31.

38 Cunningham 1990, 124.

39 Allen 1992.

40 Allen 1992, 215.

occurred on pastoral farms. With the disappearance of the small "family farms" women also lost this source of income, which meant that the "opportunity costs" of working rather than raising children decreased substantially. As Cunningham points out, in the predominantly agricultural regions, women and children were often unemployed or underemployed; only industry, where it existed, was an important source of female employment in the countryside.[41]

Consequently, the enclosure movement and the disappearance of the small family farm undermined the bargaining power of women and children in the labor market. These changes were fundamental, but they were supplemented by changes in the seasonal demand for labor. Snell has demonstrated that the seasonal demand for female labor changed immensely in the eighteenth and early nineteenth centuries: women's role during the harvest probably diminished, and instead their work was concentrated in the spring,[42] which led to a decline in female participation and earning capacity. Snell shows in detail how this change caused a decrease in the relative wages of women, especially in the eastern part of the country (confirming other research, as noted).[43]

The decline in demand for female labor was mainly concentrated in the regions specializing in arable farming; in the livestock-farming districts, demand was much more stable. A fundamental change in the technology of the harvest played a significant role here. In the late eighteenth century, the sickle was replaced by the scythe and the bagging hook, as Collins has shown.[44] The sickle had been used by both men and women, and the wages of female reapers were traditionally subject to wage setting (see table 5.1). The scythe, however, was the domain of men because it required much more hard labor.[45] While the work during harvest time had paid relatively well, now it fell as a result; and if the data published by Snell are correct, the peak in women's annual work cycle switched to the lower-paid work of weeding during spring.[46]

It has been argued by Crafts that what was peculiar about the Industrial Revolution in England was that it was coupled with a rapid decline in agricultural employment—and at a much more rapid pace than was "normal" in the rest of western Europe.[47] He links this phenomenon to changes in the structure of agriculture—particularly the rise of large, capital-intensive (and labor-extensive) farms. It was especially the demand for female labor that suffered

[41] Cunningham 1990.
[42] Snell 1981.
[43] Snell 1981, 420.
[44] Collins 1969.
[45] Snell 1981, 425.
[46] Snell 1981, 428–429.
[47] Crafts 1985, 48–70.

a decline, and this is particularly evident in England as opposed to the rest of western Europe, where family farms persisted.

The Impact of Changing Labor Markets on Population Growth

Women's relative wages declined by half during the early modern period as a result of the falling demand for their labor, especially in agriculture, the result of the enclosure movement and the disappearance of small family farms. In large parts of England, there were no alternative employment opportunities—proto-industry and services were often too small in scale to compensate for this. What were the consequences of these changes for demographic behavior and human capital formation?

It is one of the central ideas of the new home economics that emerged with the pioneering work of Gary Becker and others that the relative remuneration of men and women plays an important role in decision-making concerning fertility.[48] In this view of the determinants of demographic behavior, marriage is in essence an act of specialization; and the larger the differences between men and women—in terms of their pay and human capital—the more benefits they can derive from it. Relative remunerations also affect behavior within marriage. Having and raising children is a time-consuming activity, in which women have a "natural" advantage. But time is scarce and therefore costly, and the opportunity costs of a woman's time—her (relative) wage—is a determinant in Becker's view of fertility.

That is, when the wages of women are relatively high, they will have a strong incentive to allocate a large part of their time to wage earning and less time on reproductive activities (having and raising children); alternatively, when women's relative wages are low, their fertility will be high. In recent research, this concept has turned out to be a robust relationship, in particular when the expected wage for women is viewed as a proxy for their level of human capital.[49] That is, when women are highly schooled and are expected to earn high incomes, their fertility is lower than for women who have received almost no schooling. Figure 1.4 (chapter 1) illustrates this link for the developing world in the 1950–2000 period: when women did not receive any schooling, their fertility was as high as 5.5 to 8 children; when the average years of schooling is as high as 8 to 10, their fertility declines to 1 to 3 children. The figure shows quite clearly the switch

[48] Becker 1973, 1991; Galore and Weil 1996.

[49] Schultz 1997.

from "quantity" to "quality" and is an important part of the approach developed by Becker.[50]

Economic development normally leads to a movement to the right along the regression line shown in figure 1.4: from low levels of schooling/high levels of fertility, to high levels of schooling/low fertility. That it is the level of schooling of women that is crucial in limiting fertility has been demonstrated by T. Paul Schultz, among others, who have found that more schooling for women indeed has a strong negative effect on fertility, and that higher levels of human capital formation for men has a contrary effect, tending to lead to higher "demand for children," as explained in chapter 1. This view is consistent with the expectations based on the Beckerian model; that is, higher wages for men lead to more specialization within the household and more time for women for reproductive activities.[51]

With this knowledge, it is now possible to address that puzzle in English demographic history: Why did the population begin to grow so rapidly during the second half of the eighteenth century? We will ignore the role mortality plays in this story—which was limited—and concentrate, as Wrigley and Schofield have done, on the determinants of fertility and nuptiality.[52] In fact, the demographic acceleration of the post-1750 period was, as Goldstone has argued, caused by a number of changes that had begun much earlier.[53] Fertility within marriage did not change much during the entire 1550–1800 period; the most important driving factor was the change in the age of marriage.[54]

Wrigley and Schofield have, in their seminal study on the English demographic history of this period, stressed the links between real wages and reproductive behavior; but as argued by Goldstone and Lindert, this view does not appear to explain these changes sufficiently.[55] The mean age at marriage of women—the key variable in the Wrigley and Schofield analysis—shows a consistent decline from, according to one study, 26.7 years in 1554/1578 to 22.6 in 1779/1804.[56] In every cohort, women (and men) married somewhat earlier than before; only in the first half of the seventeenth century was this trend interrupted (in 1616: 25.6; and in 1641: 26.7). The decline was particularly marked after about 1700, when in one century the average marriage age dropped by almost four years (from 26.4 in 1691 to 22.6 in 1791).[57]

[50] Becker 1973.
[51] Schultz 1997.
[52] Wrigley and Schofield 1981, Wrigley 1983.
[53] Goldstone 1986.
[54] Wrigley and Schofield 1981, 254; Wrigley 1983, 131.
[55] Goldstone 1986, Lindert 1998.
[56] Schofield 1985.
[57] Schofield 1985.

During the seventeenth century, marriage age seems to have remained more or less stable, but it declined greatly from the early 1700s onwards, a decline that drove the "baby boom" that began in the second half of that century. This decline in the age at marriage was, we believe, the most important change in demographic behavior of this period. But it is difficult to explain on the basis of the real wage estimates that Wrigley and Schofield used: in the first half of the eighteenth century, when the mean age at first marriage was already falling substantially, real wages were going up; in the second half, when real wages declined—or at best stabilized—the process of declining marriage age continued. Thus, there does not appear to be a link between the real wages of men and the average age at marriage. Note: it also does not "work" during the second half of the sixteenth century, when again the mean age at first marriage declined, but real wages fell.[58]

Two other explanations have been suggested in the literature. On the basis of research into the demographics of proto-industrial villages, it has been suggested that this particular form of family employment created a strong demand for the labor of young children, and therefore led to a rise in fertility. The fall in the age at marriage may therefore have been driven by a rise in proto-industrial activity—that is, by more, instead of less, employment for women and children.[59] But the problem with this interpretation is that, as remarked by Smith, the same decline in marriage age that can be found in proto-industrial villages is also present in agricultural parishes.[60] Goldstone therefore suggests that it was not proto-industry that mattered but, rather, proletarianization—the growth of a class of wage workers who were "able to marry at younger ages than traditional labourers."[61] This latter group "still probably required a certain period of accumulation before marrying," as a result of which they were sensitive to fluctuations in real wages.

We think these explanations are not entirely convincing, because they attempt to explain the behavior of women (their mean age at marriage) by using real wage (and employment) data that only refer to men. The decline in the relative wages of women compared to men is a much more convincing explanation for the fall in mean age of first marriage between the 1560s and the 1800s. Firstly, because these processes coincide in time, although the decline in marriage age is stronger in the eighteenth century, whereas the decline in relative wages started well before 1700.

Secondly, the link with wages is suggested by theory: it is exactly what the Becker model predicts would happen if such a drastic change in relative incomes occurs; that is, the larger the wage gap, the more both partners profit from

[58] see Goldstone 1986, and Lindert 1998 for detailed critique along these lines.

[59] Levine 1977.

[60] Smith 1983.

[61] Goldstone 1986, 24.

specialization within marriage, and the more profitable the marriage will be, the earlier that marriage will take place. This does not imply that the female wage rate drives everything; the link between real wages of both men and women and the possibilities for acquiring the assets necessary for setting up a household (stressed by Hajnal in his seminal paper, and analyzed in detail by Wrigley and Schofield) may indeed have played a role as well.[62]

Perhaps the rise in mean age at marriage that occurred during the sixteenth century may be explained in this way (see also chapter 8). It is, however, much more difficult to explain the strong decline in the age at marriage during the eighteenth century in a similar way, because real wages did not go up (they did a bit during the first half of the century, but they go down again during the second half), and the general impression is that living standards did not really improve during the Industrial Revolution (as is also clear from the information derived from women's heights[63]).

The "baby boom" that took place during the second half of the eighteenth century was quite exceptional: demographic growth in England was much faster than elsewhere, and given the poor employment prospects of women and children, particularly in the agrarian parts of the country, it led to the emergence of a labor surplus that was so characteristic of industrializing England.[64] On the one hand, the labor input of men increased, but we do not know what happened to women's labor input; part of the increased effort by men may have been a rational response of the "family economy" to the growing disparities in earnings between the sexes.[65]

Human Capital Formation: A "Failure" of Eighteenth-Century England?

Another striking feature of English industrialization that is linked to these wage and fertility changes is the "failure" of human capital formation in this period. This development has been diagnosed in a number of ways. Crafts, for example, demonstrates that, when comparing English economic growth with the "normal" patterns of European industrialization in the nineteenth century, human capital formation in England lagged enormously; that is, school enrollment was only a third of the level of other European countries with similar levels of economic development.[66] The low degree of literacy and school enrollment in

[62] Hajnal 1965, Wrigley and Schofield 1981.
[63] Nicholas and Oxley 1993.
[64] Wrigley 1983, Allen 1992.
[65] Voth 2000.
[66] Crafts 1985, 63.

nineteenth-century England was largely the result of the slow growth in human capital formation during the long eighteenth century. This has been pointed out by Mokyr and Allen, and is used by them to argue that human capital formation was not a major source of economic growth or a cause of the Industrial Revolution.[67]

It is clear from the research into the development of literacy in this period that a literacy levels stagnated.[68] A social decomposition of these trends has been given by Stone, who shows that literacy among farmers and craftsmen continued to grow, but that for "laborers and servants," it stagnated at a level of about 45% (data for Gloucester and Oxford).[69] Nicholas and Oxley found, in their study of convicts, a decline in literacy among men and women in the late eighteenth and early nineteenth centuries.[70] There is similar evidence that in the industrializing regions such as Lancashire, where population growth was especially rapid, there was a decline in literacy between about 1750 and 1820.[71] De Pleijt demonstrates that average years of education, which rose rapidly during the sixteenth century's "educational revolution," stagnated or even fell during much of the eighteenth century.[72] This is consistent with the "deskilling" of the agricultural and industrial labor force that occurred during the same period, according to De Pleijt and Weisdorf.[73] Finally, the history of book production and book consumption suggests that, after a very fast growth in the demand for books in England in the sixteenth and seventeenth centuries, this proxy of human capital stagnated during much of the eighteenth century.[74]

The failure of human capital formation during the eighteenth and early nineteenth centuries is closely linked with the weak economic position of women during this period—a period that led to earlier marriage, less time for human capital formation for women, and a switch back to "quantity" at the expense of "quality." This is the supply side of the phenomenon; from the demand side, there were similar changes. To begin with, early industrialization was probably skill saving as, for example, spinners and weavers became industrial laborers.[75]

[67] Mokyr 2002, Allen 2003.

[68] Stephens 1990, Mitch 1993.

[69] Stone 1969, 109–111.

[70] Nicholas and Oxley 1993.

[71] See the discussion in Mitch 1993, 276–280.

[72] De Pleijt 2016b.

[73] De Pleijt and Weisdorf 2017.

[74] Van Zanden 2009, 177–204; see also St. Clair 2004.

[75] De Pleijt and Weisdorf (2017) use the HISCO classification to measure skill levels; in it, spinners and weavers are classified as skilled and industrial workers as unskilled, so industrialization by definition implies a reduction of skill levels, although it is not really clear that the actual work these people did—operating complex machines in industrial mills—required fewer skills.

Perhaps even more important was the transformation of English agriculture in the eighteenth century resulting in the decline of family farms (those operated by a skilled farmer) and the rise of large estates operated by unskilled wage laborers.

Returning to the supply side, we find that the educational level of women was not only of crucial importance for their own fertility and their age of marriage but also for the educational opportunities of their children and, via the "grandmother effect," on their fertility again.[76] This new literature argues that it is basically women's empowerment that drives fertility decline and the increase in human capital formation during the "demographic transition." In early modern England, a combination of socioeconomic developments, via an undermining of women's economic position and a halving of their relative wage, caused the Malthusian intermezzo.

Explaining the Great Conundrum

Here we have offered a new explanation for the "great conundrum," or the eighteenth-century "baby boom" mentioned at the start of this chapter. First, we stressed that it was not only population growth that was "different" in England but also the stagnation of literacy and of human capital in general, which seems to be an anomaly in this period. This "great conundrum" has been explained as follows: it has been demonstrated that in England, the gender wage gap increased substantially during the early modern period, which was brought about by: (1) the switch from the post–Black Death labor scarcity to a labor surplus, which in particular harmed the economic position of women; and (2) changes in the structure of agriculture, leading to the rise of large-scale, capital-intensive and labor-extensive farms, which had limited demand for female (wage) labor. This is also suggested by the result that on the continent (in the Netherlands), there was a much smaller decline in female wages, as family farms continued to be quite important (additionally, the period of high demand for labor during the Dutch Golden Age may have increased the relative pay of women[77]).

Moreover, the decline in English wages had important effects on its demographic development. This offers an explanation for the decline in the average age at marriage, particularly for women, between 1600 and 1800, and the related increase in fertility that occurred in this period, which resulted in a much faster

[76] Baizan and Camps 2007, Field and Ambrus 2008.
[77] Nederveen Meerkerk 2010.

rate of population growth after 1750 than elsewhere in western Europe. It also helps to explain the stagnation in human capital formation that occurred during the eighteenth and early nineteenth centuries, again a feature peculiar to English development in these years. The explanation of the "great conundrum" is, therefore, closely linked to the changing position of women in the labor market and within marriage.

6

The "Dark Side" of the EMP?

*Testing the Nuclear Hardship Hypothesis**

In chapter 2, we introduced the nuclear hardship hypothesis suggested by Peter Laslett that suggests the EMP resulted in smaller and therefore more fragile and less resilient households.[1] In this chapter, we develop this hypothesis in further detail and test some of its implications empirically by focusing on one particular group in society—namely, the elderly. We start by first explaining the differences between household and family in order to avoid any confusion.

Laslett's hypothesis has to do with two important units of analysis: the *household*—and in particular, the size and internal organization of it—and *marriage*, especially the degree to which it is postponed. The size of the household determines the "critical mass" of people available to support needy members of the family or household; the internal structure of the household is based on a hierarchy, on which we will elaborate later. Marriage decisions about timing and location—hence, the link with marriage patterns—influence the degree to which generations are available to help each other.

To refine the debate in this chapter, we keep both aspects separate, whereas in the past the debate seems to have covered them together. After having clarified this, we explain how the changing course of households and families within EMP areas led to what has been termed the "squeeze" situation. Our focus on one particular group—such as the elderly—allows us to evaluate the nuclear hardship hypothesis better than when if we looked at society as a whole. If we consider that the nuclear hardship led to a particularly difficult situation for the elderly, one would expect them to suffer substantially; this suffering would normally have an effect on their life expectancy. As we will demonstrate, however,

* This chapter has been based on Bouman, A., J. Zuijderduijn, and T. De Moor. 2012. "From Hardship to Benefit: A Critical Review of the Nuclear Hardship Theory in Relation to the Emergence of the European Marriage Pattern." CGEH Working Paper Series, No. 0028.

[1] Laslett 1988.

life expectancy for the elderly in northwestern Europe was *not* lower when compared to that in areas where family ties were stronger and the elderly were taken care of by family. On the contrary, life expectancy in northwestern Europe was as high as elsewhere and sometimes even higher. Additionally, the vulnerability of EMP regions to external shocks such as harvest failures may even have been lower than in other regions. In other words, there are no indications that a dominance of the nuclear household has a negative effect on the quality of life of the elderly (supposing that this would be directly related to life expectancy).

The question that arises, then, is whether this difference can entirely be attributed to top-down care, as is suggested by Laslett (a story that will be picked up again in chapter 8). Here, we focus on explaining the apparent paradox: Why did EMP regions not suffer from the "dark side" of the European Marriage Pattern?

Conceptualizing Family and Household: Extended versus Nuclear

The work of Hajnal, as well as that of Laslett, suffers from a lack of concise definitions of what is meant by the terms "family" and "household." In fact, both authors use the term "family" intermittently to indicate households consisting of family members, as well as extended family that does not share a household. Although it is true that most households do consist of persons related through family ties, a household is not—per definition—a family, and a family does not necessarily share a household.[2] Household formation, however, cannot be seen as completely independent of family ties, whether those ties are biological or a social construct. For the purpose of our argument, we therefore make a clear distinction between "family" and "household," based on the work of Jack Goody. Whereas Goody sees the family as focused on reproduction, he distinguishes the household as primarily focused on production, which he subdivides into distribution, preparation, and consumption.[3] This distinction in terms shows how "family" and "household" are related. Most of the other attributes of families and households follow from this basic distinction.[4]

As mentioned, people belonging to the same household do not necessarily live under the same roof. They can live side by side, in houses or huts, as is the case, in some African contexts, on compounds. They usually share assets and eat together, and the work of the household members tends to support and protect

[2] Yanigisako 1979.

[3] Goody 1958.

[4] cf. Yanigisako 1979; Fortes 1978.

Table 6.1 **Differences Between Family and Household**

Family	**Household**
• Based on reproduction • Aims to regulate sexuality • Serves as the primary social group • Regulates relationships and support • Uses different kinship systems throughout the world to indicate family members • Dissolves when reproductions fails and all members have died	• Based on production: distribution, preparation, consumption • Provides support and protection for members; • Is residential, though not necessarily under one roof • Is formed at marriage or by splitting and joining • Dissolves as the result of splitting: when production, protection, and/or support fails, or when members die

the other household members,[5] though it is not necessary that they all work together (see table 6.1).

Households might include people who are not kin, such as tenants, lodgers, maids, and apprentices; these people are part of the household for various reasons. They might pay (or be paid for by relatives) to be part of the household, or they might be paid to be so, as is the case of servants.[6] Live-in maids and servants who have their own income, support themselves, and cook for themselves can be counted as separate households, although they share the same roof and activities. For instance, in Dutch *hoofdgeld* sources of 1623 (tax revenues that mention all household members per village), servants are often mentioned as live-in, either cooking for themselves (*buiten de kost*) or eating with other household members (*in de kost*), which was also the case for lodgers (*thuisliggers, kostkopers*). All these categories are mentioned as part of the household under a household "head," but sometimes they are counted separately (1 *hoofd*), indicating their independent status. A few exceptions mention the live-in servants as not being counted, referring to them as counted as part of their parents' households in the same or in a distant village. This shows that sometimes people were seen as living in one household but belonging to another—for instance, when they migrate on a seasonal basis.

Similar to the way that people can belong to more than one household, they can also belong to more than one family—for example, married persons are

[5] But even here we see components like gender influencing the extent to which support and protection are expected.

[6] Hajnal 1982.

members of their parent's family and their spouse's family. Although singles do form households, they are always considered part of a larger family. Obviously, families dissolve when there is a lack of offspring. Households are formed by either marriage or splitting, and they split or dissolve when their members die. Whereas death dissolves both families and households, marriage unites. Importantly, families and households are involved in regulating access to property.[7] Needless to say, control over marriage choices is a powerful instrument for controlling the exchange of property, both in the past and today.[8]

Both Hajnal and Laslett write of "household formation." In doing so, Hajnal distinguishes "simple household systems" (consisting of only one married couple, or none at all), which he claims are only found in northwestern Europe; and "joint household systems" (consisting of two or more related couples), found "elsewhere in the world." Apart from these terms causing confusion,[9] "elsewhere in the world" is an oversimplification. In fact, there is a great deal more to it. In many parts of the world, couples do not exist in this sense at all. Polygamous marriages, for instance, do not consist of one couple, yet they can form multiple households, each containing but "one" couple, when co-wives live in different villages.[10] Similarly, matrifocal households, which exist in Africa and the Caribbean, are those in which mothers live with their children and their children's children, without a spouse (or rather, without a stable bond with a live-in husband); these also do not consist of couples in the traditional sense, yet they form households.[11]

Whereas Hajnal's dichotomy presents an oversimplification of household formation on a global scale, Laslett is too specific when labeling different forms of household formation, thereby ending up with so many categories (all based on similar ideas about couples being present or absent) that a comparison between countries becomes overly complex. Even though Laslett is more specific than Hajnal, his classification is not complete enough to make a global comparison and to distinguish the earlier mentioned polygamous or matrifocal family households. Furthermore, Laslett defines the household specifically as

[7] Schweizer and White 1998.

[8] Howell 1998.

[9] The term "joint family household" strictly refers to households in which siblings and their spouses have joint property rights and often live together, whether or not with their parents; Madan 1962. A better option would be the term "extended family household," originally used to describe a vertical relationship of grandparents, parents, and children living together, but eventually used as an umbrella for both horizontal (siblings) and vertical (offspring) family members sharing a roof. A simple household system could also have been called a "conjugal" or "nuclear family household" system; Murdock 1949, 2.

[10] Zeitzen 2008.

[11] Blackwood 2006.

a residential group, when he states that "a person can belong to one household only, even if, . . . that person slept in one household, the one to which we shall allot him, and worked in another household."[12]

For the purpose of this chapter, we use anthropological definitions of "family" and "household." A basic division of different household forms throughout Europe includes the conjugal, nuclear, joint, and extended family. The conjugal family household consists of a couple without children, whereas the nuclear family household consists of a couple with or without children. The extended family, as discussed earlier, contains not only parents and children but also several vertical generations, which includes grandparents and/or grandchildren. The term "extended family" is also used to include what should be called "joint family," but strictly speaking it consists of horizontal relationships—those between siblings, their spouses, and offspring.[13]

The "stem-family" household, mentioned in regard to European households,[14] is basically an extended family household. But here we can observe only one married sibling remaining at home, with his or her parents, who takes over the household headship, plus all the work this represents. Stem-family households are extended family households of a specific kind, formed on the basis of impartible (*inter vivos*) "inheritance," often based on primogeniture (the right of the first born). So, to classify households for use in this chapter, we use four categories:

1. Joint/extended family households (including stem families)[15]
2. Conjugal/nuclear family households[16]
3. No-family households
4. Solitaries

No-family households are not based on kinship relations and cannot be continued on the basis of reproduction. They are interesting, but are, at least in medieval Europe, anomalies rather than a recurrent household pattern.[17] Solitaries constitute an interesting category. Besides households forms by never-married-singles,

[12] Hajnal 1982, 513.

[13] Holy 1996; Keesing 1981; Murdock 1949.

[14] Fauve-Chamoux and Ochiai 2009; Wall 1983b.

[15] Which include Laslett's multiple family households, complex family households, stem-family households, frerèches, and multigenerational households.

[16] Which include the simple family households.

[17] Convents, however, are no-family households. The ties between the inhabitants of a convent are reinforced by spiritual kinship and the use of kinship terms referring to this spiritual kinship—"father," "mother," "brother," "sister," and "child"—are similar to the terms used for biological kinship terms.

these households only form on two occasions: when a spouse (without children living at home) dies in a conjugal or former nuclear family, or as the result of a dissolution of marriage. This is, for instance, the case with the northwestern European singles.[18] For the purpose of reconsidering nuclear hardship, we focus on the distinction between extended/joint family households, which are formed at splitting, and nuclear/conjugal family households, which are neolocal and formed at marriage.[19]

The Influence of Timing and Location of Marriage: The "Squeeze" Hypothesis

The European Marriage Pattern is characterized by, among other elements, high marriage ages for men and women, high percentages of singles among men and women, and the formation of a new household upon marriage. This combination of elements leads to a gap between generations. The time during which children set up their own households and start having children of their own coincides with the time during which their parents are getting old and needy, and likely to become widowed. The EMP not only affects the physical presence of members of the household but also has an impact on the economic lives of both the parents and their children.

Basically, the accumulation of wealth slows during three "squeezes": the early adulthood squeeze, when a household is to be set up; the middle adulthood squeeze, caused by the costs of raising adolescent children; and the retirement squeeze, when household members stop working. As a result, the wealth accumulation of households does not progress linearly or exponentially.[20] Instead, some periods in the life cycle are more difficult than others, and during these squeezes, households may depend on arrangements that offer financial security or physical help.

For any nuclear family household, the availability of financial help depends partly on the financial situation of "supporting households," such as parental households. The parents ideally offer support during the squeezes. But when the squeezes occur simultaneously in the life cycles of both households, either's offering support becomes difficult, and nuclear hardship may emerge. In extended

[18] Hajnal defined the "large number of singles who never married at all" as a characteristic of the EMP. However, it is not clear whether those singles were actually forming households, since most of them were part of the households in which they lived and worked as servants; Hajnal 1965.

[19] Since conjugal families are in fact nuclear families, we use the term "nuclear families" to indicate both forms.

[20] Di Matteo 1998, 300.

families, where different generations share the same household and marriage is earlier, these squeezes do not coincide, and the grandparents are able to help. In turn, when the grandparents hit the "retirement squeeze," the children are able to support them.

Figure 6.1 shows that age at marriage determines to a large degree whether the squeezes in the households of parents and children will coincide. In the EMP areas, late marriages increased the risk of parents becoming widows or widowers at the same time as their children started parenting their own children. This may have reduced possibilities for assistance: both households might have struggled simultaneously with a lack of both financial and physical support. When the age of marriage was lower (as in the non-EMP scenario shown in figure 6.1), the squeezes in the households of parents and children were less likely to coincide.

These are general models. The bottom line, however, is clear: late marriage increased the chance that households were parenting children at a time when grandparents were no longer able to lend financial or physical support. This also worked the other way around: when grandparents experienced the retirement squeeze, their children were feeling the early adulthood squeeze. And even if family ties did not wither over time, this unfavorable timing of wealth cycles within nuclear family households made it virtually impossible for generations to give each other mutual support.

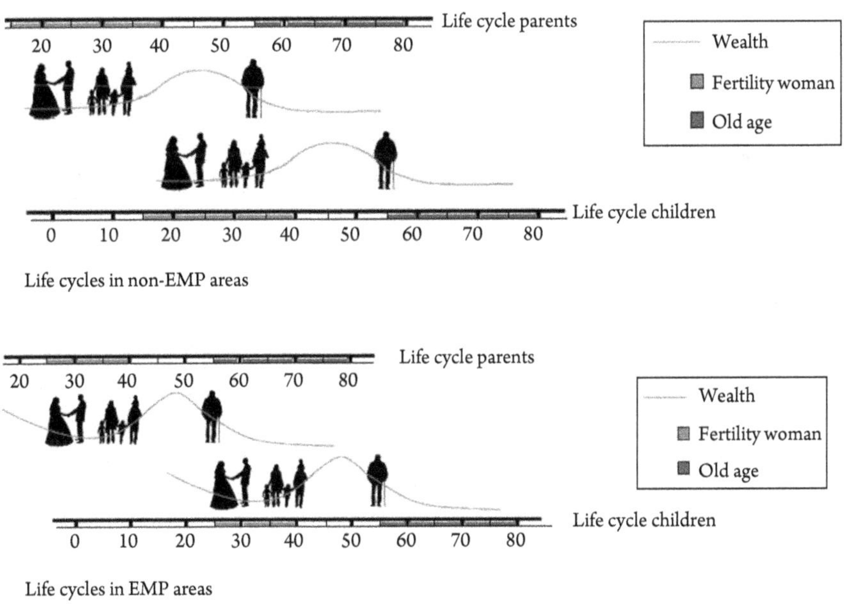

Figure 6.1 The squeeze hypothesis: life cycles in EMP and non-EMP areas.
Source: Previously published in Boele, Bouman, and De Moor 2014, 21–46.

Another feature of the EMP that influences security for the elderly is the small age gap between spouses.[21] In non-EMP areas, the age gap is larger. The "younger" women in non-EMP areas are able to look after their ageing spouses. On the other hand, those women are more likely to be widowed at an early age, unlike women in the EMP areas. For this reason, societies in non-EMP areas are likely to have more widows than widowers. But since they are also likely to share their households with their children, widowhood might not be as problematic as it would be in EMP-areas. In addition, a premature death of a husband would present young widows with the possibility to remarry (provided they are allowed to do so) or become/remain active in the labor market. All in all, this leaves widowed women in EMP areas in a potentially more vulnerable position than women in areas with larger age gaps.

But we should not jump to conclusions: as argued in chapter 2, the position of women in EMP areas was, from the late Middle Ages onward, substantially more advanced than elsewhere, leading to higher labor and capital market participation. Moreover, inheritance rules concerning a deceased husband's property or capital might also have been decisive, making rich widows at the expense of rich sons.

The age gap between spouses has yet another effect. In EMP areas, we see a clear demarcation of generations—a generation gap—that is absent in non-EMP families. This generation gap adds to the difficult position of the elderly and the impossibility for offspring to support them, whether those elderly parents are living with the offspring (which they are obviously not) or living apart. Figure 6.2 demonstrates why ties between parents and children, in EMP areas, no longer provide security for elderly parents. The key to this enigma lies in the age gap at marriage.

Let us take a closer look at the implications of figure 6.2. For the purpose of our argument, we have taken a mean age gap of ten years (non-EMP spouses). Now, with the age gap of ten years, and girls marrying in their teens, both a girl and her mother are (possibly) simultaneously at a childbearing age, which gives them the opportunity to share the care of the children. Furthermore, her parents and the parents of her spouse will not age simultaneously, which diminishes the burden of care for them. In EMP areas, however, where spouses are of the same age, whereas their parents would also have been of the same age at their marriage, all parents age simultaneously. Apart from having four elderly parents that likely require care, the children, being young, equally require care.

[21] Saller 1987.

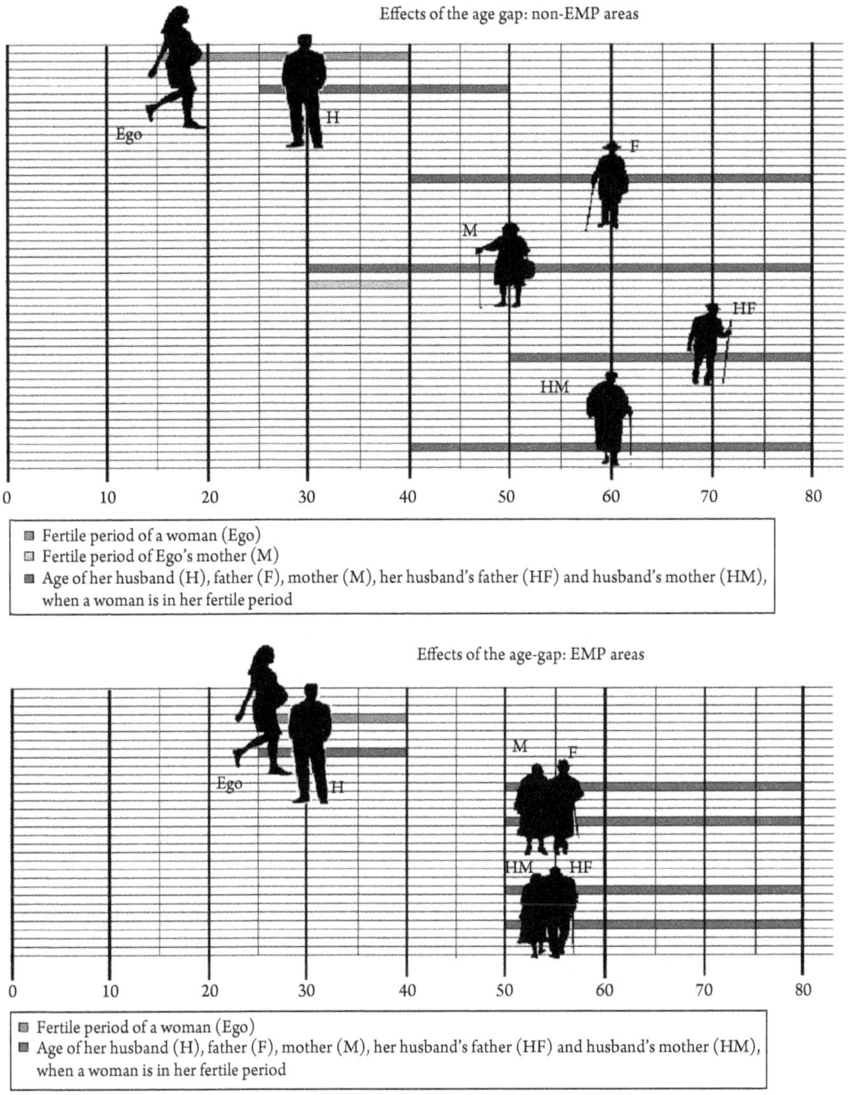

Figure 6.2 Effects of the age gap

On the other hand, the period before marriage, as well as the period after the children have left home, during which the parents might have died, would mean the couple would have no one relying on them for care or for financial help. This would open up the possibility for the couple either to save for household formation or to invest and make provisions for their own old age. If we assume that couples start having children right after marriage, the pattern for those first children reveals an even stricter pattern, diminishing the possible ages of all parents. Parents in EMP areas would thus have been between 50 and 65 years of age at the birth of their first grandchild, whereas in non-EMP areas the pattern would have been (using the terms defined in figure 6.2):

F 40 – 65
M 30 – 55 (M would be able to take care of her husband F)
HF 50 – 75
HM 40 – 65 (HM would be able to take care of her husband HF)

Taking this into account, it is possible to see that the life cycles of non-EMP family members do not diverge as much. As we have already stated, this pattern shows an overlap of time during which both a daughter (Ego) and her mother (M) were having babies simultaneously, blurring the lines between generations somewhat more.

Whereas we have taken a ten-year mean age gap for non-EMP areas, an age gap between spouses in, for example Africa, might be much greater. Since men there can have multiple wives, as well as divorce and remarry, they continuously produce offspring. An elderly man might thus have a new wife with a baby while his son and grandson also have babies. In that case, it becomes very hard to discover a pattern of generations such as can be found in EMP areas. Neolocality might only partly have been responsible for the weakening of family ties. A high marital age for women, and a small age gap between spouses, certainly attributes to a generation gap.

Effects on Life Expectancy at Old Age

Peter Laslett's concept of nuclear hardship assumes that people living in EMP areas were worse off than people living in non-EMP areas. In theory, a relative lack of care should have caused high mortality in EMP areas, particularly during the retirement squeeze. All other things being equal, this should have resulted in high mortality among the elderly in EMP areas, and if this was the case, this should have had an effect on the life expectancy of the elderly as well.

In general, life expectancy at birth increased in preindustrial societies, from 25 years in the late Middle Ages to 30 years in the seventeenth and eighteenth centuries.[22] However, since this figure includes (the many) instances of infant mortality, it is better to use the life expectancy of adults at a specific age—in particular, after the age of 30. Wrigley and Schofield, when calculating life expectancy

[22] Wrigley and Schofield 1981.

Table 6.2 **Life Expectancy in the First Half of the Fifteenth Century**

	At birth	*Age 20*	*Age 30*
England	23.8–32.8	29.4–27.7	24.1–25.0
Italy	29	25.4	21.8

Notes: England: life expectancy for 1401–1425 and 1426–1450, based on Russell (1948) data—the table gives both. Italy: based on Herlihy (1967) data on the small town of Pistoia (1427).

Sources: Acsádi and Nemeskéri 1970, 256; Herlihy 1967, 283–286.

at age 30 in England, arrived at approximately 30 years,[23] which means that the "risk" of growing old and becoming dependent was not imaginary.

Retrieving preindustrial information on life expectancy is difficult, as not many studies provide such data. Although historical demographers have studied mortality for many regions in Europe, they have focused on varying time periods, localities (e.g., towns and/or villages), and social groups. Table 6.2 presents some (scanty) evidence on England and Italy, which suggests that life expectancy tended to be slightly higher in England than in Italy—although we must stress that these data can only serve to give the most general of impressions. Still, they suggest that there was no adverse effect on life expectancy at a later age caused by the specific characteristics of the household in an EMP area. These estimates are confirmed in recent research by Cummins, who created a large dataset to reconstruct the life courses of the European elite, including their life expectancy. He also finds a "little divergence" occurring in western Europe during the late Middle Ages: life expectancy in the North Sea area developed more favorably than in the rest of the continent.[24]

Part of the explanation for the favorable development of longevity in the North Sea area may be found in the disappearance of famines in this region after the Black Death. This has been well documented for the northern Netherlands, where the Malthusian links between harvest failures and high prices for food led to famines, which led to peaks in mortality, gradually disappeared. In the seventeenth century—a period for which we have consistent data to test the link between fluctuations in the price of rye flour and mortality in the city of Rotterdam—this link no longer appears.[25] The causes of this are complex. International trade in foodstuffs (such as rye and wheat from the Baltic) expanded rapidly during this time, making the region less dependent on its domestic supply. Market integration more generally resulted in less violent

[23] Wrigley and Schofield 1981, 250.

[24] Cummins 2014.

[25] Noordegraaf and van Zanden 1995, 428–429; see also Curtis et al. 2017.

fluctuations in cereal prices, as surpluses and deficits could more easily compensate for each other. And rising real incomes created larger buffers against such exogenous shocks. Institutional changes—such as the growth of poor relief—may also have played a role. But the long-term effect of these developments was that Dutch society in the seventeenth century was less vulnerable to harvest failures—and may even have profited from them, as high cereal prices meant more business and larger profit margins for Amsterdam merchants.[26]

In England, similar changes resulted in a gradual delinking of market prices with mortality peaks. Weir, for example, found that such a link still existed in the period before 1740, but disappeared afterwards.[27] Summing up, the evidence suggests that the EMP regions of western Europe may have been more resilient and less fragile than non-EMP regions, contradicting the predictions of the nuclear hardship hypothesis.

Conclusion: The Welfare Paradox of the EMP

The question therefore is: why did the emergence of the EMP not bring about the kind of negative welfare effects that the nuclear hardship hypothesis predicted? We have explained in detail that such effects might be expected, but in historical reality they do not show up. We suggest three explanations for this. First, as will be explained in detail in the next chapter, the system of servanthood that emerged in the same period, and that was intimately related to the EMP (and even considered by some to be a key feature of the EMP), partially counterbalanced the greater exposure to external shocks that would have come from the reduced size of households. Second, institutions responded, as we explained previously in chapter 2. (We deal with this issue more extensively in chapter 7.) But a third, very tentative explanation may also be suggested. In extended families, with many members and strong hierarchies, free-rider problems may play a role, resulting in less commitment toward the common good and even shirking of responsibilities. In small nuclear families, this problem is probably much less pronounced, and men and women (and children) are more willingly committed to working hard, as they directly profit from the increased income. Perhaps the small nuclear family of the EMP was a precondition for the industrious revolution, with its increased labor productivity per capita, particularly in market-related activities. And extended families perhaps did not have the incentive structures to further such "industrious" activities. We now know

26 As suggested by De Vries 1978.

27 Weir 1984; more recently, Campbell and Ó Gráda 2011.

that the number of working hours in, for example, England increased sharply during the early modern period.[28] It is therefore, we argue, no coincidence that the productivity gains that are found in the North Sea area in the early modern period, which cushioned the exogenous shocks, materialized here. The EMP also improved the incentives for commercialization, specialization, and hard work. This increased productivity also allowed these EMP households to start saving on a regular basis for old age—and to use the capital market (discussed in chapter 4) to increase their resilience.

[28] Allen and Weisdorf 2011, Voth 2000.

7

The Institutional Effect

Alternatives for Family Ties, the Role of Trust, and the Emergence of the Commercial Household

What About Vulnerable Groups?

In chapter 6, we explained that although the elderly must have experienced substantial problems in a society with the European Marriage Pattern (EMP), this apparently did not have a negative effect on their life expectancy or on the vulnerability of EMP societies to external shocks. This chapter deals with a number of solutions that may have helped people to deal with this paradox in the early modern period. Was the nuclear hardship discussed in chapter 6 solved with the emergence of care supplied by top-down institutions, driven by charity? If so, it is likely that we see a difference in such institutional arrangements between areas with extended families and those with nuclear families. If we cannot find such differences, then there must have been other arrangements for the elderly to deal with the hardships of growing old.

Another answer could have been servanthood, which may have offered a flexible solution for households in EMP societies. We demonstrate that the institutional diversity of the EMP areas allowed the elderly to develop sufficient "agency" to deal proactively with problems of care. In this, northwestern European society differs substantially from southern European society.

We look at the different options the elderly could rely upon when they no longer received support or care from their children, possibly in combination with the "servant solution." In a way, the elderly were the social group that lost most as a result of the rise of the EMP, making it necessary to introduce certain institutional arrangements to compensate. But we demonstrate that many problems were solved by their proactive behavior (savings, investments via capital markets) by which they achieved "agency," which distinguished the EMP area from the rest of Europe (and the rest of the world). Thus, a view of agency

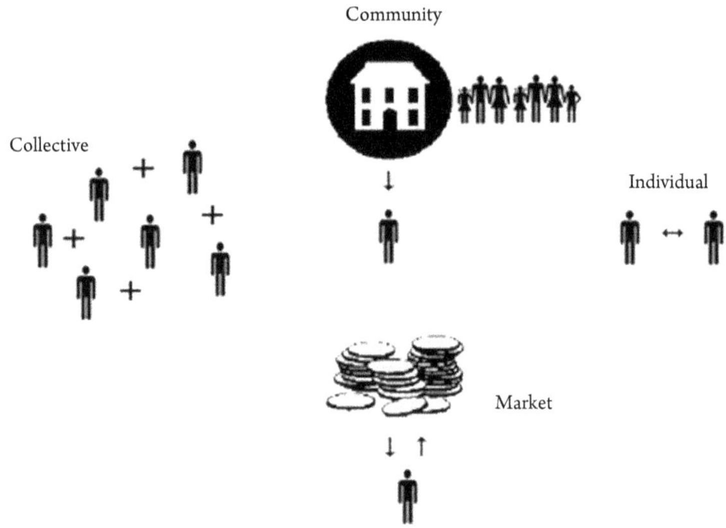

Figure 7.1 Security arrangements for the elderly. Source: Previously published in Boele, Bouman, and De Moor 2014, 21–46.

can complement the discussion of solutions for the nuclear hardship, which goes back to Laslett's claim that family and collective institutions "always imply each other"[1]: "the more widespread the nuclear family, and the more strictly neolocal rules are applied, the more important collective institutions will be for the security of the individual."[2]

We distinguish four "types" of arrangements, showing the interactions between them as one of the characteristics of the EMP area. For each of these types, we explain how it worked in the EMP area and to what extent it could also be found in southern Europe, where the EMP was not characteristic or was much less prevalent during the early modern period. Furthermore, we estimate to what extent these arrangements "solved" the problems caused by the EMP. Indeed, one of the distinguishing features of the EMP area is the early emergence of these four arrangements and—even more important—the degree to which they interacted. As we show, capital market arrangements became a normal part of the community provisions, and this was clearly due to the early development of the capital markets in northwestern Europe (see figure 7.1).[3]

A careful study of these arrangements in EMP areas reveals the way in which individuals dealt with each other and the way in which the capital market was integrated into other forms of care. In our discussion of the

[1] Laslett 1989, 133.
[2] Laslett 1988, 156.
[3] Zuijderduijn, 2009b.

available literature on this subject, we focus on changes at the individual level and on the influence of the capital markets on these solutions and the collective arrangements.

Differences in Individual Arrangements: Family, Neighbors, and Strangers

Though altruism and moral obligation might have been drivers for individual care arrangements, such arrangements were rarely documented. More formal arrangements between individuals, however, were in some cases well-documented. A close reading of the literature reveals the existence of pension plans and retirement contracts in use throughout western Europe.[4] These retirement contracts were drawn up by people with their kin, as well as with strangers. Parts of them were concluded between parents and their children.

The oldest retirement contracts stem from thirteenth-century England, Denmark, and France. Clark links the emergence of pension plans in England to a lack of family support: the devastating effects of the plague left many adults childless, thus creating a situation whereby three-quarters of all post-plague contracts had no explicit filial tie between the pensioner and his or her benefactor.[5] These pension plans served to provide not just financial security in old age but also arrangements such as clothing, bed linens, and fuel such as wood for the fireplace. In some contracts, the elderly might demand a private room to live in, a field to cultivate, or an oven for baking. Others included funeral provisions for the adults and the assurance of prayers being said for their souls. The bottom line was clear: "they wanted assurance that their needs would be met."[6] Additionally, different forms of retirement contracts between individuals, who were not necessarily family, can be found elsewhere in northwestern and northern Europe, dating from a quite early time.

[4] Brunel 2010; Moring 2010; Fusè 2008; Vogt 2008; Dribe, Lundh, and Nystedt 2007; Morin 2006, 389; Dribe and Lundh 2005; Lundh and Olsson 2002; Poska 2000; Brettell 1991, 448; Gaunt 1983; Clark 1982; Held 1982; Mitterauer and Sieder 1982.

[5] Clark 1982, 316.

[6] Clark 1982, 312; Pat Thane links the existence of retirement contracts to the "landholding class," suggesting that retirement contracts were bound to land. Even if land (in the English case) was not owned, it was "leased" by a lord, who profited from the contracts, by fees levied for him. According to Thane, retirement contracts demonstrate that the elderly tried to preserve their independence: "They display old people carefully planning the maximum use of resources available to them"; Thane 2000, 75.

The *contrat de placement*,[7] an arrangement between neighbors, is found as early as 1290 in northern France.[8] Long before the Black Death, at least since 1200, the elderly no longer stayed with their relatives but, rather, looked for contractual solutions to deal with their hardships. In Douai and Cambrai, a system of *gouvernance* existed, by which the *gouvernant* received goods from an individual or couple in exchange for food, clothing, and shelter.[9] Contracts were also made between children and parents, or parents-in-law, demonstrating that care provided by children was not, or no longer, customary.

The *fledføring* (literally, "a person to be led into another household") emerged in Scania and Zealand (in Denmark), as well as in part of Sweden[10] at the end of the twelfth or the beginning of the thirteenth century. *Fledføring* is a legal term, referring to a kind of retirement contract in which the elderly or sick who can no longer provide for themselves could offer themselves and all their property to a heir (not a stranger) at the *thing* (the local court), in exchange for food and shelter. A *fledførte* person would lose his or her legal status and personal rights, and the heir would become his or her legal guardian.[11] *Fledføring* probably resulted from the introduction of new laws (and changing taxes on the land) based on "canonical teachings about degrees of consanguinity."[12] The new, rigid definition of kinship (and as such, the new inheritance laws) made it difficult for individuals to dispose of their property in the way they preferred.

Similar practices seem to have existed throughout the area where Germanic laws prevailed: in Scandinavia, notably Sweden (*sytning, undantag, föderåd*); Austria and Germany (*Ausgedinge, Auszug, Ausbehalt, Ausnahme, Austrag, Altenteil, Leibzucht, Leibgedinge, Winkel*); Czech Republic (*výměnek*); Finland (*syytinki*); and Norway (*kår, kårstue, hold, kost, føderåd, framførsle*).[13] However, retirement contracts in those countries seem to be from a later date than the ones in Denmark, France, or England. Gaunt explains that children in Scandinavia were not obliged to take care of their parents;[14] thus, in a way similar to the *fledførte*, the elderly presented themselves at the local court to those relatives who were willing to take care of them in exchange for their property—which often meant children risked being disinherited. However, Swedish laws

[7] In the literature, the term *contrat de placement* also refers to a contract between parents and wet nurses concerning the nursing of children.

[8] The uniqueness of this contract, between Raoul de Picard and his neighbors Drouard Basin et Sibille seems clear; Brunel 2010.

[9] Brunel 2010.

[10] Gaunt 1983, 252.

[11] Vogt 2008, 273; Gaunt 1983, 251.

[12] Gelting 2000.

[13] Gaunt 1983, 251.

[14] Gaunt 1983.

(enacted by Earl Birger in the mid-thirteenth century) prevented parents from totally disinheriting their children.[15] Gaunt sees these retirement contracts with relatives as a kind of alimentation system, rather than a real property transfer and calls them "anticipated inheritance."[16] In Denmark and Sweden, such "anticipated inheritances" were common from the early sixteenth century onward, whereas in Austria and Germany, similar retirement contracts made with kin date from the second quarter of the seventeenth century until the nineteenth century.

Elsewhere in Europe, especially south of the "core" EMP area, the arrangements for caregiving differed in various ways. Not only did the caregiving entail a physical presence in the household, whether family or not, but it also was not always specified in a contract. If there was a contractual agreement, it usually involved a transfer of property from one generation to another.

Early modern Spanish law did not specifically authorize retirement contracts. In many cases, retirement arrangements appeared as conditions in dowry contracts, in which the dowry was contingent on the newlywed's acceptance of the responsibility of caring for the parent or other adult who provided the dowry. The arrangements were also integrated into legal documents known as *escritura de mejora*.[17] A person could formulate a document that provided a gift to another, a *donacion entre vivos*, before the death of the provider, but it often depended on certain conditions. Finally, the texts of many wills either reasserted the terms of retirement contracts or compensated tacitly contracted care with testamentary bequests.[18]

Brettell describes similar Portuguese strategies to influence intergenerational property transfer: *dotes de casamento*, or marriage bequests; *doaçoes*, or general bequests; *testamentos*, or wills; and *partilhas*, or land divisions.[19] These documents could include retirement clauses by which parents ensured that someone would care for them in their old age. The *dote* should thus be considered as a marriage transaction that sets up an obligation, reinforcing, rather than dispensing with, the relationship between parents and children.[20] *Doaçoes* could also be used to

[15] Gaunt 1983, 252.

[16] Held, however, who writes more specifically about the Austrian *Ausgedinge*, sees them as an alternative to the stem-family system, having more to do with the continuance of the house and household itself; Held 1982.

[17] "The *mejora*, an additional one-third plus one-fifth of the estate bequeathed to a favored child, was widely used in some areas of Galicia to supplement partible inheritance. The bequest created a reciprocal relationship between the person creating the mejora and the recipient in which the receipt of the additional portion of the postmortem estate was dependent on the fulfillment of the old-age demands made by the provider"; Poska 2000, 317.

[18] Poska 2000, 317.

[19] Brettell 1991, 448.

[20] Brettell 1991, 450.

secure care for childless couples or for unmarried men and women; they could provide nieces and nephews with parts, or all, of their possessions.[21] Similar to the practices Poska perceives in Spain, parents used wills and bequests in order to leave money and property to unmarried daughters, in gratitude for their service and care.

Although the contractual arrangements vis-à-vis retirement deserve further comparative study, some general conclusions can be drawn. Individual arrangements differed in northwestern and southern Europe: the EMP center reveals more contracts in which family members were bound by their obligations toward their families, but even more striking is that it was not uncommon to negotiate such contracts with strangers.[22] In the Spain (seventeenth century) and in Portugal (nineteenth century), retirement contracts as such did not exist; [23] however, the elderly could negotiate their care, with the contractual arrangements usually in conjunction with existing agreements on the transfer of property—that is, dowry contracts or wills. These contracts seem foremost to be arranged between relatives.

The explanation for the form of arrangement should not only be sought in the actual strength of family ties but also in the household life cycle; that is, in non-EMP areas, the marriage of the first child was well before the parents reached retirement age, whereas in EMP areas, the marriage of the first child coincided, or may even may have been later than the time when the parents started thinking about their need for care and support in old age. Even when old age was still far ahead, the parents may have wanted to secure future caregiving, so they bound the children to this obligation—for who knows how the relationship between the children and their parents might change in the meantime? On top of this, the intergenerational exchange of property *inter vivos* in non-EMP areas was for women (in the form of dowry)—more important than the post-mortem exchange (inheritance)—which thus offers more incentive to link the conditions for such a transfer to the dowry contract.

[21] Brettell 1991.

[22] We cannot completely ignore that the situation in northwestern Europe might have been different to start with; that the retirement contracts were not so much the result of the breakdown of family ties as the effect of a goal of laws to define rules regarding kinship rights (possibly under influence of the canon laws), as Vogt suggests when discussing the *fledføring* contracts of Denmark. Similarly, the accounts of Gaunt and Clark are not so positive on the treatment of the elderly, whether by strangers or by their children. Gaunt even suggests that the treatment of the elderly depended on their landholding; Gaunt 1983.

[23] Brettell remarks on changing dowry in Portugal: "Here too reciprocity and respect for the elderly are primary guiding principles. Conversely, where young people can find alternative sources of wealth and therefore independence from parental inheritance, the status of the elderly may be eroded"; Brettell 1991, 461.

Following a similar line of reasoning, we should not disregard the institution of the dower. The dower, or morning gift,[24] was a western European marital payment stemming from Germanic law and dating back to the twelfth century. It seemed to serve a similar purpose of securing a livelihood for widows.[25] The dower was decided upon at marriage. The actual transfer of money or goods, however, took place when the husband died, and could amount to a third of his possessions.[26]

Whereas both the dower and the dowry were used to ensure livelihoods for old age, the customs differed substantially. First, the dower was a gift from a husband to his wife, whereas the dowry was a gift from the parents to the daughter.[27] Second, the dower did not secure physical care; it provided a widow with property so as to remain independent. In contrast, the dowry arrangements we see in Spain, Italy, and Norway, for example, served to secure the ties between relatives and ensure care and accommodation for elderly family members, as well as for the couple (or unmarried female relative) who offered this care. The differences between EMP and non-EMP areas thus have not only to do with the frequency of contracts between parents and children (or other partners) but also the type of transfers between parents and children, whether these address issues of caregiving in old age or not.

The Influence of the Market on Caregiving Institutions

Private and public charity institutions were omnipresent in most of early modern Europe. Charity had been an important form of wealth "redistribution" since the "charitable revolution," between 1130 and 1260.[28] What makes charity different from other forms of support is the fact that it was not demand driven but, rather, supply driven; that is, charity-granting institutions were set up by the church, by local nobility, or by the state (especially from the sixteenth century onward). And although demand—the need for leprosaria (leper colonies), for instance, was clearly linked to leprosy—could have offered an initial incentive to set up

[24] The dower is also called *douaire, dour, morgengabe, morgengift, morgengave*. In England, noble widows were called "dowagers." Their dower could consist money, a house (hence the term "dowerhouse"), or land.

[25] Haskins 1948–49.

[26] Buckstaff 1893.

[27] Goody and Tambiah 1973.

[28] Vauchez 1978.

an institution, the charitable institutions could (and continue to) exist without a demand for services.[29]

Top-down charitable initiatives sometimes became redundant over time and some even started life as redundant—for instance, if the benefactor's prime motive was to display charitable intentions rather than to provide actual aid. This is evident in some of the hospitals that Italian families built to intensify their ties with the villages where their ancestors had lived; lacking a demand for care, these buildings served more as *lieux de memoire* than as hospitals.[30] To be sure, other motives may also have played a part, such as religious belief[31] and genuine compassion. This does not mean that hospitals did not accommodate the needy, but it means that looking at hospitals as immediate responses to socioeconomic shifts—such as the emergence of nuclear hardship—is problematic. In this respect, these and other top-down initiatives differed from bottom-up initiatives; the latter, whether individual or based on collective action, were directed toward the immediate stakeholders in a situation that was clearly different from how the charitable institutions were formed.

The potential influence of nuclear hardship in the EMP areas becomes visible when we look at the way in which the elderly started negotiating their care. In western Europe in the twelfth century, single women sought admittance to hospitals and even leprosaria. Thus, "sound and healthy" women were competing for a place in St. James Hospital, in Canterbury as early as 1160.[32] Here, we see how the changing demand for care caused new groups to enter existing institutions. These top-down institutions were willing to grant them access because the women were seen as paying customers, and also because the number of lepers seems to have declined from the thirteenth century onward.[33]

This was a general development visible in large parts of northwestern Europe: hospitals, leprosaria, and convents were increasingly confronted with people who were willing to pay for shelter, food, and clothing. In Paris, authorities began to worry "that it is unfitting that the number of the healthy living there exceed those of the sick and of pilgrims."[34] In the west of the German empire, in Soest, the medieval hospital was gradually divided, with one part aimed at caring for the sick and the other at caring for women.[35]

[29] Cf. supply and demand for charity: Borsay and Shapely 2007, 1.

[30] Goudriaan 2008, 199; Gavitt 1997; Henderson 1994, 353; Goldthwaite 1981, 11.

[31] Spaans 2002, 256; Spaans 1997, 25–27.

[32] Rawcliffe 2006, 297–298. Cf. Omre and Webster 1995, 35–36.

[33] Cullum 1991, 4. Cf. Power 2010, 206–207.

[34] Brodman 2007, 128–129.

[35] Fleck 2007, 26.

The *corrody* originated in fourteenth-century England. It was initially used by kings and bishops to reward servants for their service and to provide for the aged, sick, and poor. Corrodies "would protect those who, because of their vocations, were denied a family to care for them in their old age."[36] But the corrodies soon changed into a sort of retirement contract that provided the elderly with food and weekly, monthly, or annual cash payments in return for a specific one-time contribution.

These corrodies (*Pröven* in German, *kostkopers* or *proveniers* in Dutch) were accepted by charitable institutions, perhaps those coping with vacancies or unable to function without this external funding, which thus began to offer "commercial care." In the northern Low Countries, this was visible in the early fourteenth century; specialization occurred in the sixteenth century, when *proveniershuizen* emerged—commercial institutions specializing in care for the elderly.[37]

In England, northern France, and the Low Countries leprosaria, but also guesthouses, hospitals, and monasteries took in paying "guests" (not necessarily ill, handicapped, or old) to be taken care of, as early as 1314.[38] Brunel describes the existence of such institutions (*modalités de placement des vieillards*) in northern France. In the village of Laon, at the start of the thirteenth century, *les bourgeois*—Brunel does not mention whether they are all elderly—gave all their property to the *hôtel-dieu* in exchange for the best care thinkable.[39] Where the popularity of this practice resulted in a surcharge for the *hôtel-dieu*, these hospitals started providing pension plans, including food and wine delivered to the home, or paid the pensioners an annual rent so as to secure their subsistence (similar to an annuity). Brunel quotes Alain Saint-Denis, who describes how this *système d'assurance à la carte* was gradually replaced by usufruct contracts.

It was only in the Netherlands that the leprosaria, once incidents of leprosy had declined, gradually took in more and more paying elderly, turning the institutions into a kind of home for the elderly that accepted single men or women, and sometimes couples. The elderly generally paid a sum to be admitted, and they had to sign a contract that stated they would leave all or part of their possessions to the institution. In some cases, they had to bring a certain amount of possessions with them, which was carefully documented (clothing, a bed). In return, they were provided with care, meals, clothing, and even money. This "allowance" was called a *preuve* or *proven*, from which they got the title *proveniers*.

[36] Harper 1983, 97.

[37] De Moor 1994, 112; Kossmann-Putto, 261–62; Danneel 1995, 401.

[38] De Moor 1994, 112.

[39] Brunel 2010.

Indeed, once leprosy was eradicated in the Netherlands, several leprosaria were turned into *proveniershuizen*, focusing solely on the elderly.[40] This "institutional flexibility," whereby an institution transitioned to meet a new demand instead of simply closing its doors, is a remarkable phenomenon. How flexible these institutions were is demonstrated by the leprosery of Amsterdam, *Sint Jorishof*. Initially it was located outside the town walls, but this changed when the town expanded in the fifteenth century. As a consequence, the lepers had to be moved to a new location outside the new city walls. Meanwhile, the function of *Sint Jorishof* changed to that of a *proveniershuis*. Although they were not affordable for everyone, almost every town in the Netherlands had such a *proveniershuis*.

The development of capital markets also offered the possibility to make (financial) provisions for long-term care, as we mentioned in chapter 4. Money and property were given to secure care for the elderly. Although we have noticed contracts with relatives and neighbors, the elderly also relied on anonymous forms of (financial) security and care provided by institutions. Among the medieval financial instruments, the life annuity was regarded as one choice for people looking for security in their old age. Investors purchased a life annuity (annual pension), which was to be paid until they died. As an alternative, couples could buy a joint life annuity, which would be paid until both partners had died. The yields for life annuities were about 10% for single and about 12% for joint life annuities. This meant that investors had to live for eight to ten years to reach the breakeven point (i.e., the point at which they would receive more money than they put in and would start to profit from their investment). Data on the age of buyers of life annuities are relatively scarce. But there are reasons to believe that life annuities ought to be regarded as a provision taken for old age, or as a type of investment by which people could speculate on the age they (or their children) would reach.[41]

However, such market dependency posed a problem: people who received a sum from an annuity still had to purchase food, firewood, clothing, and shelter. They had to be physically able to do this; and even if they were, they still ran risks of diminishing returns, owing to inflation. One solution, which appeared early on, was to express life annuities and redeemable annuities in kind (grains, such as rye and wheat).[42] Another solution meant no investments in the capital market, but to use savings, property, or real estate to pay for board in a monastery

[40] This happened, for instance, to the leprosaria of Rotterdam, Schiedam, and Gouda, and to the Sint Nyclaes gasthuus, also called "hospitael van Onser Vrouwen ende Sinte Nyclaes" or Sint Anthonis Gasthuus of Amsterdam, as well as to the St. Jorishof of Amsterdam.

[41] Van Gerwen and van Leeuwen 1998, 143.

[42] Annuities in kind are, for instance, to be found in the late medieval Low Countries—such as in Kampen (fourteenth century)—but also in the north of France, where they became increasingly popular in the sixteenth century (Kossman-Putto 1955; Schnapper 1957, 80–81.

or hospital.[43] This could be done by paying a lump sum—a "package" of food, shelter, and care. In England as well as in the Low Countries, such "packages" were offered by guesthouses and monasteries, and curiously also by leprosaria.

Did extended family households participate to such an extent in capital markets? Many of the incentives, described here, were missing; without neolocality, fewer people would have to borrow large amounts. That is, when several generations lived together, the early adulthood squeeze may have been less severe, since grandparents could help out. Additionally, the retirement squeeze might have been absent: younger women cared for their aging spouses, parents and parents-in-law did not age simultaneously, and children living in the home could provide the necessary care. All in all, the extended family provides fewer incentives to either save or dissave.

As shown in chapter 6, the nuclear neolocal families in EMP areas, where the age gap between spouses was small, could profit from the generation gap, an opportunity that seems to have been absent in non-EMP areas. In the period before starting families, individuals could save in order to set up households upon marriage. Additionally, when both spouses no longer had to take care of children, they could continue to participate in the labor market, giving them additional chances to save. A large age gap between spouses, together with live-in parents such as we see in many extended family households, did not cause a generation gap in this sense. Indeed, the blurring of generations did not result in a squeeze (with the incentive to save for bad times), but neither did it provide a period during which adults were free to participate in the labor market simultaneously, making it possible for them to save.

But what about the medieval Italian dowry funds—the *monte delli doti*—that existed in early fifteenth-century Florence, whereby parents could invest their money in a fund, to have their principal returned with interest when their daughters were to be married? These dowry funds could, in principle, also be seen as investing or saving behavior. The incentive, however, was not so much the idea of saving for old age as the ability to marry off one's daughters, which was a costly affair. Also, the dowry funds were created by the government seeking the fiscal means to finance war. While dowry funds can be seen as encouraging investing behavior, they essentially amount to (*inter vivos*) a financial transfer from parents to daughters. If we take into account the idea that dowries can be used to enforce status mobility,[44] we see that parents were not so much interested in saving for difficult times as in buying status with a onetime investment at or shortly after the birth of their daughters. As such, these dowry funds are

[43] Van Eeghen 1941, 42–43. Gaunt refers to this practice as the Augustinian soul gift; cf. Gaunt 1983, 254.

[44] Bell 1998.

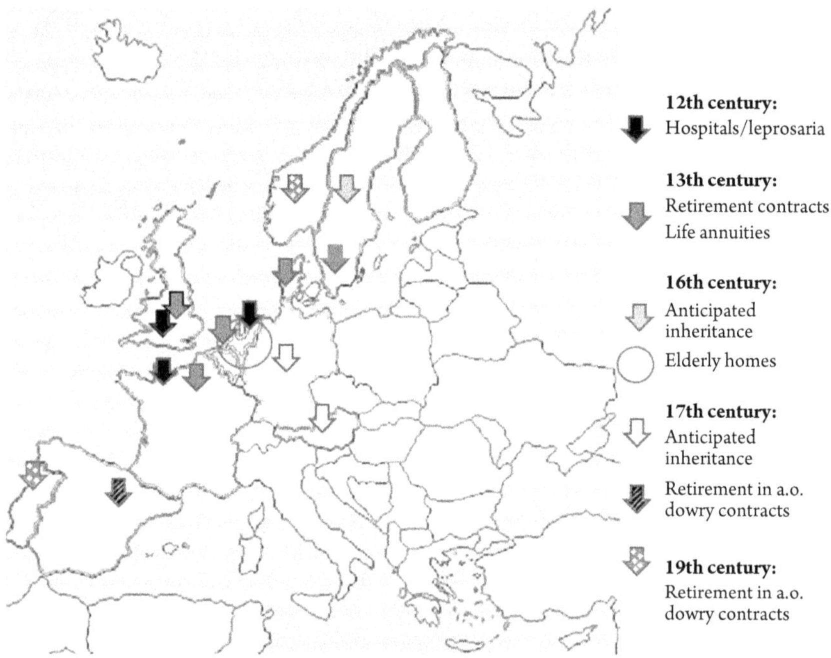

Figure 7.2 Solutions for elderly care in Europe during the early modern period

fundamentally different from the life annuities discussed earlier. Dowry funds provided their funders with status, whereas life annuities provided their funders with agency. Clearly, the north and south followed different "strategies" toward helping their elderly.

Figure 7.2 portrays the emergence and spread of the different types of contractual institutions regarding elderly care from the twelfth to the nineteenth century for Europe. The option of individual solutions, with one-on-one care given by nonrelatives, might have been based on altruism or moral obligation. These solutions also might have been enforced, as we have seen, by retirement contracts, whereby individuals surrender their goods in exchange for places to live, food, clothing, and/or care. Such exchanges have an effect on inheritance systems, of course. These contracts are drawn up between relatives or with strangers; moreover, the idea to draw up a contract, to ensure oneself of care by relatives, presupposes an inherent distrust of family members. In extended and hierarchical households in North Africa and the Middle East, this idea would be considered outrageous and unthinkable, since norms and values in these regions dictate that parents be taken good care of (whether this is done or not is another question), as we see in extended families all over the world.[45]

[45] Harral and Amoss 1981, 99.

An alternative to looking toward relatives for elderly care was that of top-down care. In fact, this form of care might be needed through the ages in places where pension plans are not generally available. Elderly without children, without land or property, need this form of support to get by. We see, however, that increasingly these institutions become part of market-based arrangements. As mentioned earlier, individuals could buy themselves into monasteries, hospitals, and guesthouses, where they would receive food and care for the rest of their lives. The Dutch *proveniershuizen*, aiming entirely at the elderly, represent the first homes for the aged. This arrangement was different from retirement contracts. Contracts no longer needed to be negotiated with (familiar) individuals but, instead, were made with institutions. This shows, on the one hand, people's trust in such institutions and thus in their contracts; it might, on the other hand, also indicate that relatives were either absent or incapable of providing such care (whether paid or unpaid).

The fact that we find rather "modern" ways of securing relief for the elderly, whereby the agency and capital of this group played a large role, at such an early time in areas where the EMP would develop first, adds strength to the idea of there being nuclear hardship brought about by a loosening of family ties. Increasingly there was a demand for these services, not only from the poorer parts of society but also from the middle class. Live-in servants were one way to deal with this problem of aging, but buying help via the corrodies was another way. This links up with the squeeze hypothesis discussed earlier. As mentioned in earlier chapters, under the EMP, older parents became widowed more or less at the same time as their children started having children of their own. And as there was little or any age gap between spouses, the parents and parents-in-law got old simultaneously. These different strategies employed by the elderly to secure care for themselves are an indication of how and when these loose family ties, linked to the EMP, spread across Europe.

It is clear that these solutions could not have been equally available to all elderly. Not all of them were able to buy life annuities or to buy their way into an institution—these steps required at least some money or property to be traded. A focus on nuclear hardship might show but one side of this coin. Hardship has always been present, and family ties could not always provide the safety net. With this as the starting point the focus shifts to the imperatives for an alternative safety net, which departs from the relationship between parents and offspring, as this relationship forms the most obvious difference between northwestern European households with their EMP and other parts of Europe. The specific problems of the elderly, therefore, hold a key to understanding these alternative safety nets. Where Laslett focused on solutions like poorhouses and poor relief, we have shown that the reality held more options.

Families do provide a safety net, but that is primarily when there is enough to share. However, in extended families, the members always take their share, a situation that does not encourage saving money for times of scarcity. Furthermore, when family members' life cycles diverge, relatives are there to take turns caring and providing. In other words, there is no need to save—in fact, it is even useless to save. Practice shows that nuclear families are obligated to provide care generally only in instances where there are contracts. Whereas extended family household members seem to exchange most of their property *inter vivos*, nuclear family household members seem to prefer a post-mortem exchange, the latter being a logical response to neolocality, where parents and married offspring are no longer members of the same household. Diverging life cycles, fewer claims of relatives on property, and post-mortem exchanges contribute to our conclusion that property accumulation is more likely to occur in nuclear families.

Our most important conclusion here is that the EMP provided the elderly with a choice—with agency to decide how to dispose of their property for their own benefit. The possibility to save and the freedom to invest what has been saved boosted the capital market as well. So the EMP might not only have caused "nuclear hardship" but also provided "nuclear opportunities" or, indeed, "nuclear benefits."[46]

Servanthood and the Commercialization of the Household

As mentioned throughout this book, the EMP of northwestern Europe is generally believed to have given rise to substantially smaller households. Such households would have concentrated around a single/widowed/married head of household, his or her spouse and/or children: what is termed the nuclear family household.[47] This is in contrast to non-EMP areas, where the extended household remained dominant.[48] Owing to the limited number of generations in the household, nuclear households have, in general, fewer adults to contribute financially and/or to provide care. In addition, as the age gap in EMP areas is smaller, and young people get married relatively late, the life courses of spouses at different generational levels coincides. Young adults with children might not be able to provide for their children and their aging parents at the same time, a problem referred to as the three life-cycle

[46] Of course, we have to keep in mind that the premises for agency did not just include possibilities to save, but also the existence and availability of notaries and laws to make and reinforce contracts.

[47] Lundh 1995; Hajnal 1965.

[48] Reher 1998; Macfarlane 1980, 3.

squeezes described in chapter 6.[49] Those young, unmarried adults would have had time to move away from their parents and earn money as live-in servants or apprentices before getting married—this is referred to as "life-cycle servanthood."[50] Similarly, parents whose children had left the household but were not yet "old" could have enjoyed a double income, which in turn made it possible for them to save for old age. This latter possibility might have stimulated savings as well as investing, both before marriage and after their children had left the household.

So far, servanthood has been mainly considered as a process preceding new-household formation, owing to its contribution to premarital savings and its influence on the postponement of marriage. Studies on this subject have primarily focused on the (quantitative) importance of servants within a society as a whole, with conclusions that service was a much more common practice in the north of Europe than in the south—or, for that matter, the Mediterranean region.[51] Other studies have focused on the servant–master relationship, mainly based on qualitative analysis of ego-documents, such as diaries, memoirs, travel logs, and so on.[52]

However, servanthood has hardly been studied from the perspective of the "receiving" households' formation processes and servants' role in facilitating the changes that such households could go through. In fact, quite to the contrary: in the research, servants are usually not even considered as making any difference in the classification of households, and often are not counted as "real" household members. Yet families in EMP areas could have solved "nuclear hardship"[53]—at least temporarily—with such commercial solutions that essentially extended their families. Thus, by "commercializing" a position in the household—either by "buying labor" (servants) or "selling space" (lodgers)—nuclear households could overcome temporary hardship of a financial or physical nature. Therefore, these non-kin extended households should be considered an important aspect of the European Marriage Pattern.

Indeed, if young adults were counted as part of the households they were working in—and northwestern European households included strangers who were paid to be part of the household (servants), or had to pay to do so (lodgers), or were paid for by charity (orphans, widows, or the poor)—then we could say that the EMP may have led to a new form of household formation,

[49] Bouman, Zuijderduijn, and De Moor 2012; Laslett 1988, 169; Van Dusen and Sheldon 1976; Oppenheimer 1974; Gove et al. 1973.

[50] Laslett 1988, 155.

[51] Viazzo 2003; Reher 1998; Laslett 1965.

[52] E.g. Light 2007.

[53] For a discussion of the term "nuclear hardship," see Bouman, Zuijderduijn, and De Moor 2012.

what we might call a temporary "commercial household."[54] The actual size of a *family* in northwestern Europe—with a nuclear household being in principle smaller than an extended one—is in this approach of less importance, as the extensions with non-kin could make them equal to large households found in the south. *Families* might have been smaller in EMP areas, but some *households* would have remained large at some points in the life cycle, owing to the inclusion of non-kin in the count. Additionally, the relationships with extended kin that mark the extended household pattern might have been replaced by commercialized relationships, which either provided help and care in exchange for money or provided money in exchange for a meal and a roof over one's head. We argue that this commercialization was a vital aspect of the mechanisms behind the development of the EMP, although there were—as we have demonstrated elsewhere—other solutions to nuclear hardship that went beyond the realm of family or the confines of the household.[55]

In a further reflection on this phenomenon, one could also claim that such commercialization made the EMP household more flexible, in that it allowed adapting to changing internal (household composition) and external (economic hardship, other opportunities) circumstances. This included maintaining the household at a size that was optimal for family members' participation in the labor market, instead of the maximal size that characterized extended households. This situation might have been temporary, but the importance of this commercialization of the household, particularly its role in creating the preindustrial labor market, remains unclear. A few authors have offered some hints. Hareven suggests that the eventual loss of flexibility regarding the incorporation of strangers into the household started at the beginning of the twentieth century, and this loss would change the form of the household substantially.[56] Skolnick, among others, connected this flexibility to changes in the labor market.[57] We do not try to reevaluate this relationship, but we do start with the basics, identifying the size of the phenomenon (i.e., non-kin living in the household) and the mechanisms behind it.

On the basis of this reasoning, we may assume that households in EMP areas might have incorporated large numbers of non-kin *exactly because* they needed a helping hand or could use additional money, as kin were no longer

[54] Lutz Berkner 1972 points to the fact that "the family" in Germany not only included relatives but also servants.

[55] Bouman, Zuijderduijn, and De Moor 2012.

[56] Hareven 1982, 449.

[57] "Above all, the preindustrial household was an economic unit and its need for labor determined how many people lived together under one roof. Families often brought in older children and young adults as servants and apprentices, and send out their own children to work in other households if they were not needed at home"; Skolnick 1993, 48.

providing either. Thus, instead of stressing agency on the labor supply side—servants wanting to work because they needed to save for marriage—we view it from the demand side. Additionally, understanding the "commercial household" requires insight into life cycles—not primarily of servants or lodgers, as has been the focus of the servanthood debate so far, but of the households themselves. If households were able to save during specific periods, they might have had the means in other periods to "buy" the extra hands they needed, for as long as they were needed. In doing so, they created a labor market for young people, including young women, who could in turn save money so as to get married. Vulnerable households might furthermore have strengthened their position by having non-kin join the household. Widows might have shared their households to cut expenses; renting out part of their dwelling could have provided an opportunity for them to stay at home while generating an income. Understanding such mechanisms requires both a dynamic approach and information on the income levels of households, as we demonstrate next.

In order to deepen our understanding of this mechanism, we consider a number of issues, all related to non-kin living in the early modern Dutch household, hereby challenging historians, sociologists, and anthropologists with a new perspective on households in EMP areas. First, we discuss the existing literature on servants and "inmates" (in the sense of "live-in persons") regarding household formation and composition, followed by a review of the categories used to classify households. Considering the rather blurred categories some scholars have used to analyze households, this new classification assumes that recognizing the relationships between household members is necessary for understanding the phenomenon of the "commercial household." Following this theoretical section, we introduce our source—a dataset of the seventeenth-century northern Netherlands, an area at the core of the EMP—and our methodology. Furthermore, we link the analysis of household composition in early modern northwestern Europe to publications by Laslett (for England) and van der Woude (for the Netherlands), among others, comparing figures on household composition and household size. In our conclusion, we argue that most of these households were indeed nuclear family households, and that the elderly usually were not incorporated into the households of their children—which is in line with the expectations formulated in the literature on nuclear hardship. In short, our analysis demonstrates that parents were far more likely to take in non-kin than to live with their own children. We also show that the dominance of the nuclear family (at the expense of the extended family) led to a high degree of dependence on nonfamily help—"filling the gap" that could no longer be filled by the extended family.

The commercial household provided labor-market opportunities, in particular for women, and simultaneously provided opportunities for heads of households—including single female heads of households—to earn money by sharing their households with others. It also provided the elderly with the possibility to bring "strangers" into their households who could either provide care or supply much needed income.[58] This chapter can only demonstrate this arrangement for the early seventeenth century, a period when the Dutch economy was flourishing. Considering that in later centuries the phenomenon largely disappeared, the commercial household may have been an essential step in the development of a commercial economy, rather than a permanent feature of the EMP.

Connecting the Dots: EMP, Nuclear Hardship, Life Cycle Service, and Household Composition

In his nuclear hardship hypothesis, Peter Laslett claims that the increasing dominance of the nuclear household could lead to hardship among aging parents and other groups in society.[59] An essential element in our interpretation of the nuclear hardship hypothesis, then, is a lack of cohabitation by multiple generations and the extent to which commercialization filled the room left by other generations. We thus need to distinguish between the different generations, on the one hand, and kin versus non-kin, on the other.

The household classification system Laslett developed does not tell us if households included non-kin, and consequently does not tell us how many households were extended by inclusion of non-kin (see table 7.1).[60] Servants can be found in simple, extended, multiple, and indeterminate family households,[61]

[58] We are not arguing, however, that the commercial household was the only solution to hardship at old age. As we have demonstrated in Bouman, Zuijderduijn, and De Moor 2012, there were many more possibilities for the elderly, like *proveniershuizen* (elderly homes). Taking non-kin in was but one of the options.

[59] Laslett 1988; J. Smith 1984; R. Smith 1984.

[60] Already in 1967, Donald Bender described similar concerns regarding the anthropological view of households that linked residence directly to kinship based on the work of, for instance, Fischer and Bohannan; Bender 1967, 497. The references for Bender refer to Fischer 1958 and Bohannan 1963.

[61] Laslett argues that servants hardly affect the final structure of households and therefore his classifications are based solely on kinship; Laslett 1978, 29. In her critique of Chayton 1980, Harris 1982 criticizes not only Chayton but also Laslett's ideas on the inclusion or exclusion of servants in his classification of households. Harris states that the presence of servants within a household "necessarily affect[s] the degree of cooperation in different forms of labour between kin and neighbours," which would especially affect the lives of female household members and their domestic tasks. When children, furthermore, are likely to move out of the household as teenagers, Harris questions the idea of the "nuclear family household" and proposes the term "*truncated* nuclear family" (148–149). Such households might only include a couple and the younger children, as well as servants.

Table 7.1 **Categories of Households Used by Peter Laslett**

Type	*Description*
Solitaries	Households consisting of one person.
No-family households	Households consisting of two or more related or nonrelated persons living together, without a couple being present.
Simple family households	Households consisting of a couple, or the remainder of a couple (a widow or widower), with or without their (unmarried) children.
Extended family households	Households with a family member (not belonging to the nuclear family) living in, but without his or her spouse or children.
Multiple family households	Households with a secondary couple living in (i.e., when a spouse of a child is living in, or is the spouse of a parent).
Indeterminate	Households where kin linkages are insufficient for classification in any category here.

Source: Adapted from Laslett 1978, 1983

but it remains unclear how they fit into this classification.[62] Another problem with the classification based on a central couple is that it becomes impossible to determine who is living with whom (but this can also be a consequence of the restrictions created by the source material). The following example, also presented in figure 7.3, demonstrates that details about household composition are most valuable to understanding intergenerational support.

In figure 7.3, Household A, for instance, consists of a widow (Ego = head of household), with a live-in son, his wife, and their children. Household B consists of a male (Ego = head of household), his wife, their children, and his widowed mother living with them. The classification used by Laslett disguises the

[62] Laslett never fails to mention they are not considered a part of the household, but does not clarify whether he counts them separately, ignores their presence in the census data, or removes them on purpose. When Laslett presents figures on the proportion of servants in the total number of households in England, France, Serbia, Japan, and colonial North America, he specifically mentions the inmates and inmate households as being excluded from the Serbian data: "All MHS [Mean Household Size] ratios approximately correspond to uncorrected maximal mean household size . . . (ratio 3 of table 4.2) except in the case of Belgrade where it corresponds to ratio 5. . . . This ratio excludes both individual inmates and inmate households"; Laslett 1978, 76, table 1.6. In another article on household size in England, he also excludes inmates: "individual lodgers" whom he classifies as "persons outside households"; see Laslett 1969, 207, table 2.

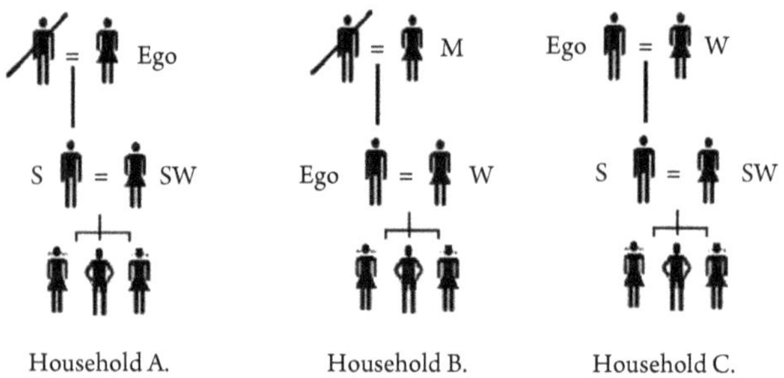

Figure 7.3 Different ways to classify households according to composition. Note: Ego is the head of household.

dependency between the members of the household. His classification labels both households as "upward extended," since the couple, rather than the head of household, is central. This is problematic if one looks for the relationship between the composition of a household and the contribution of children to elderly care. In our classification, we distinguish A and C—as downward extended households—from B—being regarded as an upward extended household. In Laslett's analysis, A and B would have been considered extended households and C would be a multiple family household.

With this example, we make clear that, in order to reveal the significance of non-kin living in the household and the absence of family members in the role of caregiver, we need a classification that does more than make a distinction between households that are simple, extended, or multiply extended—which are, in fact, classifications of family within the household. We need to see all different kinds of extensions, whether they consist of kin or non-kin, and these need to be counted starting from the household head and extending upward or downward.

Household Composition in a Core EMP Area (Seventeenth-Century Northern Netherlands): The Sources

Any research into household size or composition is destined to use census or at least census-like data, for whatever reason they may have been collected.[63] In the Netherlands, the oldest useful sources that include many of the variables we are

[63] Parish records and genealogies cannot reveal what households looked like in the past, since they do not mention live-in non-kin. And whereas there might be ego-documents that do so (such as wills, diaries, or court records), the use of such documents for this purpose is time-consuming and only provides small samples; cf. Berkner 1975.

looking for seem to be the *hoofdgeldlijsten*, or poll tax registers.[64] During the Dutch War of Independence, near the end of the Twelve Years' Truce (1609–1622), the Spanish again threatened to attack Holland with sieges of Bergen op Zoom and Breda. In need of new funds, the States-General (*Staten-Generaal*) demanded a contribution of one guilder per inhabitant of the provinces of Holland and West Friesland, to be collected by the Provincial Council (*Provinciale Staten*), both in the towns and in the countryside (*ambachten*).[65] This *hoofdgeld*, a taxation on the "heads" (*hoofden*) of all citizens regardless of age, status, or property, was intended to be raised between 1622 and 1623.[66] The resulting sources have survived for a number of large towns, such as Leiden and Gouda, and a fairly large number of villages in their vicinity.

Lodgers, students, and servants were described in our sources as members of those households. In the *hoofdgeld* sources from Leiden, the question of whether someone "belonged" to a household is addressed in an even more specific way. Here, we see how people are "accounted for" in the household while they are

[64] The sources provide us with a cross-section of a whole population in a certain area and time. However, we have to keep in mind that the data might have been meddled with to avoid taxation. The fact that names had not yet been standardized poses another difficulty. One and the same person might have been registered in different registrations under quite different names, making it hard to trace the individual in different documents that might validate the census data. Dirck Adriaenszn, for instance, might be registered as Dirk/Dirc/Dirck and Adriaensz/Arentszn/Adriaens and Arentsz. However, the fact that the data were collected by groups of men, who were themselves inhabitants of the villages or towns they registered, makes it likely they knew at least some in the households personally. In the case of Leiden, they furthermore seem to have followed a similar route that tax officers before them had taken, which gave them a point of reference. All in all, the amount of detail provided gives us confidence in the accuracy of the data.

[65] A very similar format of inquiry seems to have been used over and over again in subsequent centuries in different regions of the Netherlands. In Zeeland, we find *gemaallijsten* from 1687–88, which are in every aspect comparable to the *hoofdgeld* sources from the Zuiderkwartier. Similarly, such sources are available for the whole province of Overijssel, dating from August 1748, and are referred to as *personele quotisatie* or *hoofdelijke omslag*. Although all these sources should definitely be considered in their context (they contain similar information, on different periods and different regions, with a dissimilar historical context and dissimilar modes of production), the format is very consistent. All "poll tax sources" dating from 1622 until the nineteenth century give us similar data, including the time and region of the census, the head of household, his or her marital status, all persons related to the head of household, and live-in non-kin. Sometimes it is added that a household is not able to pay the tax.

[66] Holland and West Friesland were divided into northern and southern regions, respectively, called Noorderkwartier (with the cities Alkmaar, Hoorn, Enkhuizen, Edam, Monnikendam, Medemblik, and Purmerend) and Zuiderkwartier (with the cities Dordrecht, Haarlem, Delft, Leiden, Amsterdam, Gouda, Rotterdam, Gorichem, Schiedam, Schoonhoven, and Brielle), with a total of eighteen cities between them. Although we find several references to those records, most of the records from these cities have been lost (cf. van Dillen 1940, van der Woude 1972b. Van der Woude describes how the original records were collected by the Dutch demographer Nicolas Struyck, of whom all original data are lost (cf. Struyck 1753).

temporarily absent—for instance, if they were in the army or at sea. Others are described as living in the household but "accounted for elsewhere"—for instance, a young servant who is accounted for at a parents' house. This source even indicates who had been registered before (there must have been a version prior to the *hoofdgeld* taxation of 1622–23), but had moved or disappeared. In building our database, we decided to base conclusions solely on persons who were *present* in the households (thus excluding those living elsewhere, whether temporarily or permanently).[67]

To collect their data, interviewers followed specific itineraries going from house to house. And, in the case of the *hoofdgeld* source from Leiden, interviewers described their inquiries road by road, including addresses and household numbers. If units are mentioned separately, it is indicated if they were sharing one house (in the Leiden data this is done by adding "a/b/c" to the household number).[68] Whenever servants and lodgers provided their own provisions (*buiten de kost*), this is mentioned separately, which indicates that lodgers and servants normally might have shared in the provisions of the economic unit in which they lived.

We have used *hoofdgeld* sources from the Zuiderkwartier[69] and added specifics such as gender, the anthropological notation for the relationships within the household (on the basis of the indications given in the source), and information on, for instance, persons mentioned as living in the household and whether they were poor or not, for 41 hamlets/villages in total,[70] as well as the

[67] Literature about European households generally assumes that there is just one household head in charge, even if there is a couple present. The poll tax sources in the Netherlands confirm this idea: only the name of the first individual in the tax registers is in most cases mentioned entirely. And only in the case of widowhood is marital state added, while for married couples the spouse is mentioned second, sometimes even without her proper name ("the spouse of . . . "). John Hajnal considers the fact that married males are appointed household heads as a specific rule of normal household formation in northwestern European households: "After marriage a couple are in charge of their household (the husband is head of household)"; Hajnal 1982, 452.

[68] Whereas the different units within a dwelling might have been called "a/b/c," we have not automatically assumed household "b" to be living with household "a". We have only considered people to be living in if this can be inferred from the source itself. However, we see an overlap that might implicate that the "b/c" etc. units lived in with households mentioned as "a". This sometimes becomes clear if households could not have been completely independent: their dwelling might be referred to as a room, a cellar, an attic, or even the kitchen itself.

[69] To construct our database, we have gratefully used the transcriptions provided by Hogenda, the Hollandse Genealogische Databank, and more specifically the sources collected and transcribed by F. J. A. M van der Helm, as well as their transcriptions of the *hoofdgeld* data of Leiden.

[70] Aarlanderveen, Achtienhoven, Benthoorn/Hoogeveen, Hoogmade, Vrije Bouchorst, Vrijenhoeff, Alphen, Berkel en Rodenrijs, Stompwijk/Leidschendam/Wilsveen, Hazerswoude, beider Katwijken en 't Sant, Leimuiden, Rijnsaterwoude, Ter Aar, Voorschoten, Alkemade, Nieuwkoop, Esselijkerwoude, Lisse, Wassenaar, Zoeterwoude, Calslagen, Koudekerk a/d Rijn,

town of Leiden, all dating from 1622–23. The number of households in the *ambachten* is 7,998 (36,176 inhabitants in total) and in Leiden 4,264 (18,993 inhabitants in total), making thus an overall total of 12,262 households, with a total of 55,169 inhabitants.[71] As mentioned, we need a new classification method for households that tells us how families were extended, thus also providing information on the dependency of household members.[72] Whereas Laslett chooses to call all single parents with children "widowed," and to classify all children living in a household without a spouse automatically as "single,"[73] we choose to register only the mentioned marital relationships, if indicated. We do not distinguish between single people and widowed persons—only between those with or without a spouse.[74] The "nuclear core" of a household, also called the "central nucleus" by Laslett and Hammel, consisting of a nuclear

Cuijdelstaert, Nieuweveen/Uitterbuurt, Noorden, Noordwijkerhout, Oegstgeest, Oudshoorn/Gnephoek, Swammerdam, Voorhout, Vriesecoop, Warmond, Zevenhoven/Noorden.

[71] The source on Leiden might not be entirely complete, as is indicated by the people who transcribed it. This is also clear from the list of students, who were accounted for in a separate registration, or "*bon*," that registered the different areas of Leiden that they lived in. From this source it is clear that Noort Rapenburch, Burchstreng, Overmaren Lantzijde, Hogemorsch, and Sevenhuysen might be missing. The *hoofdgeld* sources from the *ambachten* have been added as far as their transcriptions were available and usable. Therefore, the *hoofdgeld* sources from the *ambachten* are by no means exhaustive, and await historians to take up the strenuous task of making them as complete as possible. Since the sources of the Noorderkwartier have been lost, this is worth the effort. In the same period, we find the term *haardstedengeld*, referring to a tax on fireplaces or chimneys. Although in Drenthe this tax was eventually determined by counting horses, the original intention was to tax households not according to the roof they lived under but by the number of fireplaces in the dwelling. Anthropological literature on nomads in Africa also refers to the household with the term "hearthhold," which indicates a group of people who share food and not necessarily a roof (cf. De Bruijn 1997.

[72] Our database contains, apart from the numbers per source, household, and person, a number of useful elements: the relationship between the head of household and the household member, described with the anthropological notational system, his or her gender and his or her marital status (if known). For the purpose of the research, additional labels have been created for the non-kin living in, depending on the categories mentioned in the original data: servants, for instance, have been labeled "L," lodgers "Lodger," adopted children "A," students "Student," non-kin as "living in," and unspecified non-kin living in as "other."

[73] Cf. Laslett 1978, 88.

[74] It is not always indicated if persons are single or widowed. Laslett assumes all heads of household with children but without a spouse to be widowed, and classifies them as such. We need to ask ourselves if the label "single" or "widow(er)" contributes to our understanding of household formation—if some labels are lacking and attributed by interpretation. Therefore, we decided to label them only as far as they are labeled in the original source. Thus, our classification does not distinguish between singles and widow(ers). Cf. Hammel and Laslett 1974.

family (a head of household, with or without his or her spouse and/or children), is coded as follows:

F/M (Gender) – 0/1 (Spouse absent or present) – 0 – 15 (Number of children)[75]

By using the nuclear core plus extensions, we not only see if households were extended by kin or non-kin but also what kinds of nuclear cores were extended by kin or non-kin.

To make a complete overview of all the different relationships to the household head by using the anthropological notational system might become quite elaborate. In the case of our database, we counted 74 different relationships to Ego (head of household). This makes it possible to register the relationships between all household members, but makes a thorough comparison too complicated. For the purpose of household classification, we therefore grouped categories to simplify the number of possible kinship extensions. Basically, our household classification differentiates between kin and non-kin extensions. Table 7.2 gives an overview of the ways in which we grouped the households.[76]

For the different generations within a household, we use strings with a binary system: 0 = absent, 1 = present. Ego always forms the core of the string. In our database, we designed strings showing two generations upward (with parents, upward) and three generations downward (children, downward).[77] For example, 0-1-E-1-0-0 indicates a family (within a household) consisting of three consecutive generations: parents, Ego, and children.

The Role of Non-Kin in the Household: Servants versus Inmates

The data we have collected for Leiden and surrounding areas demonstrate that over one-fifth of the households were extended with non-kin (of which a

[75] E.g., F-0-4, indicating a single female head of household, without a spouse but with four children; M-1-2, a couple with two children; and M-0-0, a single male head of household without children. Both M and F with a spouse (M-1-0 and F-1-0) thus depict couples.

[76] The labels we have used should be followed by HH, indicating household composition (except in the case of solitaries, since solitaries are themselves solitary, not belonging to a family or a household). The terms "conjugal" (a couple), "nuclear" (a couple, or a widow[er] with children), "joint" (siblings living together), and "extended" (other family members that do not belong to the "nuclear core" living in) can also be used when referring to families. When we add "HH," however, we indicate household composition. If we refer to families, we always add the word "family" (conjugal family, nuclear family, joint family, extended family) to avoid confusion.

[77] The category downward is split into grandchildren and great-grandchildren. However, the number of necessary generations differs per dataset: we had only two families with live-in great-grandchildren, and no families with live-in great-grandparents.

Table 7.2 **Terminology Used in this Chapter to Classify Households According to Their Composition**[a]

Type no.	*Household Form*	*Household Composition*	*Core and/or Extension*
1	**Solitaries**	Only the head of household living in the household	**Nuclear Core** The household core consists of a head of household, with or without a spouse and with or without children
2	**Conjugal HH**	A head of household with a spouse, no children present	
3a	**Nuclear HH**	A head of household, with a spouse and children present	
3b	**Nuclear HH**	A head of household, without a spouse, but with children present	
4a	**Joint** (extended sideways) **HH**	A nuclear core with an extension sideways: siblings living together without spouses or children	
4b	**Joint** (extended sideways) **HH**	A nuclear core with an extension sideways: siblings living together with a spouse and/or children	**Kin extended** A nuclear core with kin living in, whether sideways, parental, downward, upward or in any other way related to one of the members in the nuclear core
5	**Extended HH**	Any of the combinations mentioned under 5a–5d	
5a	Extended (parental) HH	A nuclear core and a parent or several parents living in	
5b	Extended (downward) HH	A nuclear core and a downward extension (grandchildren, great- grandchildren)	

(continued)

Table 7.2 **Continued**

Type no.	*Household Form*	*Household Composition*	*Core and/or Extension*
5c	Extended (upward) HH	A nuclear core with an upward extension (no parents, though they are also upward extensions, here we only classify grandparents and great-grandparents)	
5d	Extended (other kin) HH	A nuclear core with any relative (that does not fit the parental, downward, upward category) living in	
4+5	Joint + Extended HH	Any combination of 4 and 5a–5d	
6a	**Non-Kin Extended HH**	A nuclear core with live-in servants	**Non-kin extended** A nuclear core extended by non-kin living in the household
6b	**Non-Kin Extended HH**	A nuclear core with live-in inmates	
6c	**Non-Kin Extended HH**	A nuclear core with live-in servants and inmates	
4+6	**Joint + Non-Kin HH**	A combination of 4 and 6	**Double extended** A nuclear core with both kin and non-kin living in the household
5+6	**Extended + Non-Kin HH**	A combination of 5a–5d and 6	
4+5+6	**Joint + Extended + Non-Kin HH**	A combination of 4, 5a–5d and 6	

[a] The following example, taken from our Leiden data, serves to demonstrate the classification.

Original text	Labels	Classification
Huish#: 202 Straat: Corte Raemsteech, N	1 m = Ego, male, married	**Nuclear core:** M-1-2
1 m: Malliaert Brievaert, cammer	2 v = W (Wife), female, married	(Male headed household-spouse-two children)
2 v: Lijsbeth Joosten	3 k = D (Daughter), female	
3 k: Anna	4 k = S (Son), male	**Extension:** Non-Kin
4 k: Jan	5 ap = Lodger, male	
alhier slapen ende logeren	6 ap = Lodger, male	**Therefore classifies as:**
5 ap: Gillis Duramel, uyt Artois, cammer; weeten niet beter off blijven metter woon		"Non-kin extended HH"
6 ap: Franchoys Gordain; van Atrecht, cammer		

very small number were extended by both kin and non-kin); this is a substantial part of the population (see table 7.3. But how was this related to the rest of the household composition—dominance of nuclear households and very few multigeneration households? "Renting" an extra hand to do the work children were not doing might be one way to alleviate hardship. Other non-kin living in the household, such as lodgers or boarders, might have provided other solutions. As in the English situation analyzed by Laslett, our data also shows that a substantial portion of the live-in non-kin consisted of those lodgers, though this differed significantly between town and country (see table 7.4). In the city of Leiden, about one-fifth of the households with non-kin had lodgers, and over one-third had servants, whereas in the countryside, the latter were present in over two-thirds of the households, while a negligible share had lodgers (see figure 7.4).

Some of the lodgers were referred to as simply "living in" (*woont in*), without a further reference to their role in the household; sometimes this notion is followed by the note that the live-in person is a widow or someone who is poor or *innocente* ("ignorant"), whereby some sort of financial arrangement could have been made to provide compensation for this kind of lodging. The church and other charitable organizations paid families—and widows—who accommodated the poor, handicapped, and orphans.[78] We refer to this latter category of live-in non-kin as "inmates," in line with Laslett.[79]

The inmates in our database can be divided into five categories: the lodgers (clearly labeled, for instance, as *thuyslegger* [literally "one who lies at home"]), the living in (who are mentioned as living in the household, but not clearly labeled as lodgers), temporarily or permanently adopted children (e.g., *houkint* [literally: "a child to keep"]), students (only present in the Leiden database), and others (of whom no relationship is mentioned).[80]

[78] Schmidt 2007.

[79] The term "inmates" in this case has nothing to do with people living in prisons. See, for references to inmates and household composition, Szoltysek 2008; Ogilvie and Cerman. 1995.

[80] For Italy, clearly not an EMP area, it has been claimed that having live-in servants was clearly typical for the nobility. Szoltysek displays rather different figures for the Polish-Lithuanian Commonwealth (PLC), however, from those we find in early modern Holland or Italy. Here are the percentages of live-in kin, servants, and inmates in the Polish-Lithuanian Commonwealth in the eighteenth century. Szoltysek treats inmates and lodgers separately.

Location	**% hh with kin**	**% hh with Servants**	**% hh with inmates/lodgers**[a]
West	20.8	39.4	24.4
Middle East	40.5	12.2	7.9
East	52.0	2.1	1.2

Source: Szoltysek 2008, 400.

Table 7.3 **Upward and Downward Family Extensions, Presenting Different Generations (per household)** [a]

	Nuclear Core Without Kin Extensions			*Nuclear Core with Upward and Downward Kin Extensions*							
	1 G.	*2G.**		*2G.***		*3G.**		*3G.***			*4G.*
	A. Not extended	*B. Ext. with P*	*C. Ext. with C*	*D. Ext. with GP*	*E. Ext. with GC*	*F. Ext. with P and C*	*G. Ext. with C and GC*	*H. Ext. with GC and GGC*	*I. Ext. with P and GC*	*J. Ext. with GP and C*	*K. Ext. with P, C and GC*
Ambachten N	2,137	18	5,719	1	16	47	44	2	0	10	2
Ambachten %	27	0	72	0	0	1	1	0	0	0	0
Leiden N	1,296	12	2,867	0	16	41	23	0	1	8	0
Leiden %	30	0	67	0	0	1	1	0	0	0	0
Total N	3,433	30	8,586	1	32	88	67	2	1	18	2
Total %	28	0	70	0	0	1	1	0	0	0	0

P = Parent(s), C = Child(ren), GP = Grandparent(s), GC = Grandchild(ren), GGC = Great-grandchild(ren); G = Generation; *Consecutive generations **Non-consecutive generations.

[a] Only upward and downward (kin) extensions are included here. Since we only included upward/downward related kin in this analysis, the percentages in this table differ from the percentages used to analyze household formation. Since we are talking about generations, we cannot compare those figures to the figures on household composition.

Table 7.4 **Non-Kin Divided into Different Categories**

	Leiden *(4.264 HH. – 18.918 individuals) (avg. HH size: 4,4 members)*				**Ambachten** *(7.998 HH – 36.127 individuals) (avg. HH size: 4,5 members)*			
Non-kin	*# of HH contain-ing at least one of the below (N = 4264 HH*	*%*	*# of indivi-duals per category (N = 18918 ind.)*	*%*	*# of HH contain-ing at least one of the below (N = 7998 HH)*	*%*	*# of indivi-duals per category (N = 36127 ind.)*	*%*
Servants (L)	603	14.1	794	4.2	1074	13.4	1.497	4.1
Lodgers	373	8.7	615	3.3	26	0.3	45	0.1
Living in	498	11.7	753	4.0	29	0.4	34	0.1
Adopted child[a]	54	1.3	66	0.3	175	2.2	199	0.6
Other	19	0.4	25	0.1	85	1.1	108	0.3
Student	176	4.1	396	2.1	0	0.0	0	0.0
Total	[b]	[b]	2.649	14	[b]	[b]	1.883	5.0

[a] The label "adopted child" does not actually mean adopted in the contemporary sense of the word—i.e., any legalized adoption. Here we include all the children incorporated temporarily or for a longer time in a household of nonrelatives, such as *cost-kinderen* [literally: "lodging children"] and orphans. The number in the *ambachten* is rather high, as the figure includes a school (with children living in and paying (*in de cost*), and an orphanage. Please note that these numbers do not correspond with the total household number with non-kin in the previous tables, as we now look at the households that contained any type of live-in non-kin. Some households are thus taken into account twice if they had, for example, a servant and a lodger in the household.

[b] Here we cannot merely add the numbers mentioned above, since some HH have both students and servants living in.

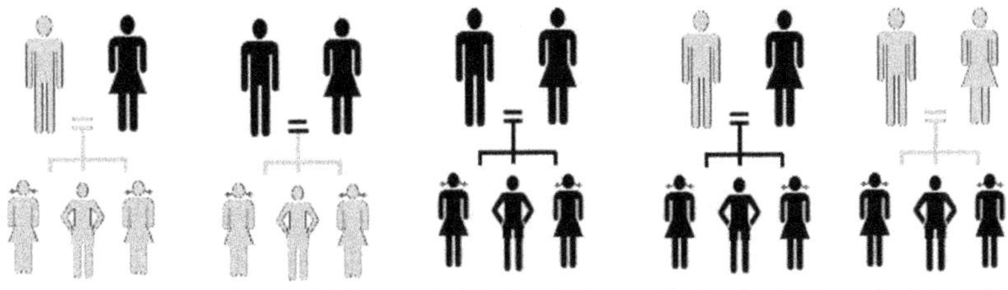

Figure 7.4 Schematic overview of types of households consisting of only the nuclear core. Note: Figures in gray refer to absent members of the household, figures in black are present. Gender is arbitrary, as is the number of children (as well as stepchildren) within a household. Therefore 1. could also consist of just a male (M-0-0), and 3b. could also consist of a male head of household (M-0-3). In household 4a. the eldest sibling is the head of household. This might similarly be a male (M-0-0). This household, a joint household, can only be included if siblings are not (yet) married. If they are married, the household becomes truly joint. We added this particular case since the data mentioned such "orphaned" households, referring to a dead parent as a household head. Source: Previously published in Boele, Bouman, and De Moor 2014, 21–46.

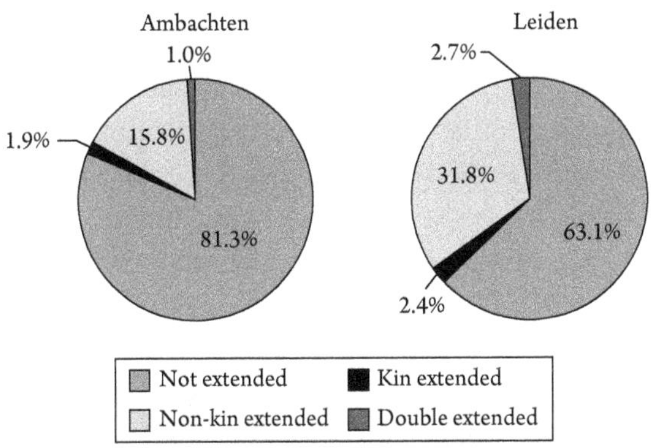

Figure 7.5 Total percentages of households that are not extended, kin extended, non-kin extended, and double extended. Source: Previously published in Boele, Bouman, and De Moor 2014, 21–46.

But how different was the EMP area as far as the presence of servants is concerned? Was having servants a typical feature of the top classes of society, as in Italy, or was it such an essential feature of the social and economic system that the practice had penetrated all layers of society? To explore whether having non-kin in the household was a common feature among early modern Dutch households, and in what manner they did so, two possible avenues of inquiry exist. On the one hand, we could check in which households servants resided: Were they in households with children, or without children? In the cases where children were still living in the household, it is quite unlikely that servants were there to take care of the elderly, but they might have helped in the care of the children or done household chores; in households with children, we might rather expect lodgers, who contribute extra cash for the family to survive temporary squeezes.

Another way to approach the question of whether the commercial household was common among all layers of society is to control for poverty. The *hoofdgeld* source indicates which households were incapable of paying taxes (*onvermogend*) and also the households that were actually poor (*arm*) or living on poor-relief (*leven van de armen, leven van de thuyssitten*).[81] Table 7.5 shows to what extent the various household types were present among the poor, which represented one-fifth of the total number of households.

Table 7.5 demonstrates that, on the whole, poor households belonged more frequently to the category of nuclear households without any extensions, but that even so, in 1 out of every 10 poorer households, non-kin were present. Here again, it can be noted that neither the poor nor the rest of society were organized in kin-extended households. The fact that the non-poor had a slightly higher number of kin living in (with kin extension and double extension) is in fact surprising, as one would expect the poor to resort to solutions within the family rather than those who could actually afford non-kin provisions.

Clearly (see table 7.6), the poor households had proportionally more paying live-in non-kin than the other households, in particular in the city of Leiden where nearly all live-in non-kin were paying instead of being paid. The reason for a more balanced situation in the *ambachten* is no doubt that these non-kin were also working in local trades or agriculture, which was less of an option in the city.

[81] Our figures are not comparable with the figures that Ariadne Schmidt presents, although she works with the same original data on Leiden. For one, she presents a much larger set of households. Secondly, she classifies the households differently and does not mention whether or not non-kin are included in her classification. Third, her categories "children" and "relatives" are not clearly defined. We are not saying her figures are not correct, just that the categories she uses are not defined clearly enough to make comparisons, even though the labels seem to suggest so. Here are her figures:

Leiden	# of hh	Poor hh	%
F Single/Widow no kids	1,216	315	25.9
M Single/Widow no kids	485	47	9.7
F Single/Widow kids	1,292	448	34.7
M Single/Widow kids	288	28	9.7
Couple, no kids	2,689	221	8.2
Couple, with kids	3,718	525	14.1

Source: Schmidt 2007, 270. Schellekens furthermore states that we do not know the exact criteria used for exempting households from paying the poll tax; Schellekens 1995, 210.

Table 7.5 **Percentage of Poor and Non-Poor Households and Total Number of Households (per category)**

	Poor (N)	*% of Poor HH in Each Category*	*Non-Poor (N)*	*% of Non-Poor HH in Each Category*	*Total N. of HH*	*Total % per HH Category*
Without extension (types 1 to 4a)*	2,117	88.4	7,077	71.7	9,194	75.0
With kin extension (types 4b to 5)	35	1.5	221	2.2	256	2.1
With non-kin extension (type 6)	241	10.1	2,375	24.1	2,616	21.3
Double extended	3	0.1	193	2.0	196	1.6
Total	2,396	100.0	9,866	100.0	12,262	100.0

*Note that we only discuss non-kin extended households, we exclude the non-kin double extended households (HH extended by both kin and non-kin)

The picture for the non-poor households is—in particular in the *ambachten*—entirely the reverse of the poor. There, the non-poor were particularly attracting servants rather than lodgers. In the city, the non-poor households were trying to get as much money out of their lodgers as possible, but a substantial number (11%) had both an inmate and a servant (see table 7.6). One could say these are the ultimate "commercial households," which were market oriented on both the demand and the supply side.

Overall, looking at city and countryside together, we see that servants and inmates are more or less in balance, with less than 10% of all households having more servants than inmates. This result demonstrates that both types of commercialization of household space were almost equally important, but that to some extent which strategy was employed depended on the economic situation and the location—that is, whether one paid someone to live in or whether the household received payment for having a lodger in the household. In a next analysis, we look more closely at those households that had servants and inmates in the same house.

In table 7.7, we see that households that included non-kin were not randomly extended. Households with couples tend to be extended with non-kin if they have no children. At a first child, this number drops slightly, only to rise again with the addition of a second child. After the second child, the number of kin taken into the household drops with every successive child.

Although single and widowed household heads were very likely to live with non-kin, we see that households with one or two children tended to be slightly more inclined to take in non-kin. Again, the number of live-in non-kin tended to drop slightly when more children were living in the household, but we see the numbers rise again if more than seven children were part of the household.

Single or widowed male heads of household form an exception. They seem to extend their households with non-kin exponentially with each successive child, but although there is a clear trend, we have to be careful not to attach too much value to it, owing to the small number of observations of households with more than five children.

This demonstrates that the higher the number of children, the less an extension of the household was needed (or the less room there was to incorporate non-kin). Furthermore, the slightly higher number of households with couples that incorporated kin at the addition of a second child makes it likely that having two children was indeed an incentive to seek a helping hand.

Table 7.6 **Poor Households Subdivided by Type of Household**

Non-kin		*Poor HH (244 total), Non-Kin Extended*				*Non-poor HH (2568 total), Non-Kin Extended*			
		Servants	*Both servants and Inmates*	*Inmates*	*Total*	*Servants*	*Both servants and Inmates*	*Inmates*	*Total*
Ambachten	N	46	3	62	111	912	43	194	1,149
	%	**41**	**3**	**56**	**100**	**79**	**4**	**17**	**100**
Leiden	N	4	2	124	130	392	140	695	1,227
	%	**3**	**2**	**95**	**100**	**32**	**11**	**57**	**100**
Total	N	50	5	186	241	1304	183	889	2,376
	%	**21**	**2**	77	**100**	**55**	**8**	**37**	**100**

Table 7.7 **Distribution of Non-Kin in Households, Related to Number of Children Present in the HH**

# of Children	*0*	*1*	*2*	*3*	*4*	*5*	*6*	*7*	*8*	*9*	*10*
Single F N	1,108	319	271	209	149	98	50	29	5	5	0
Single F extended by NK	217	72	56	35	25	9	3	4	1	1	0
Idem %	**20**	**23**	**21**	**17**	**17**	**9**	**6**	**14**	**20**	**20**	**0**
Single M Total N	608	94	96	84	56	35	15	17	3	7	3
Single M extended by NK	136	21	28	21	20	10	6	3	2	0	0
Idem %	**22**	**22**	**29**	**25**	**36**	**29**	**40**	**18**	**67**	**0**	**0**
Couples Total N	1,783	1,444	1,473	1,367	1,061	830	504	287	141	59	32
Couples extended by NK	513	366	401	328	212	163	82	43	22	3	4
Idem %	**29**	**25**	**27**	**24**	**20**	**20**	**16**	**15**	**16**	**5**	**13**

F-0 = Single female head of household, M-0 = Single male head of household, NK = Non-Kin.

Since households with more than 10 children were no longer extended by kin, we excluded them here, since the percentage of non-kin extended households adds up to 0 percent. 15 households had 11 children, 2 households had 12 children, 1 had 15 children, and 1 household had 17 children.

Source: Beguines database, *Research Group Institutions for Collective action*, 2015. See www.collective-action.info.

Summary

This chapter demonstrated that the household was much more than the "container" of potential labor-market participants: each household was, at least for some time, in preindustrial EMP Europe also a mini-market—for labor and for housing. With our large dataset on early seventeenth-century Dutch households, we demonstrated that the nuclear household was fairly dominant in this area, and that the number of kin-extended households was negligible; households extended by non-kin formed an important part of society. Both servants and inmates were present in nearly equal shares in the households, and depending on the poverty level and the location, the one or the other was more important. Although some literature refers to lodgers in EMP households, our data show that much more attention should go to their presence, especially because they may have had a role in helping the households get through periods of hardship, by way of contributions to the household budget.

We have suggested that the "commercial household" emerged as a consequence of the changes in household composition, which went hand-in-hand with the EMP and led to reduced intergenerational support. Servants may well have played a role in providing physical help, but lodgers, by way of taking the physical place of children who had left the household to set up households of their own, may have provided that little extra cash necessary to make ends meet. Our brief gender analysis of the inmates and servants showed that women were clearly very present among the non-kin. The results were far more striking than we would have expected, given the existing literature. Clearly, women lived in a society where they had the right to and the possibility to make their own living or, for that matter, determining with whom they shared a household. We do not have information about their ages, but it is not unlikely that many of these women worked as servants in the period just before marriage.

In conjunction with these conclusions, we have also demonstrated that among the extended households there were very few multigenerational households, showing that it was not common practice to take care of parents within the household. Again, this confirms earlier suppositions, made on albeit rather scanty data. Our analysis of the relationship between poverty and having non-kin in the household furthermore demonstrated that this phenomenon of the commercial household was not typical for the higher classes of society. Even in the bottom 20% of households, we found that 1 out of every 10 of these households had non-kin living in (in comparison with 1 out of every 4 among non-poor households). Unfortunately, we do not have more information about the income levels of the non-poor households so as to search for a more explicit correlation between income and the affordability of non-kin in the household.

As we suggested in chapters 2 and 6, the increasing dominance of the nuclear family brought new opportunities, the possibility to save or invest, and—together with a growing capital and labor market—increased the agency of the elderly in arranging their own care, in many cases within their home. As mentioned, this chapter demonstrates that the nuclear household led to an increased "commercialization" of the household in terms of both providing care, via lodgers and students who paid for their stay, and receiving care through the hiring of live-in servants. This commercialization was much more evident in Leiden than in the surrounding areas. Considering the number of households that engaged servants and had no children, we might expect that the elderly could indeed have had the means to resolve their hardship squeeze by incorporating non-kin into their households.

In this chapter, we have explained how the European Marriage Pattern not only influenced family ties and the strength of family safety networks but also how this went together with changes in the cycles of wealth accumulation within consecutive households, and how this affected the timing during which the households of parents and their offspring needed help. We have focused partly on the elderly and have revealed different ways in which the elderly were

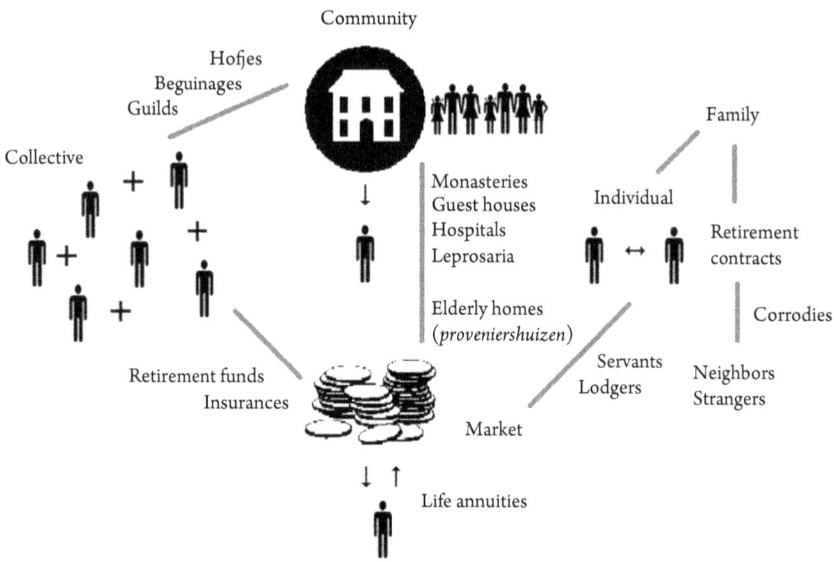

Figure 7.6 Security arrangements for the elderly, in perspective. Source: Previously published in Boele, Bouman, and De Moor 2014, 21–46.

able to secure care if their offspring were unwilling, unable, or otherwise not inclined to do so (see figure 7.6). And we have focused on singles—in particular women—who worked in "commercialized households" as servants. In the next chapter, we move on to discuss those who sought safety within the confines of a beguinage.

8

Beguines

Living Single and Safe

One of the effects of the European Marriage Pattern (EMP) was a growing number of servants in its core region, as described in chapter 7. This contributed significantly to the large number of single persons in these societies, both male and female.* Being single was, contrary to other societies, an accepted status, even for women. However, this did not mean that a woman's safety was guaranteed or that finding a job and earning an income were easy. As was demonstrated in previous chapters, a number of institutional solutions were developed to counteract the negative effects of the EMP, with the beguine movement representing one most typical of the core EMP region. This movement is a most remarkable one in the history of the Low Countries, for which the explanations given so far are largely unsatisfying. The skewed sex ratio, diminished access to convents, and religious revival of the late Middle Ages seem insufficient to explain the movement. We argue that the specific regard for women in the Low Countries that originated with the emergence of the EMP created a fertile and unique basis for the beguinages to develop: the beguinages offered women in the Low Countries safety and security should they chose to remain single. They are, in that respect, typical of the EMP that emerged in the same period.

Although the beguine movement is one of the most fascinating aspects of both religious and women's history, it has attracted relatively few scholars' attention. Over 750 years have passed since its inception, which left a substantial number of beguinages across the Low Countries, many of them recognized by UNESCO as World Heritage Sites. Even though the movement recently came to an end with the death of Marcella Pattyn in 2013, the very last beguine, much remains to be explained.[1] In this chapter, we shed new light on the rise

* Parts of this chapter appeared in De Moor 2014.

[1] See http://www.economist.com/news/obituary/21576632-marcella-pattyn-worlds-last-beguine-died-april-14th-aged-92-marcella-pattyn.

and development of the movement. We attribute a lesser role to the religious motives, emphasizing rather the social and economic motives.

First, contrary to most existing literature on beguines, we argue that the members chose their lifestyle not primarily as an alternative to life as a nun or to marriage but, rather, as a deliberate decision to remain single. Second, our findings are giving a wider perspective here: we see the beguine movement as further evidence for the prominence of the European Marriage Pattern in northwestern Europe since the late Middle Ages. Some of our arguments explain the beguinages' particular form as walled "cities within cities." We argue that the beguinages may also be viewed as female forms of "corporate" organization, much like the guilds, providing protection to individual women active in the urban economies of the Low Countries.

Since the onset of the movement in the late twelfth century, the life of beguines was marked with contradictions, making it substantially different from convent life or other (semi-)religious movements (such as the Modern Devotion) in which women could also play important roles. Beguines had vows, but only temporary ones; they lived a simple life, but some had considerable property, as they retained their right to possess—and even amass—worldly goods. Beguines kept their legal personality; they were separated from the world, but they did not live in seclusion, as in (most) convents, and they lived a life that was both active and contemplative.[2]

Geographically, the emergence of this peculiar movement was focused in the area around Liège, in present-day Belgium. It soon spread over the rest of the southern Netherlands, as well as to the north and as far east as Bohemia, as well as south to the northern part of France. The first written documentation of beguines dates back to the second decade of the thirteenth century, when James of Vitry, an ecclesiastical administrator and analyst of the state of contemporary religion, recorded the life of Mary of Oignies, a holy woman of the diocese of Liège and a model for a new variety of lay piety.[3] The core area, where every city of even a moderate size had its own beguinage or even several (such as in Ghent and Malines) would remain the area around Liège, the northern part of present-day Belgium (Flanders), and the province of North Brabant in the (present-day) Netherlands. Elsewhere in Europe, communities that described themselves as

[2] Translated from the introduction of Majérus 1997, 7.

[3] On the basis of his account, the exceptionality of her way of life for that period in history becomes clear. James of Vitry had the intention of composing a hagiographical text for use against a variety of heresies that were common in southern Europe (among others the Cathars); Neel 1989, 325–326. Even more ironic is the assumption that the name "beguine" is derived from a man called Lambert le Bègue.

beguines—but may not have had all the features just described—have also been found, but to a lesser extent.[4]

Following a period of informal gatherings of individual women, the "institutionalized" form in which the beguines started to organize as real communities with their own regulations, collective property, and identities dates from the middle of the thirteenth century. The communities varied substantially in size, from the smaller convents to the large, extensive communities that comprised virtually all the necessary functionalities of a small city. These beguinages were usually situated just outside the city walls, but were sometimes also within the walls. The most active period in the southern Netherlands for the foundation of new "settlements" was between 1230 and 1320. Almost 70% of the beguinages were founded before the Dutch Revolt of the mid-sixteenth century, most in the form of a house where multiple beguines could live, in a form much like the conventional convents. In fact, the number of contemplative women in many cases was much larger than in convents. Exceptionally large beguinages such as those in Ghent or Malines would have hundreds, and at times even thousands, of inhabitants (the beguinage of Malines comprised 1,500 to 1,900 beguines in the late fifteenth to mid-sixteenth centuries). Even the more modestly sized ones often outnumbered local nunneries, which would frequently house no more than 60 nuns.[5]

The number of beguines varied greatly, from a few in the smaller beguinages to populations that included nearly 8% of the town's population.[6] Although this was less common in the northern Netherlands, the Modern Devotion movement of the late fourteenth and fifteenth centuries also led to large numbers of women choosing to live as beguines.[7] Alternatives in the north were the communities

[4] The beguines were indeed not the only European women living an informal religious life outside of the convent; the *humiliati*, for example, became a popular lay movement for both men and women in Italy from the twelfth century onward. But as with other forms of (semi-)religious movements, what distinguishes the beguines from these other movements is that the women did not have to live in poverty: they could actually accumulate wealth, and keep and obtain property. Such rights were not available, or at least not straightforwardly so, for women in general in southern Europe. As will be shown later, their capacity to accumulate wealth explains both their uniqueness and their capacity to survive as a community, which eluded most other informal female (semi-)religious movements.

[5] Simons 1983, 60, referring to Post 1950. For a graph of the development of beguinages founded before 1566, see Simons 1983, 50.

[6] Simons gives the example of Herentals, where in 1480 the beguines accounted for 7.7% of the entire population; Simons 1983, 60.

[7] The first religious women's movement took place in the twelfth and thirteenth centuries and was characterized by many women joining already existing convents of various orders. The second, to be situated between the middle of the fourteenth century and the beginning of the sixteenth century, consisted more of women forming new convents—of which many were very small—that in the end would accept the rule of St. Francis; van Luijk 2001, 33–37.

of the *zusters van het gemene leven* (literally: Sisters of the Common Life), or the Tertiaries, convents that were part of the Modern Devotion movement. These were similar, but not the same: whereas the former did not sever contact with the lay world, they did renounce private property; the latter eventually changed from not taking any vows to following a stricter way of life, in a more cloistered form of existence, and lost their institutional independence.[8] Beguines clearly stayed more in touch with the "outer world," often providing public services such as schooling and health care, and had more freedom to accumulate and distribute their property and income gathered from participating in worldly occupations such as textile production. It is difficult to put these distinctions into figures, but clearly the beguines lived another type of life from their more contemplative sisters.

This picture clearly indicates that the beguine movement was an important part of society before the sixteenth century. The latter century was in many ways a problematic period. In the northern, mainly Protestant part of the Netherlands, most beguinages disappeared around the time of the Protestant Reformation, with the exception being those in Amsterdam and Breda, which was close to the Flemish "heart" of the movement. The sixteenth century was to some extent also an age of the return to patriarchy, during which women were restricted in their rights, behavior, and opportunities (see chapter 2). The seventeenth century witnessed a revival in the number of beguinages, following the Counter Reformation. Some of the beguinages, such as the one in Tongeren, reached their largest sizes during this period. By the end of the eighteenth century, many beguinages disappeared. Most had lost the attraction they had once enjoyed, and there were substantially fewer beguines.

The development of beguinages shows that they represented an extreme form of resilience: although many disappeared around the time of the Reformation (particularly in the northern part of the Netherlands), many individual beguinages survived for several centuries, and as a movement, they survived until the very beginning of the twenty-first century.[9] Many former houses still stand. But the architectural remains cannot be used to study the resilience of an institution. One of the more appropriate ways to explain the longstanding popularity of the movement is to reexamine the factors that may have influenced the women who chose to join a beguinage instead of a convent, or in preference to marrying, living as a lay woman with a family, or as a single person in town.

[8] Van Luijk 2001, 39–43.

[9] The last beguine in the Netherlands was Cornelia Frijters, who was a member of the beguinage in Breda; she died at the age of 81 on April 13, 1990; see "Cornelia Frijters," http://nl.wikipedia.org/wiki/Cornelia_Frijters). In Belgium, the last surviving beguine was Marcella Pattyn, who took her vows in 1942 in the beguinage of Kortrijk and died on April 14, 2013 (see also note 1).

To understand the longevity of this movement and the continuing choice of women to join it, we should focus on a period well after its beginnings. The seventeenth and eighteenth centuries not only form an interesting period because of the revival of the beguinages but also offer possibilities for gathering biographical data about individual beguines. Literature about the motives of beguines from the early years of the movement are mainly based on the *vitae* of literate and often well-off members, whereas we now know that the beguine community was socially more varied.[10]

To explain a movement that survived for such a long time we need to focus on structural factors that must have been embedded in society, rather than on temporary factors that may have influenced women for a relatively short period of time, although the latter might have contributed to its greater popularity in certain time periods. The regional exceptionality of the movement also supports the importance of focusing on structural factors. Its prevalence in the continental North Sea area and its surroundings suggests that a very specific combination of factors characterized this region, and these were probably conducive to particular choices by individuals. The fact that the female variant of this particular movement—and not the male beghard movement—became so popular, points us toward factors that conditioned female decision-making within the household sphere (e.g., a decrease in parental authority) and in society at large (i.e., their favorable position in the labor market and their ability to earn their own income).

Although the beguines formed a semi-religious movement, the religious aspects of the movement may have been overstated. Historians have not paid enough attention to the influence of social structures on the women who became beguines, as Walter Simons has stressed.[11] Although we discuss the nonreligious factors in this chapter, we do not intend to ignore or deny the importance of religious vocation in the emergence and continuation of the movement. Given the ambiguity of the beguines' lives between the religious and the secular world, and their dependence on the lay world through earned income, it is clear that a substantial part of a beguine's day was not devoted to religious activities. A woman choosing to live in a beguinage solely for religious motives may have been disappointed. Thus, she would have either not chosen this semi-religious life or have left the beguinage for a place where her vocational aspirations could have been better fulfilled. As we show on the basis of the data, a number of beguines did indeed choose to leave the beguinage for a convent, but the continuing popularity

[10] Simons 1983, 91–104.
[11] Simons 1983, 126.

of the movement until well into the eighteenth century shows that this was only a minority.

We start by exploring the traditional explanations for the beguine movement, such as the unbalanced sex ratio and the reduced access to convents, especially in the thirteenth century, which may have had a continuing effect on the growth of the movement after its foundation. We also detail a number of other factors that have received substantial attention from scholars in social and economic history, which may explain the structural differences between the area where the beguinages were formed and the rest of Europe. Even though singular examples did exist elsewhere, these institutions never developed to the same extent as in the Low Countries. In the course of this section, we study their features, making use of a large dataset of biographical data for over 13,000 beguines who lived in ten different beguinages throughout the Low Countries. This dataset, along with other data about the entry age of nuns and the marriage age of women, helps us gain an understanding of women's decision to choose a beguinage over other options in life. In the last part, we explain the major conclusions that can be drawn from the data analysis.

The Why: Two Standard Hypotheses and Our Analysis

The beguine movement is often interpreted as a solution for women who faced difficulties in finding a husband, who could not gain access to a convent, or a combination of both.[12] In the early days of the movement, it was reserved primarily for aristocratic women whose families could afford the necessary dowry.[13] Established convents were full, and this was further compounded by the decree of the Fourth Lateran Council (1215) forbidding the establishment of new religious orders.[14] Moreover, a substantial number of men had departed for the Crusades, and many others had entered the priesthood or male orders. This led scholars to suppose that medieval cities had a "surplus of women" for which the beguinages offered an attractive alternative to marriage or entering a cloister.[15]

[12] In France, Germany, and the Low Countries, there were more marriageable women than men "due to local wards, feuds, crusades . . . the large number of secular and regular clergy." See Bowie 1989, 14.

[13] See, for example, the social composition of the nuns at the cloisters of Cîteaux and Prémontré. Neel mentions the important role of these communities, founded in 1098 and 1124, respectively, in the century of spiritual activity before the registered beginning of the beguine movement. By the thirteenth century, both orders received only cloistered choir nuns into heavily endowed foundations. These nuns came exclusively from the urban patriciate and higher social groups; Neel 1989, 248.

[14] This view is supported, among others, by Greven 1912.

[15] See description of the debate on the origins of the beguine movement by Simons 1983, xi–xiii.

Similarly, the foundation of many beguinages in the thirteenth century was explained in light of the freedom that cities offered. Scholars have argued that, rather than living alone, some women preferred to live in autonomous groups where they could live a freely chosen religious life, as well as working as a teacher, spinster, or other occupation that could ensure their livelihood. In contrast to regular nuns, beguines did not take a vow of poverty.[16] They did promise to lead a humble and modest life, but this did not prevent them from following real-world occupations. And in fact, beguinages often became wealthy in the centuries after their foundation.[17]

In general, there are two major explanations for the beguine movement: one hinges on the unbalanced sex ratio (*Frauenfrage* debate) in medieval towns, and the other points to access to convents and the links with religious developments. Authors such as Greven and Philippen stress the importance of limited opportunities in the main religious orders for the emergence of beguinages. Several limitations in the growth of nunneries may have provided an impetus to the development of female communities, first in the vicinity of nunneries or hospitals and later actual beguinages.[18] The sex-ratio explanation, on the other hand, was based on Bücher's *Frauenfrage*,[19] which stressed the social role of religious movements above the religious background of the beguines, perceiving the beguinages as refuges for women of the lower classes. Simons sees the *Frauenfrage* debate as a reaction to the more religiously inspired theory.

There have been various critiques of both explanations. Access to convents was less restricted than previously thought, and there was a geographical divide between the regions with convents and those with beguinages, with each attracting different classes of women. Furthermore, access to convents probably played a role in the first period of the beguine movement, immediately after the Lateran Council in the thirteenth century, as the movement then mainly attracted women from the elite and places in the convents were indeed limited, even for them. Thereafter, women outside the nobility soon dominated the movement, since access to the convents was no longer considered an option for them.[20]

Regarding the *Frauenfrage* theory, several authors have argued that the sex-ratio imbalance may not have been significant enough to bring about a new

[16] This kind of simple life in common should also be seen as a response to the tremendous appeal of the *vita apostolica* during the fourteenth century, when many other groups—such as the flagellants, the Albigensians—that strived toward a *vita apostolica* emerged. See McDonnell 1969, 141.

[17] De Cant 2003, 60.

[18] Simons 1991, 128; Philippen 1943; Greven 1912.

[19] Bücher 1910.

[20] On the issue of class, see arguments in Milis 1992.

movement.[21] They have shown that either (1) the male surplus was not so significant in the early medieval period or (2) the female surplus was not that large in the late medieval period. Ester Koch points out that, as far as the sex ratio can be reconstructed with a sufficient number of sources for the early and late Middle Ages, there is no clear evidence that supports these hypotheses.[22]

Overall, notwithstanding their potential explanatory value for the earlier, pre-sixteenth-century developments, the arguments for both sex ratio and access to convents cannot explain the long-term development of the beguinages in the Low Countries: after a period of waning interest, in the seventeenth century there was a clear revival of the beguine movement, despite the lack of arguments claiming that either of these factors played a role in this decline and revival. Examining the later period suggests that other factors that may have played a role in the evolution of the beguine movement. No sources for the preceding period are available, but we can offer some interpretations based on the later evolution of the movement.

We focus on two major, interlinked factors that may have played a crucial role in creating fertile ground for the emergence and continuation of the beguine movement in the Low Countries. First, changes in the marriage pattern and the changing position of single women in society at large, as well as the increasing participation of women in the labor market, probably play a role. Second, the beguine movement should be seen as an institution for collective action, having more in common with other institutions such as guilds than with conventional convents. Both the changes in the marriage pattern and the development of institutions for collective action follow a similar path in western Europe, particularly in the Low Countries.[23] Here, we focus primarily on the individual motives of beguines and less on the presence of the new institutional model that thrived on self-governance and (mainly) bottom-up organization. Nevertheless, before our conclusion, we briefly touch on this aspect of the beguine movement.

We test three hypotheses directly related to the two theories on the emergence of beguinages. The main question is what the alternatives were to life as a beguine. Was it simply an alternative to marriage, to the convent, or to living single elsewhere in town, without the protection of the beguinage walls? To answer this, we look at place of birth (and the location of the beguinage) and age at taking vows (compared to the average age at taking vows in a convent or first marriage).

First, we analyze where the beguines came from to test the sex-ratio hypothesis. We take into account that the unbalanced sex ratio (more women

[21] Milis 1992, Koch 1987.

[22] Koch 1987, 162–164.

[23] See for a development of this argument, De Moor 2008.

than men) was a typically urban phenomenon. In the countryside, several factors resulted in a higher mortality among women and led to a more equal ratio, whereas in the cities an unbalanced sex ratio was more likely. Women who originally came from the country were probably able to return to get married, as it would have been far easier to find a husband there. Yet in the literature, it has long been assumed that the beguines came from the urban bourgeoisie. On the basis of preliminary analyses of more scattered data, Simons stresses that most beguines came from the areas around the town where the beguinage was situated, not from the town itself.[24] This suggests that the sex ratio might not have been an important factor in motives to move into a beguinage: if women were desperate for husbands, it would have been more logical to return to their villages to find them. For women born in an urban environment, this would have been more difficult. Thus, it would make sense that if the marriage factor played a major role, we would find primarily women with an urban background in the beguinages.

With our large data collection, we can analyze the places of origin for a large number of beguines, and we can refine our argument by looking at the age they took their vows, and then comparing it to the average age of marriage in the area. If women who entered the beguinages were generally older than the average age they took (marriage or religious) vows, they may well have considered the beguinage a last resort, indicating that their choice to join one was the result of an unsuccessful search for a groom. If profession (taking vows) occurred when women were younger than the average marriage age, it would suggest the choice was made before the point of desperation, and could indicate that it was an individual choice to remain single, without waiting for an ideal partner.

Similarly, this reasoning could be applied with respect to the nuns-manquées argument. Notwithstanding the other arguments that have been advanced to indicate that access to convents—both in entry requirements and places available—was not restricted after all, we need to take into account the argument of choice: future nuns were supposed to be trained for a certain period;[25] the beguines, too, spent on average 1.5 to 2 years in the beguinage before taking their actual vows. This entry age, which can be extrapolated for all beguines for

[24] Simons 1983, 139.

[25] According to chapters XV to XIX of the Papal Decree "On Regulars and Nuns" of December 4, 1563, issued at the Council of Trent, vows should not be made until the novice had completed a full and uninterrupted year of probation within the monastery; an additional condition was that the girl that was to take vows after this probation should be at least sixteen years of age. The chapters also contain the explicit prohibition to the family of the novice to bequeath any possessions to the monastery prior to the actual profession of the girl involved. Translated texts available at http://history.hanover.edu/texts/trent/trentall.html. For an extensive case study of the way in which women were admitted to a monastery, see, for example, Schlotheuber 2004, 104–174.

whom we know the age when they took their vows, can be compared to the age at entry into a convent. From this we can also analyze the relationship between peerage and entry into the convent by considering whether the beguines were of noble descent.

In this chapter, we propose an alternative explanation: that entering the beguinage was an individual choice to remain single (which had become normal in the Low Countries) rather than to get married. Considering that the more religious option would have been taken much earlier than the choice to get married, this difference should be reflected in the average age of profession compared to average age of taking vows in convents and average age at first marriage.

We composed a dataset with biographical information on more than 13,000 beguines (13,362 to be precise) from several beguinages in the Low Countries, mainly in the period 1550 to 1900. We also included basic data such as date of arrival at the beguinage, the date/year they took their vows, and their place and date of birth. It proved impossible to retrieve all these data about every beguine in the dataset. For the different analyses presented here, we make use of different samples of the data, so that a different set of cases is included in the various samples. We expand on the content of each sample wherever appropriate. The dataset was based on data retrieved from a number of primary and secondary sources and then linked. Most of the information is taken from profession books, burial books, and parish registers with data on beguines from a total of ten towns (Amsterdam, Breda, Dendermonde, Diest, Ghent, Hasselt, Hoogstraten, Sint-Truiden, Tongeren, and Turnhout) in the Low Countries. In some cases—such as Ghent—there were several beguinages in the city, which means it is possible that the beguines in the dataset were located in different beguinages in the same town, but this should not affect our conclusions.

Though the database can no doubt be much improved, it is the largest dataset of its kind, and it is based on a wide variety of historical sources, ranging from sources created by the beguines themselves (such as burial registers of those buried within the beguinage) to the typical sources for demographic research, such as parish registers. Given the large number of different beguinages included in the database and the large number of beguines, it is impossible to list all those sources here. Although the size of the database is considerable, the number of beguines in the Low Countries over time was much larger, and we are only looking at a sample, though a substantial one, of the whole movement.

The Geographical Origins of Beguines

The geographical origin of the beguines is interesting, for two reasons. First, it can help us understand whether there was such a thing as a skewed sex ratio in the cities; and second, it can give us a better idea of the importance of the urban bourgeoisie as a class of origin for beguines, and thus answer the question whether women became beguines because they had no other religious alternatives. As Simons has noted, the urban location of the beguinages did not prevent women from the country from choosing a life within their walls. He gives examples of estimates based on cross-sections for specific years: from 62% of the beguines in the Sint-Truiden Beguinage in 1780, to as many as 95% in the Hoogstraten Beguinage in 1619 were migrants from out of town.

These figures are far from exaggerated, as our data show. Table 8.1 demonstrates that, on average, a large majority of beguines were born in locations other than the town where the beguinage was situated. Both in the beginning and at the end of the period described, the percentage of migrating beguines was particularly high: around 95% of the total population. The number of women who had no out-of-town marriage market to rely on was thus very small. Moreover, our data demonstrate that the argument that the majority of beguines had an urban bourgeois or even noble background can also be discarded.

This runs counter to the argument that noble women were "parked" by their families in a beguinage to avoid splitting the family inheritance. One element, a rather substantial number (18%) of beguines with family members in the beguinage at the moment of profession, might suggest that there was a "family strategy" involved. But there are several possible explanations for this that do not depend on the capacity of the women's families to have planned their lives

Table 8.1 **Number of Beguines Coming from Outside the Beguinage Location**

Period	*Born Outside Beguine Location*	*Born Within Same Town as Beguinage*	*Number for Which We Know Birth Location*	*Number with Profession/ Arrival (+1) year*	*Percentage of data for Which We Have a Birth Location*
1500–1599	94.12%	5.88%	17	128	13.28%
1600–1649	69.78%	30.22%	278	943	29.48%
1650–1699	78.77%	21.23%	1,385	3,145	44.04%
1700–1749	80.27%	19.73%	1,333	2,263	58.90%
1750–1799	87.27%	12.73%	1,414	1,588	89.04%
1800–1849	89.66%	10.34%	1,141	1,187	96.12%
1850–1899	96.85%	3.15%	890	917	97.06%
1900–1977	96.75%	3.25%	277	285	97.19%
End total	85.49%	14.51%	6735	10,641	63.29%

Source: Beguines database 2012: Database on beguinages in Low Countries, Northern France and part of Germany, DataverseNL https://hdl.handle.net/10411/10102.

Table 8.2 **Distance Between Beguinage Where the Beguine Lived and Her Birth Location (in percentages of the total population, per century)**

Year of Profession of Beguine	*Distance Between Beguinage and Birth Location*					
	0	*0–20*	*20–50*	*>50*	*Total*	*#*
1500–1599	7%	40%	53%	0%	100%	15
1600–1699	21%	39%	36%	3%	100%	1,405
1700–1799	16%	54%	25%	5%	100%	2,549
1800–1899	7%	56%	33%	5%	100%	1,688
Total	14%	51%	30%	4%	100%	5,657

Source: Beguines database 2015.

for them. The work by Kim Overlaet, for example, shows that while beguines did bequeath to family members, they also did so actively to nonrelated persons.[26] This suggests that if the women were pushed by their families into becoming beguines, it was an unsuccessful financial strategy. The many women who joined a family member in a beguinage suggests that they probably considered their kin-beguine as successful examples of female "liberation" and/or independence, and that they simply sought to follow their example instead of being the subject of family intrigues and strategies.

Of course there were also beguines who were born outside of the town in which the beguinage was located, and thus would have had to move from that place to the beguinage. For nearly 5,000 beguines (4,940), both the location of birth and the location of the beguinage could be identified. A small sample of beguines came from villages that could be linked to different places; they have been excluded for further analysis. The portion of beguines who migrated to towns among the total beguinage population is very large: in some periods, more than 95% came from outside the town where the beguinage was located. Most beguines only moved less than 20 kilometers from their birthplace (see table 8.2), which means they still had the opportunity to be visited regularly by kin or visit their family, if permitted by the mistress of the beguinage. Only very few beguines originated farther than 50 kilometers from their beguinage. This analysis suggests that beguines usually did not have to lose their original kin network, nor were they cut off from their original social network, which could have also provided a husband. Returning home was not impeded by great distances.

[26] Overlaet 2012.

The rural origins of many beguines might also explain in part why the beguinage was attractive: beguinages were like small villages within cities—some even had farms and most had large pastures where the cows of the beguines grazed.[27] This particular setting probably provided a sense of familiarity and protection to women arriving from the countryside, although in itself it might have been only a secondary argument for joining a beguinage.[28]

The Marriage Possibilities for Beguines

The database also allows us to examine in a unique way the relationship between becoming a beguine and the possibility of marriage. The age we focus on is the age when the decision to stay at the beguinage was made. This is not linked to the actual entry date, but the date at which the beguine took her vows. In general, this was about one to two years after she entered the beguinage.

Because data from several beguinages could be brought together, the size of our database allows us to make well-founded conclusions for nearly every year in the period of the age when vows were taken. We focus on the ages of beguines at arrival or taking vows and their (geographic) origins. For 5,657 beguines, we know which year (and in many cases the exact date) they were born or baptized (as baptism usually followed soon after birth, these data were grouped together; see table 8.2).[29] To determine the average age when beguines chose to live in the beguinage, we relied in most cases on the year they took their vows (which we have for 9,659 beguines), and if this was not available, we relied upon the date of arrival, but added one extra year to it, as the average difference between vows and arrival was 1.5 years (in 982 cases).[30] If we combine all these data (birth/

[27] For instance, the beguinage of Louvain, founded presumably c. 1232, originally consisted of several half-timbered houses situated outside the city walls of Louvain, surrounded by meadows and streams. Later on, most of the half-timbered houses were replaced with brick houses. When the city of Louvain expanded, the beguinage was incorporated into the city, but because of its walls, the beguinage retained its secluded character; even today, the appearance of the beguinage of Louvain is described as if it were "a city within the city"; Simons 1983.

[28] In this sense, the setting of the beguinages is also reminiscent of the much later but similar format of the *tuinwijken*, or garden cities, which were fairly small, often walled communities set up in the early twentieth century to tackle social decay in many western European towns.

[29] We needed the year of birth to calculate the age at entrance/profession. For this, we checked several thousands of beguines' birth years. In some cases, we could only find the date of baptism. As is commonly known, baptism followed very closely upon birth, so the year would most likely be the same. The calculation of ages at specific moments in time is based on a combination of birth dates (in the great majority of cases) and baptism dates.

[30] The period between arrival and taking vows did not change much over time, except for the period in the first half of the seventeenth century and the first half of the eighteenth century, when beguines had to wait a little longer to be accepted officially.

baptism data with data on arrival/vows), we have a sample of 4,499 beguines for which the age at taking vows can be calculated and 540 for which we do not have the age they took vows, but we do have the age of arrival at the beguinage. This yields a total of 5,039 beguines who can be used for the analysis of the average age when they took vows (see table 8.3).[31] Our largest sample of this average age for beguines comes from Ghent (see table 8.4), which is not surprising: Ghent was one of the towns that always had large numbers of beguines.

Most of the information we have on the age of taking vows is for the period 1640 to 1781; before and after that, we have fewer than 10 records for any single year. To provide a more reliable picture of the real evolution, some outliers from figure 8.1 have been excluded.

Figure 8.1 shows that the average age of beguines on entrance and taking vows becomes progressively higher from 1580 to 1900, from around 20 years old to a little under 30. Clearly, this means that the age at which beguines entered beguinages changed over time. When they arrived, the beguines were well beyond the age of the average novice who entered a convent (see figure 8.2). In the period we studied, entrance to a convent was no longer as restricted as in the late medieval period, and could thus have been a feasible option for women choosing a religious life. The average age upon arrival and when taking vows shows that for most women the beguinage was an alternative to remaining single, not to the convent (too old), nor did they wait to reach the average marriage age (see figure 8.3).

	< 1	**1–1.99**	**2–2.99**	**Total**
Year				
1616–1650	3.23%	70.97%	25.81%	100.00%
1651–1700	3.66%	90.50%	5.83%	100.00%
1701–1750	2.12%	85.74%	12.14%	100.00%
1751–1800	5.82%	91.44%	2.74%	100.00%
1801–1850	3.19%	88.02%	8.79%	100.00%
1851–1900	1.41%	96.25%	2.34%	100.00%
1901–1965	2.05%	97.26%	0.68%	100.00%
Total	3.37%	89.79%	6.84%	100.00%

[31] When we calculated how long the period was from arrival at the beguinage to the actual taking of vows (this can be done for 2,848 cases), it became clear that in 97% of the cases this trajectory took less than 3 years (2,773 beguines). If we excluded the five extreme outliers who waited over 20 years between arrival and vows, the average period between arrival and taking vows was 1.5 years. We used this information to estimate the year of taking vows for those 540 beguines for which we only had the date/year of arrival.

Table 8.3 **Number of Beguines for Which We Have Information on Arrival/ Profession and for Which We Have Age at Profession**

Period	*Number with Profession/Arrival (+1) Year*	*Number with Age at Profession*
1420–1500	185	
1500–1599	128	15
1600–1649	943	150
1650–1699	3,145	491
1700–1749	2,263	932
1750–1799	1,588	1,195
1800–1849	1,187	1,102
1850–1899	917	879
1900–1977	285	275
Total	10,641	5,039

Source: Beguines database 2015.

A small number—and in some cases we know them by name—entered the convent after a period in the beguinage. A small number also left the beguinage to get married. It is difficult to give actual figures for these, as the availability of such data depends on whether local customs noted that. For a small sample of beguines (only 140), spread out over the entire period of study, we also have information indicating that at some point they actually left the beguinage. For half (75) of these women, the exact reason for their departure could not be retrieved. For the rest, about one-third left to enter a convent; others were considered "unfit" for the life of a beguine and were asked to leave; and still others took the initiative to leave on their own. Some of the beguines in our database were reported to have (eventually) married, but our data suggest that in most cases when they chose the beguinage, it was to escape marriage to a specific partner. This is also described by Simons, but for the pre-sixteenth-century period, and for women of noble descent in particular.[32] Apparently, the need to escape the parents' choice of partner was still present in the later period as well, but so many beguines were living a substantial distance from their place of origin that the extent of parental constraints is questionable.

[32] Simons 1983, 69.

Table 8.4 **Number of Beguines for Which We Now Average Age at Profession (per beguinage, summarized per city)**

Period	*Ghent*	*Dendermonde*	*Diest*	*Hasselt*	*Sint-Truiden*	*Tongeren*	*Breda*	*Turnhout*	*Hoogstraten*	*Amsterdam*	*Total*
1500–1599				1					14		15
1600–1649		2		6	21	20	2	12	85	2	150
1650–1699	8	7	197		36	75	88	32	48		491
1700–1749	168	55	389	26	22	123	48	34	67		932
1750–1799	551	143	239	33		53	50	36	90		1,195
1800–1849	806	102	59	4			75	12	44		1,102
1850–1899	657	79	14				58	33	38		879
1900–1977	221	11					26	5	12		275
Total	2,411	399	898	70	79	271	347	164	398	2	5,039

Source: Beguines database 2015.

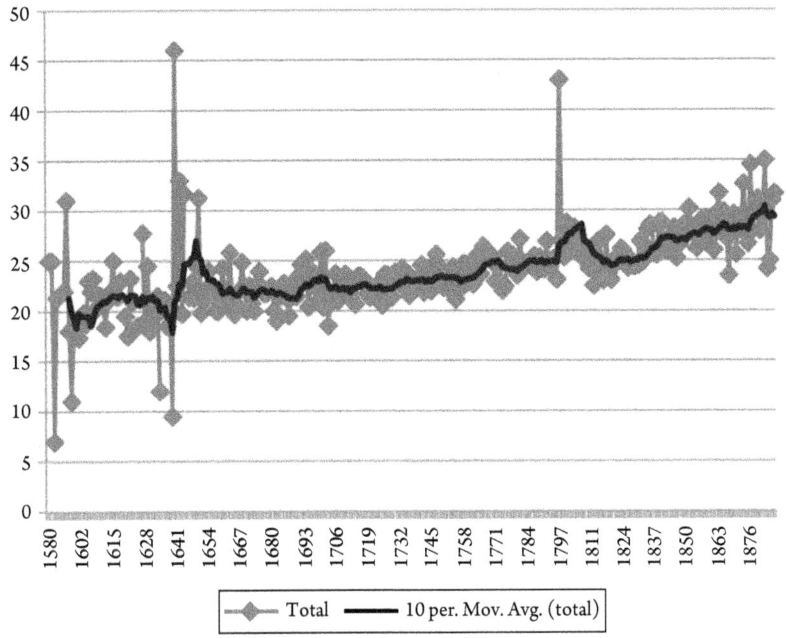

Figure 8.1 Evolution of the average age at profession of beguines, 1680–1781.
Source: Beguines database 2015. Previously published in De Moor 2014, 3–21.

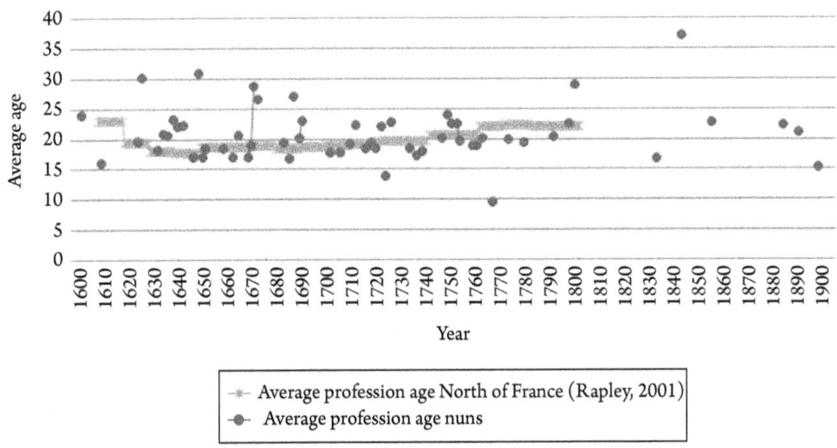

Figure 8.2 Average entry ages of nuns going into convents. Sources: Data for northern France is from Rapley 2001, 272; collection of nuns' entry ages for convents is for Brabant, Limburg, and Liège, from Berlière 1960, (180 values for the whole period). Previously published in De Moor 2014, 3–21.

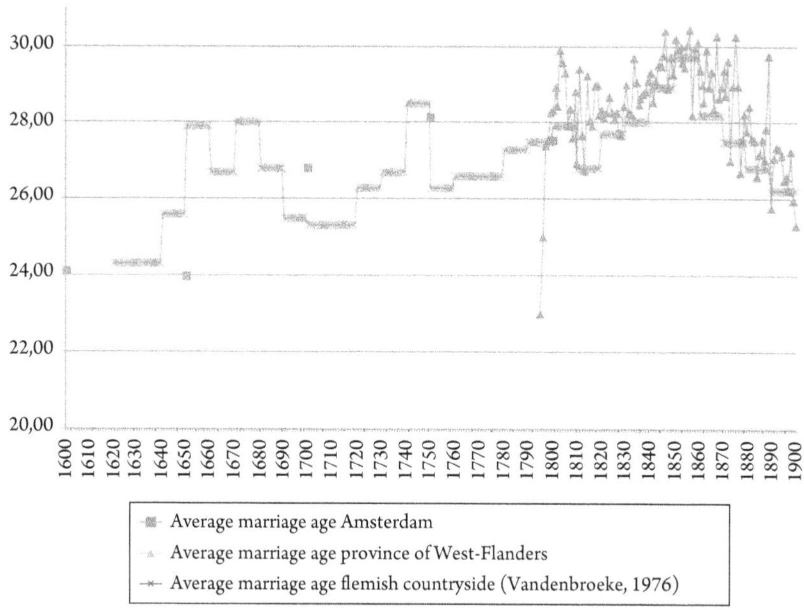

Figure 8.3 Average marriage age (at first marriage) in several locations in the Low Countries, 1600–1900. Sources: Marriage registers for West Flanders 19th century; average marriage ages for countryside (per decade) are as in Vandenbroeke 1976; samples for 1600, 1650, 1700, 1750, and 1800 of the Ondertrouwakten Amsterdam. Previously published in De Moor 2014, 3-21.

Our data do not contain sufficient information for the period before the seventeenth century, nor can we fully address the reasons for the nineteenth-century demise of the movement, leading to its final extinction at the end of the twentieth century (although the number of beguines remaining by then hardly justifies calling it a "movement"). The decline in the number of beguines from the middle of the nineteenth century seems to contradict the resurgence of monastic life in that same century.[33] It is possible to argue that potential beguines started having more intensive religious feelings, leading them to choose the convent, but our data for the nineteenth century on marriage ages suggest something else. Whereas there is a drop in marriage ages from the middle of the

[33] Between 1861 and 1868, the number of Catholic communities founded in the Netherlands rose from 200 to 500 (Wintle 1987, 48, citing Hendriks 1971, 83). The work of Wintle suggests that the relatively strong increase in the number of religious institutions emerging in the Netherlands especially in the second half of the nineteenth century seems to be the result of both past (suppression and abolition of religious institutions during the French Revolution and its aftermath) and contemporary (i.e., the struggle between Catholic, Protestant, and liberal pillars in the 1840s and 1850s) struggles between several confessional and nonconfessionals "pillars" in society, forcing "monastic sentiments" to be organized within strict, very "recognizable" formats.

nineteenth century onward, the ages at which beguines took vows remained more or less the same as before (data are only available until the 1970s), and actually surpassed the marriage ages. It might well be that in a society where staying single was increasingly accepted and possible, by the second half of the nineteenth century, women no longer sought the security and community spirit of the beguinage to help them in their plans to remain single. It might also be that the beguinage eventually became a last resort for old spinsters who had no luck in finding a man.

Summary: Free Choice, Safety, and Security

Our data analysis shows that women chose to live in a beguinage as a first choice that allowed them to stay single, rather than as a second choice to marriage or living in a convent. The fact that women were allowed to live as singles is typical for northwestern Europe, and is closely related to the other features of the EMP already discussed.[34] However, the European Marriage Pattern played a major role not only in triggering the beguine movement but also in enabling its continuation. Whereas temporary "problems," such as an unbalanced sex ratio or a lack of access to convents, may have encouraged women to choose a beguinage, they cannot explain the long-term existence of the movement, nor can they explain the geographical concentration within the boundaries of the Low Countries. The demographic regime is only part of the story, however. The particular regulation of inheritance in the Low Countries also influenced the establishment of beguinages: as women in the Low Countries were allowed to inherit, they were able to establish wills and manage their own fortunes. The beguines were thus able to take their property with them into the beguinage. Even if some of that property became the beguinage's communal property, the women would still benefit from having the right to own and acquire (through work) property of their own.

The possibility to own property is evident from the fact that some beguinages had convents for their poorer members and separate houses for the wealthier ones.[35] A description from 1328 of the beguinage of Ter Hooie in Ghent shows that there were richer and poorer women, but that the latter did manage to provide for themselves, especially with textile work: "Some women [at the Beguinage of Ter Hooie] are rich and have rents, but most own little more than their clothes,

[34] Kowalewski 1999, 40. See also her overview of average marriage ages and percentages of single women (326–328).

[35] Although much literature on beguines gives the impression that beguines—at least in the early years—came from the upper strata of society, Simons argues that from the start of the movement, the beguines had diverse social backgrounds. See Simons 1983, 91–104.

the personal belongings they store in coffers, and their beds. Yet they are a burden to no one, working with their hands, supporting themselves, napping wool and finishing cloth."[36] Simons further mentions that, besides their involvement in the textile industry and their charity work (in hospitals, leper houses, or as nurses to individuals in private homes), some beguines even "did farm work in nearby fields, herded animals, raised poultry, or grew vegetables for the urban market. Still others worked in an unspecified capacity in the city, perhaps as maids, to earn a living."[37] The EMP was the driving force behind the high female labor-market participation in the area. Linked to this was the substantial migration of rural women to early modern towns, which was exceptional compared to southern Europe, and which also accords with the many out-of-town women who became beguines. The self-sufficiency of the beguines—through production or wage labor—should not be interpreted as an exceptional phenomenon (within the context of the EMP) but, rather, consistent with the role of women in the society and economy of northwestern Europe. Women were able to earn their own living, and found support, safety, and security as a group—and the beguinage formed an excellent opportunity to achieve this. Retention of their own property and their textile production or wage labor allowed them to live autonomously.[38] The beguine movement is a powerful example (albeit only one) of how late medieval and early modern society created openings, both economically and ideologically, for women to live lives that were unthinkable in more patriarchal societies.[39]

Beguinages as Institutions for Collective Action

Because of the large numbers of single women in the Low Countries, those who had some religious vocation but wanted to remain single (and had no interest in going to a convent or marrying) could join a beguinage. This fact still does not explain why they organized themselves into beguinages. Apart from the very

[36] Citation from Simons 1983, 95, who translated an excerpt from a charter of the Begijnhof Ter Hooie, at the city archives of Ghent. The many beguines that did need charity, in particular from 1275 onward, were supported by the other wealthier beguines (104); translation Tine De Moor.

[37] Simons 1983, 85.

[38] The following comment by the Robert Grosseteste (thirteenth century), bishop of Lincoln, indicates the self-sufficient life of the beguines: "There is an even greater form of poverty and this is to work for a living, just as the Beguines do. These people have the utmost perfect and saintly form of religious life, because they live their own work, their needs never weighing on the rest of the world" (cited by De Cant 2003, 7). In some literature, the beguinages are even considered as the female versions of guilds; see, for example, Simons 1983, xi.

[39] During the fourteenth century, the Church did try to limit the expansion of the beguines.

specific form of architecture (World Heritage sites today), the internal organization also differed from a regular convent or from other groups of women who lived together and in some cases also developed into beguinages.[40] Rather than showing similarities to religious institutions, beguinages have many of the structural characteristics of secular institutions, such as guilds. In the literature they have even been called "female guilds," in relation to their work in the production of textiles. Similarities can be found in their bottom-up formation and high degree of self-governance: there was no central coordination of development, no single point of origin, no single founder.[41] Although several noble families are known to have financially supported groups of women to set up a beguinage (by donating land to build upon),[42] the women themselves were responsible for the creation of the community, and they decided (without influence of the religious authorities) how their community would be organized. In many cases, this entailed some hierarchy, but with a rotation of responsibilities among all senior members.[43] Another similarity rests in their exclusiveness and the need to become a member of the community, attained via vows.

One of the other key characteristics of institutions such as guilds and beguinages was their reliance upon economies of scale (for example, in collective provisions such as a farm on the premises) and most importantly, on risk sharing. As in guilds, beguines sought to avoid economic risks by banding together, but this also offered them the advantage of safety. Single women ran many physical risks in the early modern town; the walls around most beguinages

[40] In the city of Bergen op Zoom, for example, a community of religious women was living at the Vrijthof. In 1429, these women seem to have chosen to live a more monastic kind of life: some of them chose to live together as beguines, whereas others chose the monastic life of a *grauwzuster* (literally: "gray nun"); van Ham 2000, 393–395. The beguinage of Onze-Lieve-Vrouwe-ter-Hooie in Ghent was also originally a congregation of devout women living together; after some years, they organized according to the example of the larger beguinage of Saint-Elizabeth. The beguinage was formally recognized by the Countess of Flanders in 1262 (Majérus 1997, 883–892; Cailliau 1995, 13–17).

[41] Simons 1983, 47.

[42] For instance, both beguinages that existed in the city of Sittard were founded by donations in kind. The first one was first mentioned in archival sources in 1276 and was founded by the noble Lady of Montjoie. Archival sources also mention the existence of a second beguinage, founded by the municipal government of Sittard in 1441 on behalf of the late Lord Huprecht and his wife Kathrijne, who bequeathed their house and a rent charge as an inheritance to five poor beguines; Van Luyn 1995. For archival sources, see Euregionaal Historisch Centrum Sittard-Geleen, Bestuursarchief Gemeente Sittard, 1243–1794, toegang 163, inv. nr. 1238, and Regionaal Historisch Centrum Limburg (Maastricht), Archief van het Kapittel van Sint Pieter te Sittard, toegang 14B004, inv.nr. 7, regest 16). An example in the Flemish part of Belgium (Flanders) was the beguinage of Onze-Lieve-Vrouwe-ter-Ooie (Our Lady of ter-Ooie), which was granted the right to build a chapel, to create a graveyard, and to have its own chaplain by the Countess of Flandres; Majérus 1997, 883–892; Cailliau 1995, 13–17.

[43] Simons 1983, 143.

and gates were closed at night, offering them much-needed security. The fact that the beguines chose to organize the way they did should be no surprise: they could find many examples of institutionalized collective action around them.[44]

Choosing a collectivity to achieve safety requires an explanation. The way it was organized was similar to other collective institutions in medieval and early modern northwestern Europe, both religious and nonreligious. Of course, the religious motives of women who entered a beguinage should not be ignored. However, because beguinages have been studied in the past as particular constructs within the city, as peculiarities, or as reservoirs for nuns-manquées, the wider context has often been forgotten. That wider context was an area that differed in many ways from the rest of Europe, and as such can serve as an explanation for the emergence and continuation of this interesting movement. The choice to live collectively (in fairly large collectivities) and not as semi-religious small groupings could have been inspired by other forms of institutions that thrived on collective norms and advantages of scale through self-governance and bottom-up formation and organization. Of course, there was also the influence of the convent as a community model, but this does not hold for the organizational setting of the beguinage, which consisted mainly of small houses for those who could afford them and larger, more convent-like communities for the less fortunate.

Conclusion

In this chapter, we have given an alternative explanation for the development of the beguine movement in the Low Countries. We have described the explanations in the literature, although it should be noted that those explanations mainly pertained to the pre-1500 situation. Skewed sex ratios and the lack of other religious alternatives have been the dominant elements in this literature. After examining the importance of these factors for the period from the late sixteenth century onward, we came to the conclusion that the impetus for women to become beguines lay neither in avoiding the convent nor resisting marriage but, rather, in the possibility of choosing the life of a single woman within a safe environment.

The beguinage movement demonstrates that in the early modern Low Countries, remaining single was a real choice, and not the result of failures. Nevertheless, this does not mean that women would not want some sort of protection, both physically within the walls of their community and religiously in

[44] See De Moor 2008, 179; Lynch 2003.

their choice to lead a religious life, although in the case of the beguines they could achieve this without the usual constraints of living in a convent.

The decision to live the life of a beguine reflects an exceptionally high level of agency among single women in northwestern Europe. Women there had a substantially larger say over their own future, thanks to the conditions of household formation in the European Marriage Pattern, their right to inherit and to own and accumulate property, and their presence in the labor market. This enabled them to achieve, through their own income, relative independence from a male breadwinner or their parents, but it also left them in a safety vacuum that was not easy to resolve. For those women, the beguinage formed a safe haven.

Although the beguine movement may seem peculiar to us today, in its contemporary context it was not so bizarre at all. It simply accommodated single women's needs, not shielding them from a society that was hostile but, rather, offering them a unique opportunity to direct their future in a society that tolerated spinsterhood as a way of life.

9

Conclusion

The EMP in Eurasian Perspective

Broadening the Debate

In this book we have, mainly employing data and literature related to the North Sea area, developed a new interpretation of the European Marriage Pattern (EMP). The key idea is that the EMP is a marriage system based on consensus and neolocality, and that the basic features of the EMP, as famously distinguished by Hajnal, are the result of these underlying institutions. We have presented a tentative analysis of its emergence in late medieval Europe, stressing the role played by the doctrine of the Catholic Church that consensus is the basis for marriage; and by social and economic developments and institutions that enhanced the bargaining power of young women (and men), such as women's access to labor markets and their share in inheritances (instead of a dowry). A large part of the book was devoted to analyzing the long-term consequences of this marriage system: on human capital formation, on capital markets, on labor markets, and on the well-being of those involved, testing the nuclear hardship hypothesis as developed by Laslett.

In a nutshell, we found, first, that in the Low Countries in the fifteenth and sixteenth centuries, levels of human capital as measured by numeracy (via the age-heaping method) of women (and men) were already remarkably high and clearly higher than in other parts of Europe. Second, that in the North Sea area in the centuries after the Black Death, the gender wage gap (measuring the degree to which women earned less than men for similar work) was remarkably low: quite often women earned the same wage or almost the same as male unskilled laborers. This small gender wage gap points to the strong position women held in northwestern Europe in the labor market. In other parts of Europe—France, Spain, Italy—unskilled women in the late Middle Ages earned about

50% of the wages of unskilled male laborers. There, participation by women in the labor force was probably much smaller than in the North Sea area.[1]

But in the North Sea area, that favorable position for women changed in the sixteenth and in particular the seventeenth and eighteenth centuries. Then, the gender wage gap increased from about 20% to 40% to 60%; in particular in England this change was quite dramatic.[2] Third, as our case study of Edam and De Zeevang illustrated, women in the Low Countries in the late medieval and early modern period had good access to an efficient capital market, which must have strengthened their economic position (and in its turn also reflects their autonomy). Finally, we found no evidence that nuclear hardship affected households during this period, and we tested various ideas related to institutional responses to the possibly increased fragility of households in the EMP. Our study showed that, on various levels and via various "partnerships," societies that were characterized by the EMP developed coping mechanisms to deal with the consequences of the higher marriage ages, such as the double squeeze we have described. These coping mechanisms had a fundamental impact on society, such as through the "commercialization" of the household sphere.

Moreover, we situated the debate about the EMP in discussions in economics and development studies about the importance of female agency for economic development. We, by and large, corroborated the view developed in this literature about the favorable long-term consequences of family systems such as the EMP that allow women greater autonomy.

In this final chapter, we broaden the debate in various ways, having already sketched the implications for the present-day in more general terms in the introduction. After focusing on the core area of the EMP, the North Sea, for most of our study, we now move to the broader European and even the Eurasian level. We do this by analyzing two datasets: related to marriage systems in Europe and in Eurasia as a whole. Moreover, these new data make it possible to test more systematically whether the EMP mattered.

These new perspectives were triggered by a critical evaluation of the EMP hypothesis by two scholars, Tracy Dennison and Sheilagh Ogilvie, who have tested the hypothesis that the EMP enhanced economic development in western Europe, but who arrived at negative conclusions.[3] According to the data they collected, there was no link between the EMP and economic growth in the North Sea area. We respond to this by first reanalyzing their data, which allows us to create a European map of the EMP that makes it possible to test a number

[1] De Pleijt and van Zanden 2016, which compares wages for men and women who have similar jobs, either unskilled workers in the building industry, or harvest workers in agriculture.

[2] Humphries and Weisdorf 2015.

[3] Dennison and Ogilvie 2014.

of ideas of the EMP debate: Is there a Hajnal line (does eastern Europe—to the east of the line from Petersburg to Triest—have a different marriage system? Is the North Sea area different from the rest of the subcontinent?).

Next, we argue that their data do not really address the EMP as we see it. As we have explained extensively in this book, the high age of marriage of women in the EMP regions is the result of underlying institutions, such as neolocality and consensus. When analyzing the effects of the EMP, we should concentrate on these institutions, which we map—making use of data collected by anthropologists—for Eurasia as a whole. This allows us to test the EMP hypothesis more accurately, and to confirm the expectations of our version of this hypothesis: that in western Europe between 1300 and 1800, family systems with high levels of female agency enhanced economic growth.

Our interpretation of the EMP fits into a larger debate on the relevance of institutions for explaining long-term economic performance. The debate is dominated by the representatives of New Institutional Economics (NIE), such as Douglass North, Avner Greif, and Daron Acemoglu and James Robinson, who have argued that institutions are the main drivers of economic change, and more specifically, that certain western European institutions help to explain the "Rise of the West" in the centuries between 1000 and 1800.[4] But this assessment has not gone unchallenged. Sheilagh Ogilvie, in particular, has criticized these views in a number of important papers and books.[5] Her main point is that we should not assume that "whatever is, is right," or more specifically, that institutions that exist in dynamic economies necessarily contribute to development.[6] She has particularly concentrated on the (dis)advantages of the guilds (and other trade-related institutions) to make this point; but recently—in the paper co-authored with Tracy Dennison—has focused on the European Marriage Pattern, in a similar critique.[7]

Dennison and Ogilvie essentially follow the Hajnal interpretation that the EMP can be identified on the basis of a number of distinctive features: high age of marriage for women, a high percentage of singles, and a low percentage of complex households (as most households are nuclear).[8] Hajnal found these features in Europe west of the famous Hajnal line, running from Trieste to St. Petersburg. The EMP has resurfaced in the recent discussions of the institutional determinants of the Great Divergence as one of the factors contributing to the

[4] Acemoglu, Robinson, and Woren 2012; Greif 2006a; North 1981.

[5] Edwards and Ogilvie 2012; Ogilvie 2007.

[6] Ogilvie 2007.

[7] Dennison and Ogilvie 2014; Ogilvie 2008.

[8] Hajnal also mentioned a large share of the population working as life-cycle servants and a low age gap between marriage partners; Hajnal 1965.

long-term economic performance of the region. In various ways, it was argued in chapter 2, this institution (or interrelated set of institutions) enhanced economic growth: by restraining population growth (the classical argument found in Hajnal's original contribution), by strengthening the position of women, by enhancing human capital formation (of women and their offspring), and by encouraging their access to labor and capital markets.

Dennison and Ogilvie test these ideas by looking at the correlation between the mentioned features of the EMP and the pattern of economic growth in early modern Europe. When looking for this correlation, they subdivide countries into three categories: pure, moderate, and extreme forms of the EMP. For each single indicator (mean age of marriage of women; share of singles; and share of complex households), they establish if the economically most progressive countries (England, the Netherlands) are also "leading" in this respect. Unsurprisingly—given measurement errors and small sample sizes—they find many exceptions; in other words, the correlation between the economic modernity and the three dimensions of EMP is far from perfect. This leads them to conclude that the institution as such does not seem to matter.

We have two problems with their analysis. First, we think their analysis of the three separate indicators of the EMP—age of marriage, share of singles, and share of complex households—misses Hajnal's point that the EMP is a "pattern." The three criteria should not be seen in isolation but, rather, interpreted as expressing an underlying pattern (of the values and norms). This requires another approach to the data collected by Dennison and Ogilvie: the underlying pattern can be identified by applying factor analysis aimed at finding the common denominator in the three indicators for which they present the data. As we show here, such an analysis also has the advantage that it is possible to estimate margins of error for the reconstructed "latent variable" EMP, and to identify those countries that in certain centuries are clearly different from the European mean—in two directions: having the typical EMP characteristics or diverging in the opposite way. On the basis of this analysis, it can easily be demonstrated that the most dynamic countries in Europe were also the most EMPish.

Second, their paper is an attempt to test Hajnal's original hypothesis, but they do not deal explicitly with the new interpretation of this hypothesis that is presented in this book (and has been presented in various papers).[9] We first present their findings—their estimates of the regional variation in the age of marriage, the share of singles, and the share of complex households—asking

[9] Carmichael and van Zanden 2015; Carmichael, De Moor, and van Zanden 2011a; De Moor and van Zanden 2010a.

the question to what extent their findings confirm the established Hajnal view of the European variation in marriage patterns. Next, we discuss what is wrong with this view, and we suggest a better proxy for the differences in family systems within Europe (and Asia). Finally, we test the hypothesis that there indeed was a connection between marriage patterns and economic growth in Europe between 1300 and 1800.

Refining the Analysis of EMP Characteristics

Instead of analyzing the spatial patterns in the three features of the EMP on which Dennison and Ogilvie focused in their paper, we argue here that we are interested in the underlying pattern—in the EMPishness of a country in a certain time period, which can be read from the combination of these three features. Given the weaknesses of the dataset put together by Dennison and Ogilvie, it is not possible to rely on data for individual characteristics, but the combination of the three features is a more reliable guide to the EMP. This does justice to Hajnal's idea that the various features of the EMP form one interrelated system, and has the added advantage that margins of error can be estimated, which makes explicit the fact that we are dealing with data of uncertain (and far from perfect) quality.

The common denominator in the three datasets of average age of marriage of women, share of singles, and share of complex households can statistically be established by using factor analysis. This is a formal test: Are there systematic patterns in the data indicating that age of marriage is positively related to share of singles, and negatively linked to share of complex households? Do the features of the EMP suggested by Hajnal indeed show a clear pattern?

The factor analysis confirms the EMP hypothesis: the latent variable EMP index that can be estimated is a function of a positive mean age of marriage, a positive share of singles, and a negative share of complex households—and all variables contribute significantly to the EMP index. Standardizing the estimates reveals that the SMAM (singulate mean age at marriage) has the strongest contribution, followed by the celibacy rate, and finally the percentage of complex households. The EMP index for the eighteenth century is presented in figure 9.1 (we focus on this period, as the margins of error for the earlier centuries are often so large that no clear pattern can be established). It clearly shows the Hajnal line from Triest to St. Petersburg, and with the most "extreme" versions of the EMP in the Netherlands and Denmark.

This approach does fit the data for most countries well, but the results for especially Italy and (to a lesser extent) Spain are less consistent. In particular, for Italy this classification is somewhat problematic, as the regional differences

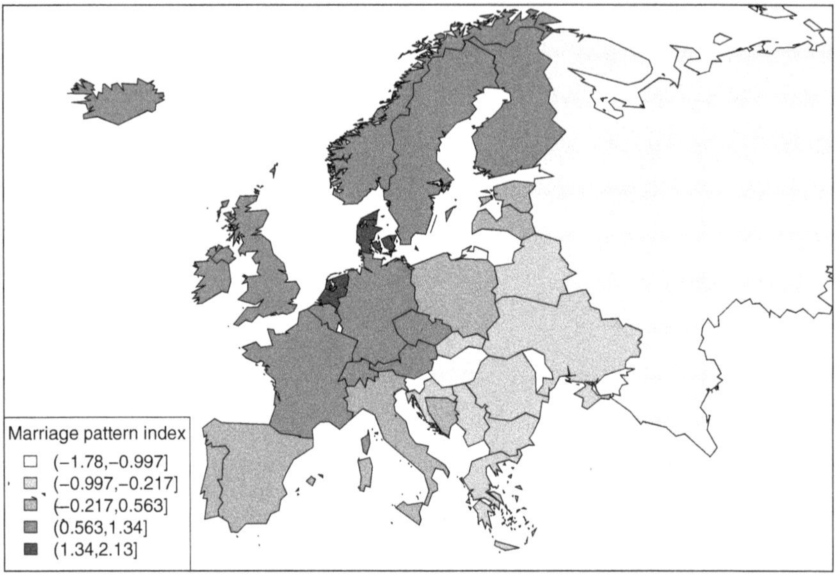

Figure 9.1 European Marriage Pattern, eighteenth century. Data source: Carmichael 2011.

in marriage patterns and household structures do not necessarily follow the classical dimensions of the EMP, and are affected by variations in agricultural systems (sharecropping in the central area of Tuscany/Umbria; large-scale agricultural estates in combination with a large rural proletariat in the south). The links between age of marriage, share of singles, and complex households may be different in those regions.[10]

We also present the development of the EMP index for different geographic units (see figure 9.2). The division of Europe between countries to the west and to the east of the Hajnal line is quite clear from these figures. Countries that significantly diverge "negatively" from the European mean are, for example, Russia (eighteenth and nineteenth centuries), Hungary (eighteenth and nineteenth centuries), and almost all other central European and eastern European states; but for most of them only the nineteenth-century data are good enough to make the divergence significant.

In the west, England and Sweden (sixteenth to nineteenth centuries), the Netherlands, Denmark, Belgium, northern France, and Scotland (seventeenth to nineteenth centuries) are the clearest examples of the EMP, later to be joined by other northern and western nations. The gradual narrowing of the margins of error in almost all cases points to the fact that the statistical basis for these

[10] See for example, Curtis 2015; Dalla Zuanna et al. 2012; Finzi 2012; Beningo 1989.

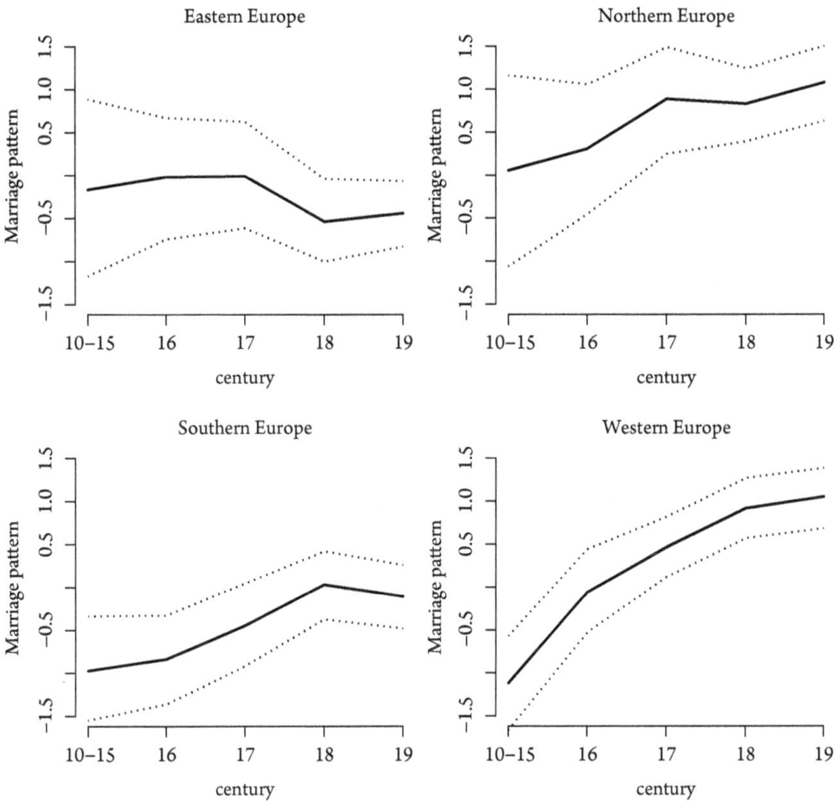

Figure 9.2 European Marriage Pattern by region. Data source: Carmichael 2016.

estimates becomes firmer when moving from the sixteenth to the nineteenth centuries. This creates the impression that the EMP is gradually emerging in Europe, consolidating itself during the early modern period, and becoming more prominent with the passage of time, but this may simply be due to the improving quality of the data.

Overall, this analysis of the data by Dennison and Ogilvie shows that their results are in fact consistent with the picture that arises from the often more qualitative literature on the EMP: the Hajnal line is there, the North Sea area is clearly distinct, and southern Europe (Italy in particular) is probably characterized by a somewhat different marriage system that does not entirely fit the classification scheme as developed by Hajnal. It also appears that the EMP gradually consolidates itself—and that countries like England and the Netherlands only develop these features during the sixteenth and seventeenth centuries, respectively. At this point we disagree, however. Is this EMP index—and the underlying mean age of marriage for women—indeed the right indicator of the EMPishness of a country?

Is Age of Marriage the Right Index?

There is another strand of literature that analyzes the EMP as a "homeostatic regime," which not only limits population growth (via the postponement of marriage by women to ages 23 to 27, and through a large group of single women), but also stresses that age of marriage (and share of singles) responds to economic pressures.[11] Couples have to save for setting up a household after marriage (as neolocality is the norm); when real wages are high and the demand for labor is great, age of marriage will be lower than when wage levels are low. In other words, the degree of economic stress faced by men and women active in the labor market will affect the outcomes of the "system." Demographic behavior will adapt to a situation of high pressure (low employment and low real wages, land scarcity) as much as to one of low pressure (land abundance and high real wages). The interaction between real wages and age of marriage tends to stabilize the economy at a relatively high equilibrium, helping to explain the relatively high income levels earned in the region between the Black Death and the Industrial Revolution.

This perspective on the EMP is relevant for understanding what went wrong with the attempt by Dennison and Ogilvie to test the hypothesis that the EMP contributed to the economic development of western Europe before the Industrial Revolution. They assume that the EMP is a system with high average age of marriage for women, a large share of singles, and nuclear (noncomplex) households, and that the degree to which these features appear makes a country more EMPish.[12]

[11] Clark 2007a; Wrigley and Schofield 1981.

[12] To begin with, we have serious reservations about the coverage and the quality of the data used, the weights used, and more generally how data have been processed to get the country-wide averages they present and analyze. But we did not get access to their dataset for reasons that remain rather unclear. We regret this, and think this conflicts with the open access and data-availability policies adopted by leading academic institutions and journals, and more generally with good academic practices. However, despite this obstacle we do have some specific criticisms of the way that the data in the Dennison and Ogilvie database have been used. For some countries the observations in given years are based on a few, even solitary observations. Of the 40 regional units they cover, over a quarter have 10 observations or fewer for female age at first marriage. They also do not seem to have weighted the observations for the population density of a given region to come to a national value. The earlier, working paper version presented a more complete set of summary statistics than the published paper does, but it is unclear what has changed between the calculations in the working paper and those in the final version. Their paper presents a far-ranging, but at the same time patchy, summary of the numbers available in the literature. However, they do not appear to cover the proliferation in recent years of databases of demographic information at the individual level, often made available online (such as the Mosaic, Napp and Ipums, and the EHPS network).

We think this interpretation of the data is based on a serious misunderstanding of the literature. Perhaps it is possible to interpret Hajnal's version of the EMP as arguing that the EMPishness of a country increases with the average age at marriage and the share of singles in the population (although such an interpretation is already doubtful). But as Dennison and Ogilvie wish to test hypotheses from the recent literature about the consequences of the EMP for economic development, this "simple" interpretation is plainly wrong. The key issue is that the average age at marriage is the result of two factors: whether or not marriage is based on the underlying institutions analyzed in chapter 2 (primarily consensus and neolocality), and the standard of living of the population, potentially resulting in further postponement of marriage. If an economy is highly successful in generating economic growth and raising standards of living, thanks to the EMP, this will result in relatively low ages of marriage—that is, low within the context of marriage behavior based on consensus—that is, around 20 years.

This was the situation in the late Middle Ages after the Black Death, when (we argue) consensus became the norm for large parts of the population of northwestern Europe, but real wages and employment opportunities were such that it was relatively easy to marry. The available data show an average age at marriage of 18 to 21 years for both England and Holland.[13] The sixteenth-century price inflation brought an end to this favorable situation; although real wages in the Netherlands and England declined less than those elsewhere in western Europe, they did go down. There is substantial evidence pointing to a strong rise in age at marriage during the sixteenth century—not because marriage institutions became more EMPish (which they did not; in fact, the Reformation and the Counter-Reformation strengthened the position of parents), but because of the increase in economic stress resulting in the deterioration of living standards.[14] From our agency-based perspective, the rise in age at marriage owing to the decline in real wages in the sixteenth century was not a strengthening of the EMP but, rather, a weakening.

A similar example can be derived from the emigration experience of men and women in early modern Europe. When emigrants from the North Sea area settled in the Cape Colony or North America, they did not change their values

[13] See Dennison and Ogilvie 2014, 662; also find a significant lower age of marriage for the sixteenth century.

[14] Dennison and Ogilvie 2014 also present fifteenth-century evidence that points in the same direction: the average age of marriage of the fifteenth-century studies is 18.8 years; for the sixteenth century, this is 21.8 years; and for the seventeenth century, 24.8 years, confirming the rise in age of marriage during the period in which real wages decline steeply; see for this link also Wrigley and Schofield 1981.

and norms concerning marriage behavior (consensus remained the central notion), but they soon began to marry much earlier owing to the different economic circumstances; in these parts of the world, land was abundant and real incomes were relatively high. In the Cape Colony, for example, the mean age of marriage for women was as low as 19 to 20 years during the eighteenth century (perhaps it is not a coincidence that this is comparable to the level found in late medieval Europe).[15]

In other words, women's average age at marriage is influenced by both the economic circumstances and the underlying institutions. The introduction of consensus marriage must have resulted in a strong rise in the age of marriage (say, from 12 to 16 years to 18 to 30 years), but within the EMP, a lot of variation was possible, dependent on the employment prospects and the real incomes of the working population. The other indicators (share of singles and of complex households) used by Dennison and Oligvie suffer from the same problems: they are endogenous and measure both the presence of the institutions underlying the EMP and the large degree of variation within the EMP. It is therefore no accident that Dennison and Oligvie do not find a correlation between economic growth and marriage age—it is exactly what we would expect. Economically successful regions with EMP institutions will have relatively lower marriage ages than stagnating EMP regions. The growth spurt that began in England after 1650 and that brought about the Industrial Revolution of the late eighteenth century resulted in a long-term decline in marriage age, whereas at the same time, when the Dutch Golden Age turned into a silver age in the eighteenth century, the age at marriage went up.[16]

Summing up, then, the age of marriage is not a correct proxy for the degree to which a region has adopted the EMP, as it is (also) endogenous, affected by living standards and real wages. The same applies, of course, to the other measures used by Dennison and Oligvie. We have to analyze the underlying institutions to really get a grip on the EMPishness of societies. This is what we do in the next section.

Testing the EMP hypothesis

Hajnal's hypothesis of the EMP can be seen as a special case of the more encompassing theory of the family system. This broader theory—mainly developed by ethnographers, sociologists,[17] and demographers—maintains that there

[15] Cilliers 2013.

[16] Wrigley and Schofield 1981; van der Woude 1980b.

[17] Such as Todd 1987, 1985.

are important international (and regional) differences in the norms and values that determine behavior at the micro level concerning marriage, family, reproduction, and upbringing, which tend to persist over time and change only slowly and in a highly path-dependent way. Family life in central Africa is differently organized from that in China or western Europe, and the various institutions (as "rules of the game") determining behavior at the micro level are to some extent interdependent and form a coherent whole. In patriarchal societies, women usually do not inherit (or even own) property, for example (except for their dowry). This clustering of institutions makes it possible to use the concept of a family system to describe such sets of more or less coherent institutions (about which more below). These sets of rules have a substantial impact on behavior at the micro level: it matters if marriage is arranged and girls marry at age 12, or if it is based on consensus and marriage is at age 25. One of the links between the family system and such "societal outcomes" is the degree of agency (autonomous decision-making power) women have in a family system. In chapter 2, it was argued that the EMP, as it was based on consensus and neolocality as the two core institutions, resulted in and was a reflection of a relatively high degree of female agency, and that, by contrast, in most premodern family systems, female autonomy is quite limited. Consensus, introduced by the Catholic Church as a norm, meant that the young woman (and obviously also the young man) had to agree to the choice of a marriage partner or were actually engaged in the search for a partner, which strengthened the position of (young) women. Neolocality meant that partners set up an independent household after marriage, and they were not living with either set of parents; again, this created a lot of opportunities for autonomous decision-making by the man and wife.

This brief review of the debate regarding the links between family systems, agency, and economic development makes it possible to suggest an alternative way of testing the hypothesis that the EMP was beneficial for economic growth. Obviously, we have to focus on the underlying institutions, and try to measure them, but that is not an easy job. In the paper "Towards an Ethnographic Understanding of the European Marriage Pattern," Sarah Carmichael and Jan Luiten van Zanden have tried to do this.[18] They have redefined the EMP in ethnographic terms and used ethnographic information (Murdock's database and Todd's studies) to classify the societies of Eurasia on various marriage and family-related institutions, such as monogamy, consensus, female inheritance, exogamy, and neolocality).

All these institutions have a "female friendly" version: monogamy is from this perspective to be preferred to polygamy; consensus to arranged marriage;

[18] Carmichael and van Zanden 2015.

Table 9.1 **Scoring for the FF Index**

Variable	*Lowest Score*	*Intermediate Scores*	*Highest Score*
Domestic organization	Extended – 0	Stem – 0.5	Nuclear – 1
Cousin marriage	Endogamy – 0[a]		Exogamy – 1
Monogamy	Polygamy – 0		Monogamy – 1
Marital residence	Patrilocal and Virilocal – 0	Avunvulocal – 0.25 Ambilocal – 0.5 Neolocal – 0.75	Matrilocal - 1
Inheritance	Patrilineal – 0	Children daughters less – 0.5	Children equally – 1 Other matrilineal – 1

[a] Assigning a score to the extended family variable and the endogamy is complicated as in some cases living in extended, endogamous families can be beneficial to women, as it keeps their natal kin close by and can provide a support mechanism in times of need. An argument could therefore be made for assigning a half point for the combination of the two; however, for simplicity sake this has not yet been implemented here (moreover it has only a marginal effect on the Eurasian distribution).

female inheritance to systems without them; exogamy to endogamy (which restricts the choice of marriage partners to kin-members), and neolocality to patrilocality. An easy and transparent way to classify societies is to let them score on all five dimensions; societies that are monogamous score one point here, and societies with polygamy do not score a point. Female inheritance, exogamy, matrilocality, and consensus all score similar points.[19] The scoring is presented in table 9.1.

The data used for this table is derived from a combination of three sources. First and foremost, we use Murdock's *Ethnographic Atlas*. The atlas was featured in *Ethnology* from 1962 to 1980; in 1967, the data was compiled into a book.[20] It contains data on 1,267 societies for a wide range of characteristics. These were then translated to country-level indicators by Jutta Bolt, using the *Atlas Narodov Mira*.[21] The dataset used here is largely as classified by Murdock, with a number of corrections made on the basis of comparing his categorizations to those of

[19] See for full details Carmichael and van Zanden 2015.

[20] A revised *Ethnographic Atlas* was used that has been published by *World Cultures* journal. The data are available at intersci.ss.uci.edu/wiki/pub/XC/EthnographicAtlasWCRevisedByWorldCultures.sav.

[21] Bolt 2012.

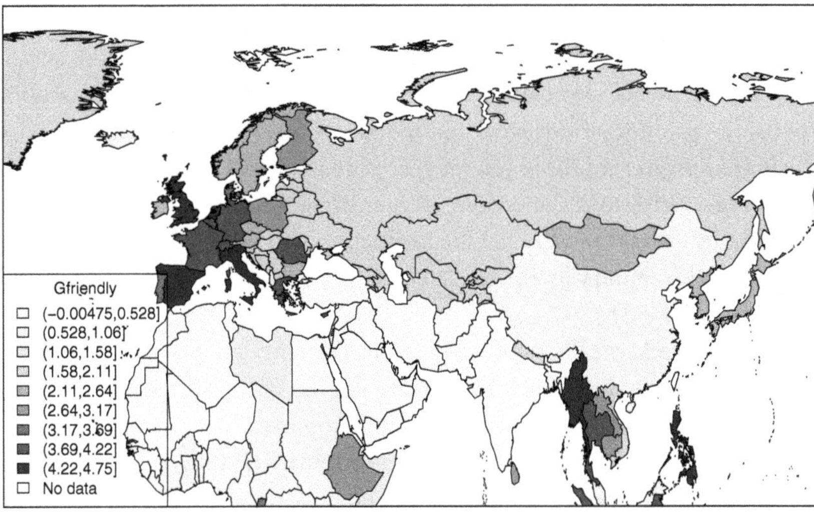

Figure 9.3 FF index mapped for Eurasia. Data source: Rijpma and Carmichael 2016.

Emmanuel Todd. This is only relevant for the domestic organization and cousin marriage variables.[22]

Using this index, the "female-friendliness" (FF index) of family systems in Eurasia can be established: the more points a country scores on the range between 0 and 5, the more its institutions favor female agency. It is a bit arbitrary to weigh all institutions in the same way, but we do not have a method to differentiate the impact of different marriage and family-related institutions. This results in the map presented in figure 9.3, showing that Europe to the west of the Hajnal line is clearly very female-friendly, but so is Southeast Asia.[23] When looking more closely, they find that in the other margins of the Eurasian landmass—in south India (Kerala is a famous case), Sri Lanka, and Japan, family systems also allow for female agency. The map presents this visually at the country level for Eurasia.

Shifting the focus to Europe, we find, with the exception of Romania and Greece, the pattern is remarkably similar to the Hajnal line, with Poland, the Czech Republic, and Austria displaying an intermediate pattern and the UK and the Netherlands, along with Italy and Spain, attaining the highest scores. A somewhat similar "patriarchy index" was constructed by Siegfried Gruber and Mikołaj Szoltyzek; the methodology is rather different, constructed as it is of

[22] For further details on the derivation of country-level variables and the process of checking and correcting, see Rijpma and Carmichael 2016.

[23] In Carmichael and van Zanden 2015, qualitative information confirming this pattern is presented.

large micro-datasets concerning demographic behavior, measuring 14 different dimensions, such as "familial behavior, including nuptiality and age at marriage, living arrangements, postmarital residence, power relations within domestic groups, the position of the aged, and the sex of the offspring."[24] Their results, which are however available for only 12 countries and can therefore not be used for the regressions shown here, demonstrate the same west–east gradient in patriarchy as was found in the reconstruction of the FF index. Their results, averaged at the country level, correlate strongly, but obviously negatively, with our index ($R2 = .53$).[25]

Another check can be conducted using the correlation with current day measures of gender inequality. For this we use the Historical Gender Equality Index developed by Dilli, Carmichael, and Rijpma.[26] This measure captures gender differences in life expectancy, labor-force participation, infant mortality, educational attainment, marriage ages, and political participation. Again, the FF index is correlated with contemporary measures of gender inequality, although the correlation is far from perfect ($R2 = .33$); Sweden, for example, is currently world leader in gender equality, but it does not score very high on the FF index.

We think this measure for female agency within the family system is a good proxy for testing the "Girlpower" version of the EMP hypothesis, as it is clearly based on the underlying institutions. We focus on the question of whether this index can help to explain the Little Divergence within Europe, which is (implicitly) also the issue addressed by Dennison and Ogilvie. In another paper, De Pleijt and van Zanden have tested the various hypotheses for explaining the divergent development of the North Sea area between 1300 and 1800.[27] The results of that paper indicate that political institutions and human capital formation were the main underlying causes of economic growth in this period. We add to this analysis here by directly testing the EMP-Girlpower hypothesis, building on those previous results.[28]

The key independent variable in our regression is the FF index, which shows substantial differences between European countries: northwestern Europe, notably England and the Netherlands, had institutions favoring more female agency than countries located in southern and central Europe. We regress this on two sets of dependent variables. First, the latest estimates of per capita GDP

[24] Gruber and Szoltyzek 2015.

[25] Here the Turkish sample has been excluded, as it is based solely on Istanbul. Similarly, Italy is based on only one location (Legano) in 1430, and therefore has also been left out of this correlation.

[26] Dilli, Carmichael, and Rijpma, forthcoming.

[27] De Pleijt and van Zanden 2013.

[28] In De Pleijt and van Zanden 2013, we performed Random-Effect/Two-Stage least-square regressions, whereas here we have estimated a linear regression model.

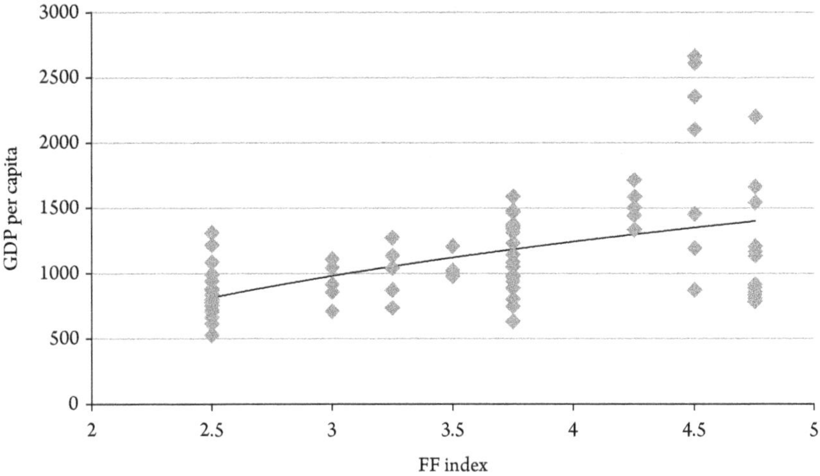

Figure 9.4 Basic correlation between FF index and GDP per capita. Data source: Carmichael and van Zanden 2015.

for these European countries in the period 1300 to 1800.[29] Second, to evaluate the robustness of our results, we follow earlier studies by taking the urbanization ratio as an alternative dependent variable.[30]

The unit of observation are countries at intervals of approximately a century. The years included are 1300, 1400, 1500, 1600, 1700, 1750, and 1800. Observations for 1300 and 1400 are only available for Spain, Italy, England, and the Netherlands. Germany, France, Austria, Poland, Belgium, Switzerland, Denmark, Ireland, and Norway enter the dataset in 1500; Sweden and Portugal enter the sample in 1600. The FF index is related to per capita GDP and the urbanization ratio by estimating a simple linear regression model.[31]

Figure 9.4 shows the basic correlation between the FF index and per capita GDP. The figure nicely illustrates a strong positive relationship between the

[29] For an overview, see Bolt and van Zanden 2014.

[30] For example, Bosker, Buringh, and van Zanden 2013; Acemoglu, Johnson, and Robinson 2005.

[31] The model is:

$$\ln \mathbf{Y}_{it} = \alpha_i + \alpha_t + \mathbf{X}_{it}\beta + \gamma_1 \mathbf{GF}_i + \varepsilon_{it} \tag{1}$$

where Y_{it} denotes GDP per capita or the urbanization rate of country *i* in century *t*, GF_i is our main variable of interest, the FF index. X_{it} is a vector of control variables related to economic development, α_i is the country-specific effect, and α_t denote the century-specific effects. We include a full set of country and century dummies to allow for unobserved country-specific and century-specific heterogeneity. ε_{it} captures all other unobserved (or unmodeled) variables related to economic growth, and we assume that it is uncorrelated with the FF index. Standard errors are clustered at the country level to control for serial correlation in the unobservables.

Table 9.2 **Female Agency and Economic Development, 1300–1800**

	(1)	*(2)*
Estimator	*OLS*	*OLS*
Dependent variable	*Ln GDP*	*URB*
FF index	0.22***	0.05***
	(0.03)	(0.01)
Century dummies	YES	YES
Country dummies	YES	YES
Constant	6.05***	-0.22***
	(0.25)	(0.07)
R2	0.78	0.81
No. of observations	81	81

Notes: Standard errors are clustered at the country level to control for serial correlation in the unobservables. Standard errors in parentheses. *, **, *** denote significance at the 10%, 5%, 1% level, respectively.

two: countries with female friendly institutions were also the ones with the highest levels of per capita GDP and urbanization.

Table 9.2 presents the baseline estimation results including the set of country and century dummies. The regression results in column (1) suggest a strong and positive effect of female-friendly institutions on per capita GDP (denoted Ln GDP): the coefficient on the FF index is highly significant at the 1% level. Column (2) shows that this result is robust to the inclusion of the urbanization ratio as the dependent variable (denoted URB). The coefficients on the index again enter with the expected sign and are statistically significant.

To check for the robustness of our results, the next step is to control for other important determinants of economic growth. The control variables capture the development of political institutions, the role of international trade and shipping, the spread of Protestantism, and the incidence of warfare. We now turn to a brief discussion of the various variables that we include.

Research stresses the importance of political institutions in "constraining the executive" as a root cause for early modern growth.[32] To proxy the quality of political institutions, we use the activity index of Parliaments of van Zanden, Buringh, and Bosker.[33] The activity index is defined as the number of years

[32] cf. North and Weingast1989; Acemoglu, Robinson, and Woren 2012.

[33] Van Zanden, Buringh, and Bosker 2012.

Parliaments were in session during a century, and it varies from zero, when no Parliament convened, to 100, when the Parliament met every year during a given century. The idea is that in republican systems with a strong Parliament (such as England after the Glorious Revolution of 1688), property rights were more secure than in states ruled by absolutist kings (such as France). Active Parliaments, constraining the actions of the sovereign, are therefore expected to have contributed to economic development between 1300 and 1800.

As a second variable capturing political institutions, we include the share of cities with self-government.[34] The communal movement that started in the eleventh and twelfth centuries is important for economic growth, as it created a stable system of property rights in cities.[35] Between 1100 and 1500, many European cities obtained city rights, but they could also lose their status as a result of conquest by another city or by the abolishment of their independent status by absolutist rulers. The share of cities with self-government is therefore argued to proxy the "republican" nature of the polity as self-government constrains the executive.

Another body of literature stresses the significant contribution of international trade and shipping to preindustrial development.[36] To measure the impact of international trade on per capita GDP and urbanization, we make use of the tonnage size of the merchant fleet.[37] This measure has the advantage that it is available for a large set of European countries and for a long period of time. Moreover, to account for the contribution of colonies to economic growth,[38] we introduce "Colonial Realm" in the regressions. This variable captures the size of the colonial population compared to the population of the colonizing country.[39]

To control for the effect of religion on growth, we include a dummy variable for Protestantism. The variable equals 1 for countries that became Protestant after the Reformation; it takes value 0.5 for states that were about 50% Protestant; and, finally, it equals 0 for countries that remained fully Catholic. Since it is strongly related to human capital formation, we also include the number of universities per capita in the regressions.[40] The number of universities per capita may also directly have contributed to economic progress, as it measures advanced levels of human capital.[41]

[34] Bosker, Buringh, and van Zanden 2013.

[35] Stasavage 2014.

[36] For example, Acemoglu, Johnson, and Robinson 2005; Allen 2003.

[37] De Pleijt and van Zanden 2013.

[38] Acemoglu, Johnson, and Robinson 2005; Daudin 2004; Pedreira 1993.

[39] Bosker, Buringh, and van Zanden 2013.

[40] De Pleijt and van Zanden 2013; Becker and Woessmann 2007; Universities: van Zanden, Buringh, and Bosker 2012.

[41] De Pleijt and van Zanden 2013.

A final set of control variables included in the regressions is related to the effect of warfare. Research has found an important effect of war on state formation and subsequent economic development.[42] We therefore first add the average years of war during the previous period (a century or half-century).[43] Second, we control for the Thirty Years' War by including a dummy variable that equals 1 for Germany during the century after the war.[44] Table 9.3 reports the results of the regressions, including the set of control variables.

Although the standard errors become slightly larger, the coefficient on the FF index does not become statistically insignificant. Interesting is the finding of a strong relation between political intuitions and our measures of economic development: the coefficients on the Parliamentary activity index and on the share of cities with self-government enter with the correct sign and are highly significant in all regressions. Regarding international trade, the coefficient on the size of the merchant fleet is insignificant, suggesting that female agency and political institutions were more important drivers of economic growth between 1300 and 1800. The regression in column (2), however, suggests a positive relationship between colonial realm and urbanization, which indicates that the growth of overseas land contributed to city growth. Although Protestantism enters with the correct sign, it is never found to be significant in the regressions. This finding suggests that religion had no direct effect on economic outcomes, but that it worked via other channels such as human capital formation.[45] With respect to warfare, we indeed find a weak negative effect of the Thirty Years' War on economic growth in Germany. The outcome reported in column (1) furthermore shows that average years of war did not contribute to per capita GDP; it was, however, positively related to the process of urbanization (column (2)).

Concluding Thoughts

This chapter aimed to summarize the debate about how to establish a clear link between the EMP and economic growth in western Europe between 1300 and 1800, also responding to the critical assessment of our ideas about such a connection by Dennison and Ogilvie. We show that their data are clearly consistent with the original Hajnal hypothesis. However, we argue that they have in our view misunderstood the EMP hypothesis about the relationship between this family system and economic development.

[42] Tilly 1990.

[43] Acemoglu, Johnson, and Robinson 2005.

[44] Baten and van Zanden 2008.

[45] De Pleijt and van Zanden 2013; Baten and van Zanden 2008; Becker and Woessmann 2007.

Table 9.3 **Female Agency and Economic Development, 1300–1800, Controlling for Other Determinants of Economic Development**

	(3)	(4)
Estimator	*OLS*	*OLS*
Dependent Variable	*Ln GDP*	*URB*
FF index	0.25***	0.05*
	(0.07)	(0.03)
Ln Parliamentary	0.09*** (0.03)	0.01*
		(0.00)
Share cities self-government	0.85***	0.16**
	(0.15)	(0.07)
Ln size of merchant fleet	0.00	0.00
	(0.00)	(0.00)
Colonial realm	0.04	0.03*
	(0.06)	(0.02)
Protestantism	0.10	0.03
	(0.10)	(0.03)
No of universities p/c	–0.09	–0.01
	(0.12)	(0.03)
Years at war	–0.04	0.02*
	(0.06)	(0.01)
Thirty Years' War	–0.10**	–0.02*
	(0.05)	(0.01)
Century dummies	YES	YES
Country dummies	YES	YES
Constant	5.84***	–0.21*
	(0.28)	(0.11)
R2	0.91	0.92
No. of observations	81	81

Notes: Standard errors are clustered at the country level to control for serial correlation in the unobservables. Standard errors in parentheses. *, **, *** denote significance at the 10%, 5%, 1% level, respectively.

Hajnal does not postulate that there is a simple, linear relationship between the basic features of the family system (age of marriage, share singles, and share of complex households) and economic development. It is immediately clear from the fact the (for example) age of marriage is also determined by the standard of living of the population, that this relationship is not linear. So their failure to find a clear link between these features and economic development is exactly what might be expected.

In addition, we have suggested a test of the link between the EMP and economic development in early modern Europe, starting from the alternative interpretation of the EMP as a system that allows a lot of female agency. We argue that this new conceptualization of the EMP—stressing the underlying institutions and in particular the most remarkable feature of this marriage system, the high degree of female agency—also makes it possible to properly test this link between EMP and the Little Divergence. However, the "simple" measure of average age of marriage does not make it possible to establish such a link, although it cannot be denied that a high marriage age is an important feature of the EMP as such.

In making this point we mapped the various features of the EMP according to the female friendliness of various components of their family systems. Summing up, this chapter aimed to contribute to the debate about how to establish a clear link between the EMP and economic growth in western Europe between 1300 and 1800, also responding to the critical assessment of our ideas as those mentioned in the last chapter. We showed that data such as those of Ogilvie and Dennison are clearly consistent with the original Hajnal hypothesis. However, we argued that they have in our view misunderstood the EMP hypothesis about the relationship between this family system and economic development.

In this book we have brought together ideas about the importance of the European Marriage Pattern for the social and economic development of western Europe in the period between 1300 and 1800. We developed a new way to interpret the EMP, and analyzed the implications for demographic behavior, market participation, and human capital formation, making use of much new data on these aspects of long-term development of the region. It was also an attempt to add the gender dimension to one of the core debates among economic historians—about the Little Divergence and the deep roots of the Industrial Revolution—by demonstrating its importance for understanding development in the very long run. As we explained in the introduction, the aim was also to test and refine similar ideas current in development studies, inspired by Sen's thinking on capabilities and freedom.

This book has applied these theories to western Europe in the late medieval and early modern period. In a parallel research project, "Agency, Gender and Economic Development of the World Economy, 1850–2000," the same questions were addressed for the world as a whole in the period after the Industrial Revolution. This resulted in a second study, authored by Sarah Carmichael, Selin Dilli, Jan Kok, Lotte van der Vleuten, Auke Rijpma, and Jan Luiten van Zanden that developed a more detailed conceptualization and classification of family systems and female agency rooted therein, and systematically tested various versions of the Sen hypothesis (i.e., *female agency furthers economic development*) at the level of the world as a whole and at the regional level (for India).[46] The availability of much better data made it possible to use refined econometric techniques to demonstrate the impact of female agency (in its various dimensions) on growth and political modernization.

The other extension of this study is, obviously, to move back in time. Did the EMP really emerge in the late Middle Ages, or does this family system have much older roots—going back to Germanic or even Celtic influences? Where does the Eurasian distribution of family systems that we showed in figure 9.3 come from? Why did and do the core areas of Eurasia (the Middle East, northern India, China), which were also the original centers of the Neolithic Revolution and the regions where the first ancient civilizations emerged, have relatively patriarchal family systems and why do we find "female friendly" systems in the periphery (as suggested by Todd 2011)? And how did these family systems interact with the religions of Eurasia, given, for example, the impact that Latin Christianity had on the EMP but also the supposedly negative link between female agency and Islam? And finally, how unique was European girlpower seen from this wider and longer perspective? These are some of the questions to which future research may turn to uncover the deep, gendered roots of modern economic development.

[46] Van Zanden, Rijpma, and Kok 2017.

REFERENCES

Acemoglu, D., S. Johnson, and J. Robinson. 2005. "The Rise of Europe: Atlantic Trade, Institutional Change, and Economic Growth." *American Economic Review* 95(3): 546–579.

Acemoglu, D., J. A. Robinson, and D. Woren. 2012. *Why Nations Fail: The Origins of Power, Prosperity and Poverty*. New York: Crown Business.

Ackerberg, D. A., and M. Botticini. 2000. "The Choice of Agrarian Contracts in Early Renaissance Tuscany: Risk Sharing, Moral Hazard or Capital Market Imperfections?" *Explorations in Economic History* 37(3): 241–247.

Acsádi, G. and Nemeskéri, J. 1970. *History of Human Life Span and Mortality*. Budapest: Akadémiai Kiadó.

Adams, A. J. 1997. "The Three-Quarter Length Life-Sized Portrait in 17th-Century Holland: The Ideological Function of 'Tranquillitas.'" In *Looking at Seventeenth-Century Dutch Painting: Realism Reconsidered*, edited by W. Franits, 158–174. New York: Cambridge University Press.

A'Hearn, B., J. Baten, and D. Crayen. 2009. "Quantifying Quantitative Literacy: Age Heaping and the History of Human Capital." *Journal of Economic History* 69: 783–780.

Algoet, C., and C. Vandenbroeke. 1977. "Alfabetisme in Vlaanderen en inzonderheid in zuidelijk Vlaanderen." *Vijfde Jaarboek van de Geschiedkundige en Heemkundige Kring van de Gaverstreke*: 142–178.

Alleaume, G., and P. Fargues. 1997. "La naissance d'une statistique d'État. Le recensement de 1848 en Égypte." *Histoire et Mésure* 13: 147–194.

Allen, R. C. 1992. *Enclosure and the Yeoman*. Oxford: Clarendon Press.

Allen, R. C. 2001. "The Great Divergence in European Wages and Prices from the Middle Ages to the First World War." *Explorations in Economic History* 38(4): 411–447.

Allen, R. C. 2003. "Progress and Poverty in Early Modern Europe." *Economic History Review* 56(3): 403–443.

Allen, R. C., and J. L. Weissdorf. 2011. "Was There an 'Industrious Revolution' Before the Industrial Revolution? An Empirical Exercise for England, c. 1300–1830." *Economic History Review* 64(3): 715–729.

Amin, S., and M. Cain. 1997. "The Rise of Dowry in Bangladesh." In *The Continuing Demographic Transition*, edited by G. W. Jones, R. M. Douglas, J. C. Caldwell, and R. M. D'Souza, 290–306. Oxford: Clarendon Press.

Ariès, P. 1962. *Centuries of Childhood: A Social History of Family Life*. Translated by R. Baldick. New York: Alfred A. Knopf.

Art, J., and E. Vanhaute. 2003. *Inleiding tot de lokale geschiedenis van de 19de en 20ste eeuw*. Gent: Gent University, Mens & Cultuur Uitgevers.

Bachi, R. 1951. "The Tendency to Round off Age Returns: Measurement and Correction," *Bulletin of the International Statistical Institute* 33: 195–221

Bailey, M. 1996. "Demographic Decline in Late Medieval England: Some Thoughts on Recent Research." *Economic History Review* 49: 1–19.

Baizan, P., and E. Camps. 2007. "The Impact of Women's Educational and Economic Resources on Fertility. Spanish Birth Cohorts 1901-1950." In *Gendering the Fertility Decline in the Western World*, edited by A. Janssens, 25–59. Bern: Peter Lang.

Banarjee, A., and E. Duflo. 2012. *Poor Economics. A Radical Rethinking of the Way to Fight Global Poverty*. New York: Public Affairs.

Bange, P., and A. G. Weiler. 1987. "De problematiek van het clandestiene huwelijk in het middeleeuwse bisdom Utrecht." In *De Nederlanden in de late middeleeuwen*, edited by D. E. H. de Boer and J. W. Marsilje, 393–408. Utrecht: Het Spectrum.

Bardsley, S. 1999. "Women's Work Reconsidered. Gender and Wage Differentiation in Late Medieval England." *Past and Present* 165: 3–29.

Barron, C. M. 1989. "The 'Golden Age' of Women in Medieval London." In *Medieval Women in Southern England*, edited by K. Bate, 35–58. Reading: Reading University.

Baten, J., and J. L. van Zanden. 2008. "Book Production and the Onset of Modern Economic Growth." *Journal of Economic Growth* 13(3): 217–235.

Becker, G. S. 1973. "A Theory of Marriage: Part I." *Journal of Political Economy* 81: 813–846.

Becker, G. S. 1991. *A Treatise on the Family*. Cambridge, MA: Harvard University Press.

Becker, S. O., and L. Woessmann. 2007. "Was Weber Wrong? A Human Capital Theory of Protestant Economic History." *Quarterly Journal of Economics* 124: 531–596.

Bell, D. 1998. "Wealth Transfers Occasioned by Marriage: A Comparative Reconsideration." In *Kinship, Networks and Exchange*, edited by T. Schweitzer and D. R. White, 187–209. Cambridge: Cambridge University Press.

Bender, D. R. 1967. "A Refinement of the Concept of Household: Families, Co-residence, and Domestic Functions." *American Anthropologist* 69: 493–504.

Beningo, F. 1989. "The Southern Italian Family in the Early Modern Period: A Discussion of Co-residential Patterns." *Continuity & Change* 4(1): 165–194.

Bennett, J. M. 1981. "Medieval Peasant Marriage: An Examination of Marriage Licence Fines in *Liber Gersumarum*." In *Pathways to Medieval Peasants*, edited by J. A. Raftis, 193–247. Toronto: Pontifical Institute of Medieval Studies.

Bennett, J. M. 1996. *Ale, Beer and Brewsters in England: Women's Work in a Changing World, 1300-1600*. New York and Oxford: Oxford University Press.

Bennett, J. M. 2007. *History Matters: Patriarchy and the Challenge of Feminism*. Philadeplhia, PA: University of Pennsylvania Press.

Berkner, L. K. 1972. "The Stem Family and the Developmental Cycle of the Peasant Household." *American Historical Review* 77: 398–418.

Berkner, L. K. 1975. "The Use and Misuse of Census Data for the Historical Analysis of Family Structure." *Journal of InterdisciplinaryHistory* 5: 721–738.

Berlière, U. (1960). Monasticon Belge. Liège: Centre national de recherches d'histoire religeuse.

Berman, H. J. 1983. *Law and Revolution: The Formation of the Western Legal Tradition*. Cambridge, MA: Harvard University Press.

Bernhardt, K. 1999. *Women and property in China: 960-1949*. Stanford, CA: Standford University Press.

Beveridge, L. 1955. "Westminster Wages in the Manorial Era." *Economic History Review* 8(1): 18–35.

Bezemer, W. 1894. "Keurboekje van Edam." *Verslagen en mededeelingen van de Vereeniging tot Uitgaaf der Bronnen van het Oud-vaderlandsche recht* 2: 129–163.

Biller, P. 2000. *The Measure of Multitude: Population in Medieval Thought*. Oxford: Oxford University Press on Demand.

Birge, B. 2003. "Women and Confucianism from Song to Ming: The Institutionalization of Patrilineality." In *The Song-Yuan-Ming Transition in Chinese History*, edited by P. J. Smith and R. von Glahn, 212–240. Cambridge, MA: Harvard East Asian Monographs.

Blackburn, R. H. 2003. "Partridge, Nehemiah (1683–c. 1737)." In *Encyclopedia of American Folk Art*, edited by G. C. Wertkin. New York: Routledge.

Blackwood, E. 2006. "Marriage, Matrifocality and 'Missing Men.'" In *Feminist Anthropology, Past, Present and Future*, edited by P. L. Geller and K. Stockett, 73–88. Philadephia, PA: University of Pennsylvania Press.

Blockmans, W. 1985. "Corruptie, patronage, makelaardij en venaliteit als symptomen van een ontluikende staatsvorming in de Bourgondisch-Habsburgse Nederlanden," *Tijdschrift voor sociale geschiedenis* 11: 231–247.

Boele, A., Bouman, A. and De Moor, T. 2014. "Commerciële huishoudens? De gevolgen van het Europese huwelijkspatroon en de inzet van niet-familiale hulp als overlevingsstrategie voor ouderen in het vroegmoderne Holland (casus: Leiden)." In *Kwetsbare groepen in/ en historische demografie—Historisch-demografisch onderzoek in Vlaanderen en Nederland Jaarboek Historische Demografie 2014*, edited by Isabelle Devos, Koen Matthijs, and Bart van de Putte, 21–46. Leuven: Acco.

Bohannan, P. 1963. *Social Anthropology*. New York: Holt, Rinehart and Winston.

Bolt, J. 2012. "Quantifying Pre-Colonial Institutions in Africa: Assessing the Reliability of the Ethnographic Atlas." Working Paper, University of Groningen.

Bolt, J., and J. L. van Zanden. 2014. "The Maddison Project: Collaborative Research on Historical National Accounts." *Economic History Review* 67(3): 627–651.

Boone, M. 1998. "Netwerken in de steden." In *Prinsen en poorters. Beelden van de laatmiddeleeuwse samenleving in de Bourgondische Nederlanden, 1384-1530*, edited by W. Blockmans, M. Boone, and M. T. Caron, 232–257. Antwerpen: Mercatorfonds.

Borsay, A., and P. Shapely. 2007. "Introduction." In *Medicine, Charity and Mutual Aid: The Consumption of Health and Welfare in Britain, c. 1550-1950*, edited by A. Borsay and P. Shapely, 1–10. Aldershot: Ashgate.

Boschma-Aarnoudse, C. 2003. *Tot verbeteringe van de neeringe deser stede. Edam en de Zeevang in de late Middeleeuwen en de 16e eeuw*. Hilversum: Verloren.

Bosker, M., E. Buringh, and J. L. van Zanden. 2013. "From Baghdad to London: Unraveling Urban Development in Europe, the Middle East, and North Africa, 800–1800." *Review of Economics and Statistics* 95(4): 1418–1437.

Boswell, J. E. 1988. *The Kindness of Strangers: The Abandonment of Children in Western Europe from Late Antiquity to the Renaissance*. Chicago: University of Chicago Press.

Boswell, J. E. 2004. "Expositio and Oblatio: The Abandonment of Children and the Ancient and Medieval Family." In *Medieval Families: Perspectives on Marriage, Household, and Children*, edited by C. Neel, 234–272. Toronto: University of Toronto Press.

Botticini, M. 1999. "A Loveless Economy? Intergenerational Altruism and the Marriage Market in a Tuscan Town, 1415-1436." *Journal of Economic History* 59: 104–121.

Botticini, M. 2000. "A Tale of Benevolent Governments: Private Credit Markets, Public Finance, and the Role of Jewish Lenders in Medieval and Renaissance Italy." *Journal of European Economic History* 60: 164–189.

Botticini, M., and A. Siow. 2003. "Why Dowries?" *American Economic Review* 93(4): 1385–1398.

Bouman, A., J. Zuijderduijn, and T. De Moor. 2012. "From Hardship to Benefit: A Critical Review of the Nuclear Hardship Theory in Relation to the Emergence of the European Marriage Pattern." CGEH Working Paper Series, No. 0028.

Bowie, F. 1989. *Beguine Spirituality: An Anthology*. London: SPCK.

Brettell, C. 1991. "Kinship and Contract: Property Transmission and Family Relations in Northwestern Portugal." *Comparative Studies in Society and History* 33(3): 443–465.

Broadberry, S., B. Campbell, A. Klein, M. Overton, and B. van Leeuwen. 2010. *British Economic Growth, 1270-1870: Some Preliminary Estimates*. England: University of Warwick.

Broadberry, S., J. Custodis, and B. Gupta. 2015. "India and the Great Divergence: An Anglo-Indian Comparison of GDP per capita, 1600–1871." *Explorations in Economic History* 55: 58–75.

Brodman, J. W. 2007. "Religion and Discipline in the Hospitals of Thirteenth-Century France." In *The Medieval Hospital and Medical Practice*, edited by B. S. Bowers, 123–132. Aldershot: Ashgate.

Brucker, G. 1986. *Giovanni and Lusanna. Love and Marriage in Renaissance Florence.* London: Weidenfeld & Nicholson.

Brundage, J. A. 1990. *Law, Sex, and Christian Society in Medieval Europe.* Chicago: University of Chicago Press.

Brunel, G. 2010. "Une retraite bien preparée. Le cas du paysan Raoul le Picard à la fin du XIIIe siècle." *Histoire & Sociétés Rurales* 33: 159–180.

Bücher, K. 1910. *Die Frauenfrage im Mittelalter.* 2nd ed. Tübingen: Verlag der H. Laupp'schen Buchhandlung.

Buckstaff, F. 1893. "Married Women's Property in Anglo-Saxon and Anglo-Norman Law and the Origin of Common Law Dower." *Annals of the American Academy of Political and Social Science* 4: 233–264.

Budd, J. W., and T. Guinnane. 1991. "Intentional Age-Misreporting, Age-Heaping, and the 1908 Old Age Pensions Act in Ireland." *Population Studies* 45(3): 497–518.

Buringh, E. 2014. "The Role of Cities in Medieval Book Production: Quantitative Analyses." In *Uses of the Written Word in Medieval Towns: Medieval Urban Literacy II, Utrecht Studies in Medieval Literacy* 28, edited by M. Mostert and A. Adamska, 119–177. Turnhout: Brepols.

Buringh, E., and J. L. van Zanden. 2009. "Charting the 'Rise of the West': Manuscripts and Printed Books in Europe. A Long-Term Perspective from the Sixth through Eighteenth Centuries." *Journal of Economic History* 69(2): 409–445.

Burnard, T. 1994. "A Failed Settler Society: Marriage and Demographic Failure in Early Jamaica." *Journal of Social History* 28(1): 63–82.

Burnette, J. 1997. "An Investigation of the Female-Male Wage Gap during the Industrial Revolution in Britain." *Economic History Review* 50(2): 257–281.

Burnett, J. 2008. *Gender, Work and Wages in Industrial Revolution Britain.* Cambridge: Cambridge University Press.

Caferro, W. 1994. "City and Countryside in Siena in Second Half of the Fourteenth Century." *Journal of Economic History* 54(1): 85–103.

Cailliau, H. 1995. *'Soo geluckigh als een beggijn': het begijnhof Onze-Lieve-Vrouw-Ter-Hooie, 1584-1792.* Gent: Maatschappij voor Geschiedenis en Oudheidkunde te Gent.

Carmichael, S. 2011. Marriage and Power: Age at First Marriage and Spousal Age Gap in Lesser Developed Countries. *History of the Family* 16(4): 416–436.

Carmichael, S. G. 2016. "Marriage, Family and Gender Inequality—An Historical Exploration of the Relationship between Family Systems, the Position of Women and Development." Dissertation, Utrecht University.

Carmichael, S. G., T. De Moor, and J. L. van Zanden. 2011a. "Marriage Patterns, Household Formation and Economic Development: Introduction." *History of the Family* 16(4): 309–311.

Carmichael, S. G., T. De Moor, and J. L. van Zanden. 2011b. "'When the Heart Is Baked, Don't Try to Knead It': *Huwelijksleeftijd en leeftijdsverschil tussen partners als maatstaf van 'agency' van vrouwen.*" In *Levenslopen in Transformatie; liber amicorum bij het afscheid van prof. dr. Paul M.M. Klepi*, edited by Th. Engelen, O. Boonstra, and A. Janssens, 208–221. Nijmegen: Valkhof.

Carmichael, S. G., and J. L. van Zanden. 2015. "Towards an Ethnographic Understanding of the European Marriage Pattern: Global Correlates and Links with Female Status." Population Histories in Context. CGEH Working Paper no. 67. http://www.cgeh.nl/sites/default/files/WorkingPapers/cgehwp67_carmichaelvanzanden.pdf.

Casterline, J. B., L. Williams, and P. McDonald. 1986. "The Age Difference Between Spouses: Variations among Developing Countries." *Population Studies* 40: 353–374.

Chayton, M. 1980. "Household and Kinship: Ryton in the Late 16th and Early 17th Centuries." *History Workshop* 10: 25–60.

Chojnacki, S. 1975. "Dowries and Kinsmen in Early Renaissance Venice." *Journal of Interdisciplinary History* 5: 571–600.

Cilliers, J. 2013. "Cape Colony Marriage in Perspective." Ph.D. dissertation, Stellenbosch University.

Clarke, E. 1957. *My Mother Who Fathered Me: A Study of the Family in Three Selected Communities in Jamaica*. London: Allen & Unwin.

Clark, E. 1982. "Some Aspects of Social Security in Medieval England." *Journal of Family History* 7(4): 307–320.

Clark, G. 1988. "The Cost of Capital and Medieval Agricultural Technique." *Explorations in Economic History* 25: 265–294.

Clark, G. 2004. "The Long March of History: Farm Laborers' Wages in England, 1209-1869." Unpublished manuscript. https://core.ac.uk/download/pdf/6519027.pdf.

Clark, G. 2005. *The Interest Rate in the Very Long Run: Institutions, Preferences and Modern Growth*. London: Centre for Economic Policy Research. https://www.researchgate.net/profile/Gregory_Clark/publication/228426504_The_interest_rate_in_the_very_long_run_institutions_preferences_and_modern_growth/links/0c96052129625c34eb000000.pdf.

Clark, G. 2007a. "The Long March of History: Farm Wages, Population and Economic Growth, England 1209-1869." *Economic History Review* 60: 97–136.

Clark, G. 2007b. *A Farewell to Alms: A Brief Economic History of the World*. Princeton, NJ: Princeton University Press.

Collins, E. J. T. 1969. "Harvest Technology and Labour Supply in Britain, 1790-1870." *Economic History Review* 22(2): 453–473.

Cooper, J. P. 1976. "Patterns of Inheritance and Settlement by Great Landowners from the Fifteenth to the Eighteenth Centuries." In *Family and Inheritance: Rural Society in Western Europe, 1200-1800*, edited by J. Goody, J. Thirsk, and E. P. Thompson, 192–327. Cambridge: Cambridge University Press.

Cornell, L. L. 1987. "Hajnal and the Household in Asia: A Comparativist History of the Family in Preindustrial Japan, 1600-1870." *Journal of Family History* 12:143–162.

Craft-Giepmans, S., and A. De Vries, eds. 2012. *Portret in portret in de Nederlandse kunst 1550-2012* RKD (Nederland Instituut voor Kunstgeschiedenis).

Crafts, N. F. R. 1985. *British Economic Growth during the Industrial Revolution*. Oxford: Clarendon Press.

Crawford, K. 2007. *European Sexualities, 1400-1800*. Cambridge: Cambridge University Press.

Crayen, D. 2005. "The Relationship of Literacy, Numeracy, and Age Heaping: Patterns in Recent LDC Data." Working Paper 262, University of Tübingen.

Crayen, D., and J. Baten. 2006. "Numeracy, Inequality, Age Heaping, and Economic Growth: New Estimation Strategies for Western Europe and the US (17th-19th centuries)." Working Paper, University of Tübingen.

Cullum, P. H. 1991. *Cremetts and Corrodies. Care of the Poor and Sick at St. Leonards Hospital, York, in the Middle Ages*. York: Borthwick.

Cummins, N. 2014. "Longevity and the Rise of the West: Life-Spans of the European Elite, 800-1800." Working Paper. http://dx.doi.org/10.2139/ssrn.2496939

Cunningham, H. 1990. "The Employment and Unemployment of Children in England, c. 1680-1851." *Past and Present* 126: 115–150.

Curtis, D. 2015. "An Agro-Town Bias? Re-examining the Micro-Demographic Model for Southern Italy." *Journal of Social History* 48(3): 685–713.

Curtis, D., J. Dijkman, T. Lambrecht, and E. Vanhaute. 2017. "Famines in the Low Countries, fourteenth to nineteenth centuries." Working Paper. http://hdl.handle.net/1854/LU-7180278

Dalla Zuanna, G., M. di Tullio, F. Leverotti, and F. Rossi. 2012. "Population and Family in Central and Northern Italy at the Dawn of the Modern Age: A Comparison of Fiscal Data from Three Different Areas." *Journal of Family History* 37(3): 284–302.

Dale, M. K. 1933. "The London Silkwomen of the Fifteenth Century." *Economic History Review* 4(3): 324–325.

Danneel, M. 1995. *Weduwen en wezen in het Laat-Middeleeuwse Gent.* Leuven: Garant.

Daudin, Guillaume. 2004. "Profitability of Slave and Long-Distance Trading in Context: The Case of Eighteenth-Century France." *Journal of Economic History* 64(1): 144–171.

De Bruijn, M. 1997. "The Hearthhold in Pastoral Fulbe Society, Central Mali: Social Relations, Milk and Drought." *Africa* 67: 625–651.

De Cant, G. 2003. *A World of Independent Women: From the 12th Century to the Present Day: The Flemish Beguinages.* Riverside, CT: Herve van Caloen Foundation.

Dehaene, S. 1997. *The Number Sense: How the mind creates mathematics.* Oxford: Oxford University Press.

De Jongh, C. 1986. *Portretten van echt en trouw: Huwelijk en gezin in de Nederlandse kunst van de zeventiende eeuw.* Zwolle/Haarlem: Waanders.

Della Pina, M. 1982. "L'évolution démographique des villes toscanes à l'époque de la naissance et de l'affirmation de l'Etat régional (XVe-XVIIe siècles)." In *Annales de démographie historique,* vol. 1982/1, 43–53. Persée-Portail des revues scientifiques en SHS.

De Moor, G. 1994. *Verborgen en geborgen: het Cisterciënzerinnenklooster Leeuwenhorst in de Noordwijkse regio (1261-1574).* Hilversum: Uitgeverij Verloren.

De Moor, T. 2008. "The Silent Revolution: A New Perspective on the Emergence of Commons, Guilds, and Other Forms of Corporate Collective Action in Western Europe." *International Review of Social History* 53(Supp. 16): 179–212.

De Moor, T. 2014. "Single, Safe, and Sorry? Explaining the Early Modern Beguine Movement in the Low Countries." *Journal of Family History* 39(1): 3–21.

De Moor, T., and J. L. van Zanden. 2006. *Vrouwen en de geboorte van het kapitalisme in West-Europa.* Meppel: Boom.

De Moor, T., and J. L. van Zanden. 2008. "Van fouten kun je leren: Een kritische benadering van de mogelijkheden van 'leeftijdstapelen' voor sociaal-economisch onderzoek naar gecijferdheid in het pre-industriële Vlaanderen en Nederland." *Tijdschrift voor Sociale en Economische Geschiedenis* 4: 55–87.

De Moor, T., and J. L. van Zanden. 2010a. "Girlpower. The European Marriage Pattern (EMP) and Labour Markets in the North Sea Region in the Late Medieval and Early Modern Period." *Economic History Review* 63(1): 1–33.

De Moor, T., and J. L. van Zanden. 2010b. "'Every Woman Counts': A Gender-Analysis of Numeracy in the Low Countries during the Early Modern Period." *Journal of Interdisciplinary History* 41(2): 179–208.

De Moor, T., and C. J. Zuijderduijn. 2013. "The Art of Counting: Reconstructing Numeracy in the Middle and Upper Classes on the Basis of Portraits in the Early Modern Low Countries." *Historical Methods* 46(1): 41–56.

De Pleijt, A. M. 2016a. "Human Capital Formation in the Long Run: Evidence for Average Years of Schooling in England, 1300-1900." *Cliometrica.* https://link.springer.com/article/10.1007/s11698-016-0156-3

De Pleijt, A. M. 2016b. "The Role of Human Capital Formation in the Transition to Modern Economic Growth, 1300-1900." Dissertation, Utrecht University.

De Pleijt, A., and J. L. van Zanden. 2013. "Accounting for the 'Little Divergence':What drove Economic Growth in Preindustrial Europe, 1300-1800?" CGEH Working Paper no. 46. http://www.cgeh.nl/sites/default/files/WorkingPapers/CGEHWP46_depleijtvanzanden_0.pdf.

De Pleijt, A., and J. L. van Zanden. 2016. "Gender Income Inequality in Western Europe." Paper for Einite workshop, Milan.

De Pleijt, A. M., and J. L. Weisdorf. 2017. "Human Capital Formation from Occupations: The 'Deskilling Hypothesis' Revisited." *Cliometrica* 11(1): 1–30.

De Soto, H. 2001. *The Mystery of Capital: Why Capitalism Triumphs in the West and Fails Everywhere Else.* New York: Basic Books.

Desportes, A. 1966. "La population de Reims au XVe siècle d'après un dénombrement de 1422," *Le moyen âge* 72: 463–509.

De Vries, J. 1978. "Barges and Capitalism. Passenger Transportation in the Dutch Economy, 1632–1839." *A.A.G. Bijdragen* 21: 398.

De Vries, J. 1994. "The Industrial Revolution and the Industrious Revolution." *Journal of Economic History* 54: 249–270.

De Vries, J., and A. van der Woude. 1995. *Nederland 1500-1850. De eerste ronde van de moderne economische groei.* Amsterdam: Balans.

De Vries, J., and A. van der Woude. 1997. *The First Modern Economy: Success, Failure, and Perseverance of the Dutch Economy, 1500-1815.* Cambridge and New York: Cambridge University Press.

Dennison, T., and S. Ogilvie. 2014. "Does the European Marriage Pattern Explain Economic Growth?" *Journal of Economic History* 74(3): 651–693.

Derville, A. 1984. "L'alphabétisation du peuple á la fin du Moyen Age," *Revue du Nord* 26: 759–772.

Dickson, P. G. M. 1967. *The Financial Revolution in England: A Study in the Development of Public Credit, 1688-1756.* London: Macmillan.

Diebolt, C., and F. Perrin. 2013. "From Stagnation to Sustained Growth: The Role of Female Empowerment." *American Economic Review* 103(3): 545–549.

Diebolt, C., and F. Perrin. 2014. "The Foundations of Female Empowerment Revisited." *Revue d'Economie Politique* 124(4): 587–597.

Diebolt, C., and F. Perrin. 2016. "Growth Theories." In *Handbook of Cliometrics,* edited by C. Diebolt and M. Haupert, 177–195. Berlin: Springer.

Dilli, S. D. 2017. "The Deep Causes of Economic Development." In *Agency, Gender and Economic Development in the World Economy 1850–2000: Testing the Sen Hypothesis,* edited by J. L. van Zanden, A. Rijpma, and Jan Kok, 138–161. Oxford: Taylor & Francis.

Dilli, S. D., S. Carmichael, and A. Rijpma. Forthcoming. "Introducing the Historical Gender Equality Index." *Feminist Economics.*

Di Matteo, L. 1998. "Wealth Accumulation and the Life-Cycle in Economic History: Implications of Alternative Approaches to Data." *Explorations in Economic History* 35(3): 296–324.

Dribe, M., and C. Lundh. 2005. "Retirement as a Strategy for Land Transmission: A Micro-study of Preindustrial Rural Sweden." *Continuity and Change* 20(2): 165–191.

Dribe, M., C. Lundh, and P. Nystedt. 2007. "Widowhood Strategies in Preindustrial Society." *Journal of Interdisciplinary History* 38(2): 207–232.

Duflo, E. 2012. "Women Empowerment and Economic Development." *Journal of Economic Literature* 50(4): 1051–1079.

Duncan-Jones, R. 1990. *Structure and Scale in the Roman Economy.* Cambridge: Cambridge University Press.

Dupont, G. 1996. *Maagdenverleidsters, hoeren en speculanten. Prostitutie in Brugge tijdens de Bourgondische periode (1385-1515).* Brugge: Genootschap voor Geschiedenis "Société d'Emulation" te Brugge.

Dupont, G. 2001. "Van Copkin over Coppin naar Jacob. De relatie tussen de voornaamsvorm en de leeftijd van de naamdrager in het Middelnederlands op basis van administratieve bronnen voor het graafschap Vlaanderen, einde 14de-midden 16e eeuw." *Naamkunde* 33(2): 111–217.

Dyer, C. 2005. *An Age of Transition? Economy and Society in England in the Later Middle Ages.* Oxford and New York: Oxford University Press.

Eastman, L. E. 1988. *Family, Fields, and Ancestors: Constancy and Change in China's Social and Economic History, 1550-1949.* New York and Oxford: Oxford University Press.

Ebrey, P. B. 2003. *Women and the Family in Chinese History.* London and New York: Routledge.

Edlund, L., and N.-P. Lagerlöf. 2006. "Individual vs. Parental Consent in Marriage: Implications for Intra-household Resource Allocation and Growth." Working paper, Columbia University. http://www.columbia.edu/~le93/LoveWPJan23_06.pdf.

Edwards, J., and S. Ogilvie. 2012. "Contract Enforcement, Institutions, and Social Capital: The Maghribi Traders Reappraised." *Economic History Review* 65(2): 421–444.

Elgharabway, R. M., A. Saber Ahmed, and R. A. Alsuhaibani. 2015. "Awareness, Prevalence, and Determinants of Birth Control Methods Use among Women in Saudi Arabia." *International Archives of Medicine* 8: 1–11.

Emigh, R. J. 1996. "Loans and Livestock: Comparing Landlords' and Tenants' Declarations from the 'Catasto' of 1427." *Journal of European Economic History*, 25(3): 705–723.

Engelen, T. 2005. "The Hajnal Hypothesis and Transition Theory." In: *Marriage and the Family in Eurasia: Perspectives on the Hajnal Hypothesis*, edited by T. Engelen and A. P. Wolf, 51–73. Amsterdam: Aksant.

Epstein, S. A. 1991. *Wage Labor and Guilds in Medieval Europe*. Chapel Hill: University of North Carolina Press.

Epstein, S. R. 2000. *Freedom and Growth. The Rise of States and Markets in Europe, 1300-1750*. London: Routledge.

Fauve-Chamoux, F., and E. Ochiai, eds. 2009. *The Stem-Family in Eurasian Perspective: Revisiting House Societies, 17th-20th Centuries. Population, Family and Society*, Vol. 10. Bern: Peter Lang.

Field, E., and A. Ambrus. 2008. "Early Marriage, Age of Menarche, and Female Schooling Attainment in Bangladesh." *Journal of Political Economy* 116(5): 881–930.

Finzi, R. 2012. "Normalità climatica e mondo rurale." In *Storia economica e ambiente italiano (ca.1400-1850)*, edited by G. Alfani, M. Di Tullio, and L. Mocarelli, 117–128. Milan: Franco Angeli.

Fischer, J. L. 1958. "The Dassification of Residence in Censuses." *American Anthropologist* 60: 508–517.

Fleck, B. S. 2007. "Quellen zu Insassen Westfälischer Hospitäler im 15. und 16. Jahrhundert." In *Hospitäler in Mittelalter und Früher Neuzeit. Frankreich, Deutschland und Italien. Eine vergeleichende Geschichte*, edited by G. Drossbach, 25–39. Munich: R. Oldenbourg Verlag.

Fortes, M. 1978. "Parenthood, Marriage and Fertility in West Africa." *Journal of Development Studies* 14(4; Special Issue: Population and Development): 121–149.

Fox, H. S. A. 1996. "Exploitation of the Landless by Lords and Tenants in Early Medieval England." In *Medieval Society and the Manor Court*, edited by Z. Razi and R. M. Smith, 518–569. Oxford: Clarendon Press.

Fratianni, M., and F. Spinelli. 2006. "Italian City-States and Financial Evolution." *European Review of Economic History* 44: 257–278.

Fruin, R. J. 1866. *Informacie up den staet, faculteyt ende gelegentheyt van de steden ende dorpen van Hollant ende Vrieslant om daernae te reguleren de nyeuwe schiltaele gedaen in den jaere MDXIV*. Leiden: Sijthoff.

Fusè, L. 2008. *Parents, Children and Their Families: Living Arrangements of Old People in the XIX Century, Sundsvall Region, Sweden*. Umeå: Umeå Universitet.

Gallman, J. M. 1984. "Relative Ages of Colonial Marriages." *Journal of Interdisciplinary History* 14: 609–617.

Galor, O. 2011. *Unified Growth Theory*. Princeton, NJ: Princeton University Press.

Galor, O., and D. N. Weil. 1996. "The Gender Gap, Fertility and Growth." *American Economic Review* 86(3): 374–387.

Gary, K. 2017. "Constructing Equality? Women's Wages for Physical Labour, 1550-1759." Lund Papers in Economic History. Population Economics, no. 158, Department of Economics, Lund University.

Gates, H. 2001. "Footloose in Fujan: Economic Correlates of Footbinding." *Comparative Studies in Society and History* 43: 130–148.

Gaunt, D. 1983. "The Property and Kin Relationships of Retired Farmers in Northern and Central Europe." In *Family Forms in Historic Europe*, edited by R. Wall, 249–280. Cambridge and New York: Cambridge University Press.

Gavitt, P. 1997. "Charity and State Building in Cinquecento Florence: Vincenzio Borghini as Administrator of the Ospedale degli Innocenti." *Journal of Modern History* 69(2): 230–270.

Gelting, M. H. 2000. "Odelsrett—lovbydelse—bordsratt—retraitlignager, Kindred and Land in the Nordic Countries in the Twelfth and Thirteenth Centuries." In *Family, Marriage and Property Devolution in the Middle Ages*, edited by L. I. Hansen, 133–165. Tromsø: Tromsø University.

Giraudo, A. 2007. *L'impedimento di età nel matrimonio canonico (Can. 1083): evoluzione storica e analisi delle problematiche attuali della dottrina e della prassi*. Rome: Gregorian Biblical BookShop.

Goldberg, P. J. P. 1986a. "Female Labour, Service and Marriage in the Late Medieval Urban North," *Northern History* 22: 18–38.

Goldberg, P. J. P. 1986b. "Marriage, Migration, Servanthood and Life-Cycle in Yorkshire Towns of the Later Middle Ages: Some York Cause Paper Evidence." *Continuity and Change* 1(2): 141–169.

Goldberg, P. J. P. , ed. 1992a. *Woman Is a Worthy Wight: Women in English Society c. 1200-1500*. Wolfeboro Falls, NH: Alan Sutton.

Goldberg, P. J. P. 1992b. *Women, Work, and Life Cycle in a Medieval Economy: Women in York and Yorkshire, c.1300-1520*. Oxford and New York: Oxford University Press.

Goldberg, P. J. P., and F. Riddy, eds. 2004. *Youth in the Middle Ages*.Woodbridge: Boydell & Brewer.

Goldin, C. 2006. "The Quiet Revolution That Transformed Women's Employment, Education, and Family." *American Economic Review* 96(2): 1–21.

Goldin, C. 1990. *Understanding the Gender Gap: An Economic History of American Women*. Oxford: Oxford University Press.

Goldstone, J. A. 1986. "The Demographic Revolution in England: A Reexamination." *Population Studies* 49: 5–33.

Goldstone, J. A. 1996. "Gender, Work and Culture: Why the Industrial Revolution Came Early to England but Late in China." *Sociological Perspectives* 39: 1–21.

Goldthwaite, R. A. 1981. *The Building of Renaissance Florence: An Economic and Social History*. Baltimore: Johns Hopkins University Press.

Goody, J. 1958. *The Development Cycle in Domestic Groups*. Cambridge: Cambridge University Press.

Goody, J. 1976. *Production and Peproduction: A Comparative Study of the Domestic Domain*. Cambridge and New York: Cambridge University Press.

Goody, J. 1983. *The Development of the Family and Marriage in Europe*. Cambridge: Cambridge University Press.

Goody, J. 1990. *The Oriental, the Ancient and the Primitive: Systems of Marriage and the Family in the Pre-industrial Societies of Eurasia*. Cambridge: Cambridge University Press.

Goody, J. 1996. "Comparing Family Systems in Europe and Asia: Are There Different Sets of Rules?" *Population and Development Review* 22: 1–20.

Goody, J., and S. J. Tambiah. 1973. *Bridewealth and Dowry*. Cambridge: Cambridge University Press.

Gooszen, H. 1999. *A Demographic History of the Indonesian Archipelago, 1880-1942*. Leiden: KITLV Press.

Gottlieb, B. 1993. *The Family in the Western World from the Black Death to the Industrial Age*. New York and Oxford: Oxford University Press.

Goudriaan, K. 2008. "Die Frühgeschichte des Hospitalwesens in den Grafschaften Holland und Seeland und im Niederstift Utrecht." In *Institutions de l'assistance sociale en Lotharingie médiévale. Einrichtungen der sozialen Sicherung im Mittelalterlichen Lotharingen.: Actes des 13es Journées Lotharingiennes 12-15 octobre 2004*, edited by M. Pauly, M. Uhrmacher, and H. Pettiau, 194–255. Luxemburg: CLUDEM.

Gove, W. R., J. W. Grimm, S. C. Motz, and J. D. Thompson. 1973. "The Family Life Cycle: Internal Dynamics and Social Consequences." *Sociology & Social Research* 57(2): 182–195.

Greif, A. 2006a. *Institutions and the Path to the Modern Economy: Lessons from Medieval Trade*. Cambridge: Cambridge University Press.

Greif, A. 2006b. "Family Structure, Institutions and Growth: The Origins and Implications of Western Corporations." *American Economic Review* 96: 308–312.

Greven, J. 1912. *Die Anfänge der Beginen; Ein Beitrag zur Geschichte der Volksfrömmigkeit und des Ordenwesens im Hochmittelalter.* Münster i.W.: Aschendorff.

Gruber, S., and M. Szołtysek. 2015. "The Patriarchy Index: A Comparative Study of Power Relations across Historical Europe." *History of the Family* 21(2): 1–42.

Hajnal, J. 1965. "European Marriage Patterns in Perspective." In *Population in History: Essays in Historical Demography*, edited by D. V. Glass and D. E. C. Eversley, 101–143. Chicago: Aldine.

Hajnal, J. 1982. "Two Kinds of Preindustrial Household Formation Systems." *Population and Development Review* 8: 449–494.

Hamaker, H. G. 1875-76. *De Rekeningen der Grafelijkheid van Holland onder het Henegouwsche Huis.* 3 vols. Utrecht: Kemink.

Hamilton, E. J. 1936. *Money, Prices, and Wages in Valencia, Aragon, and Navarre, 1351–1500.* Philadelphia: Porcupine Press.

Hammel, E. A., and P. Laslett. 1974. "Comparing Household Structure over Time and between Cultures." *Comparative Studies in Society and History* 16: 73–109.

Hanawalt, B. A. 1986. *The Ties That Bound: Peasant Families in Medieval England.* New York and Oxford: Oxford University Press.

Hanawalt, B. A. 1993. *Growing Up in Medieval London: The Experience of Childhood in History.* New York and Oxford: Oxford University Press.

Hanus, J. 2006. "Bossche renteniersters. Een zestiende-eeuwse rentemarkt als spiegel van vrouwelijk investeringsgedrag." *Historica* 29(3): 18–20.

Hanus, J. 2007. *Tussen stad en eigen gewin. Stadsfinanciën, renteniers en kredietmarkten in 's-Hertogenbosch (begin zestiende eeuw).* Amsterdam: Aksant.

Hareven, T. 1982. *Family Time and Industrial Time: The Relationship between the Family and Work in a New England Industrial Community.* Cambridge: Cambridge University Press.

Harper, R. I. 1983. "A Note on Corrodies in the Fourteenth Century." *Albion* 15(2): 95–101.

Harral, S., and P. Amoss. 1981. *Other Ways of Growing Old: Anthropological Perspectives.* Stanford, CA: Stanford University Press.

Harris, O. 1982. "Households and Their Boundaries." *History Workshop* 13 (Rustin College): 143–152.

Hart, S. 1976. *Geschrift en getal. Een keuze uit de demografisch-, economisch- en sociaal-historische studiën op grond van de Amsterdamse en Zaanse archivalia, 1600-1800.* Dordrecht: Historische Vereniging Holland.

Hartman, M. S. 2004. *The Household and the Making of History: A Subversive View of the Western Past.* Cambridge: Cambridge University Press.

Haskins, G. L. 1948-49. "The Development of Common Law Dower." *Harvard Law Review* 62: 42–55.

Hayami, A. 2001. *The Historical Demography of Pre-Modern Japan.* Tokyo: University of Tokyo Press.

Heeringa, K. 1926. *Rekeningen van het Bisdom Utrecht 1378-1573.* 3 vols. Utrecht: Kemink.

Heers, J. 2003. "Montes." In *Lexikon des Mittelalters*, VI. München: Artemis en Winkler.

Held, T. 1982. "Rural Retirement Arrangements in 17th and 18th Century Austria: A Cross-Community Analysis." *Journal of Family History* 7(3): 227–250.

Henderson, J. 1994. *Piety and Charity in Late Medieval Florence.* Chicago: University of Chicago Press.

Hendriks, J. 1971. *De emancipatie van de Gereformeerden. Sociologische bijdrage tot de verklaring van enige kenmerken van het huidige Gereformeerde volksdeel.* Alphen aan den Rijn: Samsom.

Herlihy, D. 1967. *Medieval and Renaissance Pistoia: the social history of an Italian town.* New Haven: Yale University Press.

Herlihy, D. 1973. "The Population of Verona in the First Century of Venetian Rule." In *Renaissance Venice*, edited by J. R. Hale, 91–120. London: Faber & Faber.

Herlihy, D. 1977. "Deaths, Marriages, Births, and the Tuscan Economy (ca. 1300-1500)." In *Population Patterns in the Past*, edited by R. D. Lee, 135–164. New York: Academic Press.

Herlihy, D. 1985. *Medieval Households.* Cambridge, MA: Harvard University Press.

Herlihy, D., and C. Klapisch-Zuber. 1978. *Les Toscans et leur familles*. Paris: Presses de la Fondation Nationale des Sciences Politiques.

Herlihy, D., and C. Klapisch-Zuber. 1985. *Tuscans and Their Families: A Study of the Florentine Catasto of 1427*. New Haven, CT: Yale University Press.

Hilevych, Y. 2015. "Abortion and Gender Relations in Ukraine, 1955-1970." *History of the Family* 20(1): 86–105.

Hilton, R. H. 1975. *The English Peasantry in the Later Middle Ages: The Ford Lectures for 1973, and Related Studies*. Oxford: Clarendon Press.

Hoffman, P. T., G. Postel-Vinay, and J. L. Rosenthal. 2000. *Priceless Markets. The Political Economy of Credit in Paris, 1660-1870*. Chicago: University of Chicago Press.

Holy, L. 1996. *Anthropological Perspectives on Kinship*. London and Chicago: Pluto Press.

Hopcroft, R. L., and R. J. Emigh. 2000. "Divergent Paths of Agrarian Change: Eastern England and Tuscany Compared." *Journal of European Economic History* 60: 9–51.

Hoppenbrouwers, P. C. M. 1985. "Maagschap en vriendschap: een beschouwing over de structuur en functies van verwantschapsbetrekkingen in het laat-middeleeuwse Holland." *Tijdschrift Holland* 17: 69–108.

Hoppenbrouwers, P. C. M. 2001. "Mapping an Unexplored Field: The Brenner Debate and the Case of Holland." In *Peasants into Farmers? The Transformation of Rural Economy and Society in the Low Countries (Middle Ages–19th Century) in the Light of the Brenner Debate*, edited by P. C. M. Hoppenbrouwers and J. L. van Zanden, 41–66. Turnhout: Brepols.

Howell, M. C. 1998. *The Marriage Exchange: Property, Social Place, and Gender in Cities of the Low Countries, 1300-1550*. Chicago: University of Chicago Press.

Hughes, D. O. 1978. "From Brideprice to Dowry in Mediterranean Europe." *Journal of Family History* 3: 262–296.

Humphries, J. 1990. "Enclosures, Common Rights, and Women: The Proletarianization of Families in the late Eighteenth and Early Nineteenth Centuries." *Journal of Economic History* 50(1): 17–42.

Humphries, J., and J. Weisdorf. 2015. "The Wages of Women in England, 1260–1850." *Journal Economic History* 75: 405–447.

Inglehart, R., P. Norris, and C. Welzel. 2002. "Gender Equality and Democracy." *Comparative Sociology* 1: 321–345.

International Institute of Social History, n.d. "Women's Work in the Northern Netherlands in the Early Modern Period (c. 1500–1815)." https://socialhistory.org/en/projects/womens-work-early-modern-period.

Janssens, A. 2007. "Were Women Present at the Demographic Transition? A Question Revisited." *History of the Family* 12(1): 43–49.

Johnson, P., and S. Nicholas. 1995. "Male and Female Living Standards in England and Wales, 1812-1857: Evidence from Criminal Height Records." *Economic History Review* 48(3): 470–481.

Jowett, J., and Y. Li. 1992. "Age-Heaping: Contrasting Patterns from China." *GeoJournal* 28: 427–442.

Keesing, R. M. 1981. *Cultural Anthropology: A Contemporary Perspective*. New York: Holt, Rinehart and Winston.

Kirshner, J., and A. Molho. 1978. "The Dowry Fund and the Marriage Market in Early Quattrocento Florence." *Journal of Modern History* 50: 403–438.

Kishor, S., and K. Johnson. 2004. *Profiling Domestic Violence: A Multi-Country Study*. Calverton, MD: Macro International.

Klapisch-Zuber, C. 1985. *Women, Family, and Ritual in Renaissance Italy*. Chicago: University of Chicago Press.

Klapisch-Zuber, C. 1986. "Women Servants in Florence During the Fourteenth and Fifteenth Century." In *Women and Work in Preindustrial Europe*, edited by B. Hanawalt, 56–80. Bloomington: Indiana University Press.

Klasen, S. 2002. "Low Schooling for Girls, Slower Growth for All? Cross-Country Evidence on the Effect of Gender Inequality in Education on Economic Development." *World Bank Economic Review* 16(3): 345–373.

Klasen, S., and F. Lamanna. 2009. "The Impact of Gender Inequality in Education and Employment on Economic Growth: New Evidence for a Panel of Countries." *Feminist Economics* 15(3): 91–132.

Koch, E. 1987. "De positie van vrouwen op de huwelijksmarkt." *Tijdschrift voor Sociale Geschiedenis* 13: 150–172.

Koepke, N., and J. Baten. 2005. "The Biological Standard of Living During the Last Two Millennia." *Review of European Economic History* 9(1): 61–97.

Kok, J. 1990. "The Moral Nation. Illegitimacy and Bridal Pregnancy in the Netherlands from 1600 to the Present.," *Economic and Social History in the Netherlands* 2: 7–36.

Kok, J., W. S. Yang, and Y. H. Hsieh. 2006. "Marital Fertility and Birth Control in Rural Netherlands and Taiwan, 19th and Early 20th Centuries." In *Positive or Preventive: Fertility Developments in Taiwan and the Netherlands, 1850-1950,* edited by Y. C. Chuang, T. Engelen, and A. P. Wolf, 199–235. Amsterdam: Aksant.

Kossman-Putto, J. A. 1955. *Kamper schepenakten 1316-1354.* Zwolle.

Koster, P. 1929. *Hoorn in de middeleeuwen. De economische ontwikkelingsgang van een Westfriesche stad.* Amsterdam: HJ Paris.

Kotlikoff, L. J., and A. Spivak. 1981. "The Family as an Incomplete Annuities Market." *Journal of Political Economy* 89: 372–391.

Kowaleski, M. 1998. "Singlewomen in Medieval and Early Modern Europe: The Demographic Perspective." In *Singlewomen in the European past, 1250-1800I,* edited by J. M. Bennett and A. M. Froide, 38–81. Philadelphia: University of Pennsylvania Press.

Kowaleski, M. 1999. "Appendix: Demographic Tables." In *Singlewomen in the European Past, 1250-1800,* edited by Judith M. Bennett and Amy M. Froide, 325–344. Philadelphia: University of Pennsylvania Press.

Kowaleski, M., and J. M. Bennett. 1989. "Crafts, Guilds, and Women in the Middle Ages: Fifty Years after Marian K. Dale." In *Sisters and Workers in the Middle Ages,* edited by J. M. Bennett, 11–38. Chicago: University of Chicago Press.

Kreager, P., and E. Schroeder-Butterfill, eds. 2005. *Ageing without Children: European and Asian Perspectives.* Oxford and New York: Berghahn Books.

Kuijpers, E. 1997. "Lezen en schrijven. Onderzoek naar het alfabetiseringsniveau in zeventiende-eeuws Amsterdam." *Tijdschrift voor sociale geschiedenis* 23: 490–523.

Kuijpers, H. M. E. P. 2005. *Migrantenstad. Immigratie en Sociale Verhoudingen in 17e-Eeuws Amsterdam.* Hilversum: Uitgeverij Verloren.

Kussmaul, A. 1981. *Servants in Husbandry in Early Modern England.* Cambridge: Cambridge University Press.

Lagerlöf, J. 2003. "Gender Equality and Long-Run Growth." *Journal of Economic Growth* 8: 403–426.

Langdon, J. 2010. "Women and Workers on Royal Building Sites before the Black Death." Paper for the Tenth Anglo-American Seminar on the Medieval Economy and Society, Durham.

Laslett, P. 1965. *The World We Have Lost.* London and New York: Routledge.

Laslett, P. 1969. "The Household in England over Three Centuries." *Population Studies* 23(2): 199–223.

Laslett, P. 1977. *Family Life and Illicit Love in Earlier Generations: Essays in Historical Sociology.* Cambridge and New York: Cambridge University Press.

Laslett, P. 1978. "Introduction: The History of the Family." In *Household and Family in Past Time,* edited by P. Laslett and R. Wall, 1–90. Cambridge: Cambridge University Press.

Laslett, P. 1982. "Family and Household as Work Group and Kin Group: Areas of Traditional Europe Compared." In *Family Forms in Historic Europe,* edited by R. Wall, J. Robin, and P. Laslett, 513–563. Cambridge: Cambridge University Press.

Laslett, P. 1988. "Family, Kinship and Collectivity as Systems of Support in Pre-industrial Europe: A Consideration of the Nuclear-Hardship Hypothesis." *Continuity and Change* 3: 152–175.

Laslett, P. 1989. *A Fresh Map of Life: The Emergence of the Third Age.* Cambridge, MA: Harvard University Press.

Lee, J. Z., and W. Feng. 1999. *One Quarter of Humanity: Malthusian Mythology and Chinese Realities, 1700-2000.* Cambridge, MA: Harvard University Press.

Leers, S. 2003. "Vrouwen en meisjes steeds crimineler." *Nieuw Amsterdams Peil,* October 29.

Leroy Ladurie, E. 1976. "Family Structures and Inheritance Customs in Sixteenth-Century France." In *Family and Inheritance: Rural Society in Western Europe, 1200-1800,* edited by J. Goody, J. Thirsk, and E. P. Thompson, 37–70. Cambridge: Cambridge University Press.

Levine, D. 1977. *Family Formation in an Age of Nascent Capitalism.* New York: Academic Press.

Light, A. 2007. *Mrs. Woolf and the Servants: An Intimate History of Domestic Life in Bloomsbury and the Servant's Hand: English Fiction from below.* New York: Bloomsbury Press.

Lindert, P. 1998. "Poor Relief Before the Welfare State: Britain versus the Continent, 1780-1880." *European Review of Economic History* 2: 101–141.

Lucas, R. E. Jr. 1988. "On the Mechanics of Economic Development." *Journal of Monetary Economics* 22: 3–42.

Lucas, R. E. Jr. 2002. *Lectures on Economic Growth.* New Delhi: Oxford University Press.

Lundh, C. 1995. "Households and Families in Pre-industrial Sweden." *Continuity and Change* 10: 33–68.

Lundh, L., and M. Olsson. 2002. "The Institution of Retirement on Scanian Estates in the Nineteenth Century." *Continuity and Change* 17(3): 373–403.

Lyna, D. 2005. "Van Loonse stad tot Limburgse provinciehoofdplaats. De demografische, sociaal-economische en ruimtelijke ontwikkeling van Hasselt en haar positie in Limburg 1796-1846." Dissertation, Universiteit Antwerpen, Faculteit Letteren en Wijsbegeerte, Departement Geschiedenis.

Lynch, K. A. 2003. *Individuals, Families, and Communities in Europe, 1200-1800: The Urban Foundations of Western Society.* Cambridge: Cambridge University Press.

Macfarlane, A. 1980. "Demographic Structures and Cultural Regions in Europe." *Cambridge Anthropology* 6: 1–17.

Madan T. N. 1962. "The Joint Family: A Terminological Clarification." *International Journal of Comparative Sociology* 3: 7–10.

Majérus., P. 1997. *Ces femmes qu'on dit béguines. . . ..: Guide des béguinages de Belgique: Bibliographie et sources d'archives.* Bruxelles: Archives générales du Royaume.

Manzel, K. 2008. *Essays on Human Capital Development in Latin America and Spain Aufsätze zur Humankapitalentwicklung in Lateinamerika und Spanien.* Dissertation Universität Tübingen. https://publikationen.uni-tuebingen.de/xmlui/handle/10900/47891.

Mason, K. O. 1997. "Gender and Demographic Change: What Do We Know?" In *The Continuing Demographic Transition,* edited by G. W. Jones, R. M. Douglas, J. C. Caldwell, and R. M. D'Souza, 158–182. Oxford: Clarendon Press.

Mate, M. E. 1998. *Daughters, Wives, and Widows After the Black Death: Women in Sussex, 1350-1535.* Woodbridge/Rochester: Boydell and Brewer.

Mate, M. E. 1999. *Women in Medieval English Society.* Cambridge: Cambridge University Press.

Mayhew, G. 1990. "Life-Cycle, Service and the Family Unit in Early Modern Rye." *Continuity and Change* 5: 201–225.

Maynes, M. J., and A. Waltner. 2001. "Childhood, Youth, and the Female Life Cycle: Women's Life-Cycle Transitions in a World-Historical Perspective. Comparing Marriage in China and Europe." *Journal of Women's History* 12: 11–21.

McDonnell, E. W. 1969. *The Beguines and Beghards in Medieval Culture, with Special Emphasis on the Belgian Scene.* New York: Octagon Books.

McIntosh, M. K. 2005. *Working Women in English Society, 1300-1620.* Cambridge: Cambridge University Press.

Menant, F., and O. Redon. 2004. *Notaires et crédit dans l'Occidant Méditerranéen medieval.* Roma: École française de Rome.

Menning, C. B. 1993. *Charity and State in Late Renaissance Italy: The Monte di Pietà of Florence*. Ithaca, NY: Cornell University Press.

Milis, L. 1992. *Angelic Monks and Earthly Men: Monasticism and its Meaning to Medieval Society*. Woodbridge/Rochester, NY: Boydell Press.

Minchington, W. E., ed. 1972. *Wage Regulation in Pre-Industrial England*. New York: David & Charles.

Mitch, D. 1993. "The Role of Human Capital in the Industrial Revolution." In *The British Industrial Revolution: An Economic Perspective*, edited by J. Mokyr, 267–308. Boulder, CO: Westview Press.

Mitterauer, M., and R. Sieder. 1982. *The European Family*. Oxford: Basil Blackwell.

Mokyr, J. 1983. *Why Ireland Starved: A Quantitative and Analytical History of the Irish Economy, 1800-1850*. London: Allen & Unwin.

Mokyr, J. 1990. "The Great Conundrum." *Journal of Modern History* 62(1): 78–88.

Mokyr, J. 2002. *The Gifts of Athena: Historical Origins of the Knowledge Society*. Princeton, NJ: Princeton University Press.

Molho, A. 1971. *Florentine Public Finances in the Early Renaissance, 1400-1433*. Cambridge, MA: Harvard University Press.

Molho, A. 1988. "Reception and Mrriage Strategy in Renaissance Florence: The Case of Woman's Ages." *Renaissance Quarterly* 41: 193–217.

Molho, A. 1994. *Marriage Alliance in Late Medieval Florence*. Cambridge, MA: Harvard University Press.

Molho, A. 1995. "The State and Public Finance: A Hypothesis Based on the History of Late medieval Florence." *Journal of Modern History* 76 (Suppl.): 97–135.

Moran, J. A. H. 1985. *The Growth of English Schooling, 1340-1548: Learning, Literacy, and Laicization in Pre-Reformation York Diocese*. Princeton, NJ: Princeton University Press.

Moring, B. 2006. "Nordic Retirement Contracts and the Economic Situation of Widows." *Continuity and Change* 21(3): 383–418.

Moring, B. 2010. "Rural Widows, Economy and Co-residence in the 18th and 19th Centuries." *History of the Family* 15: 239–254.

Munro, J. H. 2003. "The Medieval Origins of the Financial Revolution: Usury, Rents, and Negotiability." *International History Review* 25: 505–562.

Munro, J. H. 2007. "The Usury Doctrine and Urban Public Finances in Late-Medieval Flanders: Annuities, Excise Taxes and Income Transfer from the Poor to the Rich." Working paper 288, Department of Economics, University of Toronto.

Murdock, G. P. 1949. *Social Structure*. New York: MacMillan.

Murdock, G. P. 1967. *Ethnographic Atlas*. Pittsburgh, PA: University of Pittsburgh Press.

Murray, J. 1998. "Individualism and Consensual Marriage: Some Evidence from Medieval England." In *Women, Marriage, and Family in Medieval Christendom: Essays in Memory of Michael M. Sheehan, C.S.B.* edited by C. M. Rousseau and J. T. Rosenthal, 121–151. Kalamazoo: Western Michigan University Press.

Myers, R. 1954. "Accuracy of Age Reporting in the 1950 United States Census." *Journal of the American Statistical Association* 49: 826–831.

Nederveen Meerkerk, E. 2010. "Market Wage or Discrimination? The Remuneration of Male and Female Wool Spinners in the Seventeenth-Century Dutch Republic." *Economic History Review* 63(1): 165–186.

Neel, C. 1989. "The Origins of the Beguines." *Signs: Journal of Women in Culture and Society* 14(2): 321–342.

Nicholas, D. 1985. *The Domestic Life of a Medieval City: Women, Children, and the Family in Fourteenth-Century Ghent*. Lincoln: University of Nebraska Press.

Nicholas, S., and D. Oxley. 1993. "The Living Standards of Women during the Industrial Revolution." *Economic History Review* 46(4): 723–749.

Niessen, W. J. 2005. "De Nijmeegse onroerend goedmarkt 1570-1630. Een onderzoek naar de bewegingen op en de deelnemers aan de Nijmeegse onroerend goed- en kredietmarkt." Ph.D. dissertation, Radboud University Nijmegen.

Nilsson, A., L. Petterson, and P. Svensson. 1999. "Agrarian Transition and Literacy: The Case of Nineteenth Century Sweden." *European Review of Economic History* 3(1): 79–96.

Noonan, J. T. 1973. "The Power to Choose." *Viator* 4: 414–434.

Noordegraaf, L., and J. L. van Zanden. 1995. "Early Modern Economic Growth and the Standard of Living. Did Labor Benefit from Holland's Golden Age?" In *A Miracle Mirrored*, edited by C. A. Davids and J. Lucassen, 410–437. Cambridge: Cambridge University Press.

North, D. C. 1981. *Structure and Change in Economic History*. New York: Norton.

North, D. C., and B. R. Weingast. 1989. "Constitutions and Commitment: The Evolution of Institutions Governing Public Choice in Seventeenth-Century England." *Journal of Economic History* 49(4): 803–832.

Ogilvie, S. 2003. *A Bitter Living: Women, Markets, and Social Capital in Early-Modern German*. Oxford: Oxford University Press.

Ogilvie, S. 2007. "'Whatever Is, Is Right'? Economic Institutions in Pre-Industrial Europe." *Economic History Review* 60(4): 649–684.

Ogilvie, S. 2008. "Rehabilitating the Guilds: A Reply." *Economic History Review* 61(1): 175–182.

Ogilvie, S., and M. Cerman. 1995. "The Bohemian Census of 1651 and the Position of Inmates." *Histoire Sociale* 28: 333–346.

Omre, N., and M. Webster. 1995. *The English Hospital, 1070-1570*. New Haven, CT: Yale University Press.

Oppenheimer, V. K. 1974. "The Life-Cycle Squeeze: The Interaction of Men's Occupational and Family Life Cycles." *Demography* 11(2): 227–245.

Otterbein, K. F. 1965. "Caribbean Family Organisation: A Comparative Analysis." *American Anthropologist* 67(1): 66–79.

Outhwaite, R. B. 1995. *Clandestine Marriage in England, 1500-1850*. London: Hambledon Press.

Overlaet, K. 2012. "Beguinages in Early Modern West-European Cities: Isolated Islands or Open Networks? A Reconsideration of the Social and Familial Embeddedness of Beguines for the Case of Sixteenth-Century Mechelen, a Medium-Sized Town in the Low Countries." Working Paper. Waar?

Ozment, S. E. 1983. *When Fathers Ruled: Family Life in Reformation Europe*. Cambridge, MA: Harvard University Press.

Panhuysen, B. 2000. *Maatwerk: kleermakers, naaisters, oudkleerkopers en de gilden (1500-1800)*. Amsterdam: IISG Studies and Essays 30.

Pedreira, Jorge M. 1993. "La economía portuguesa y el fin del imperio luso-brasileño." In *La independencia americana: consecuencias económicas*, edited by L. Prados de la Escosura and S. Amaral, 219–252. Madrid: Alianza Editorial.

Philippen, L. J. M. 1943. *Het ontstaan der begijnhoven: Een synthetische studie*. Antwerpen: De Nederlandsche Boekhandel.

Pitt, M., S. Khandker, and J. Cartwright. 2003. "Does Micro-Credit Empower Women? Evidence from Bangladesh." WorldBank Policy Research Working Papers No. 2998.

Piwonka, R. 1991. "Recovering the Lost Ark: The Dutch Graphic Tradition in the Hudson Valley." In *A Beautiful and Fruitful Place: Selected Rensselaerswijck Seminar Papers*, edited by N. A. McClure Zeller, 23–35. Albany, NY: New Netherland Publishing.

Pomeranz, K. 2000. *The Great Divergence: China, Europe, and the Making of the Modern World Economy*. Princeton, NJ: Pinceton University Press.

Poos, L. R. 1986. "The Pre-history of Demographic Regions in Traditional Europe." *Sociologia Ruralis* 26: 228–247.

Poos, L. R. 1991. *A Rural Society After the Black Death: Essex, 1350-1525*. Cambridge and New York: Cambridge University Press.

Poska, A. M. 2000. "Gender, Property, and Retirement Strategies in Early Modern Northwestern Spain." *Journal of Family History* 25: 317.

Post, R. 1950. "De roeping tot het kloosterleven in de 16e eeuw." *Mededelingen Der Koninklijke Akademie Van Wetenschappen, Afdeling Letterkunde, n.s.* 13: 31–76.

Posthumus, N. W. 1912. "Een zestiende-eeuwsche enquête naar de buitenneringen rondom de stad Leiden." *Bijdragen en Mededeelingen van het Historisch Genootschap* 33: 1–95.

Power, E. 2010. *Medieval English nunneries c. 1275-to 1535*. Cambridge: Cambridge Library Collection.

Prak, M. 1994. "Goede buren en verre vrienden. De ontwikkeling van onderstand bij armenzorg in Den Bosch sedert de Middeleeuwen." In *Op lange termijn: verklaringen van trends in de geschiedenis van samenlevingen*, edited by H. Flap and M. H. D. van Leeuwen, 147–170. Hilversum: Uitgeverij Verloren.

Priester, P. 1998. *Geschiedenis van de Zeeuwse landbouw circa 1600-1910*. Wageningen: Landbouwuniversiteit Wageningen.

Pullan, B. S. 1971. *Rich and Poor in Renaissance Venice: The Social Institutions of a Catholic State, to 1620*. Oxford: Blackwell.

Putnam, R. D. 1993. *Making Democracy Work: Civic Traditions in Modern Italy*. Princeton, NJ: Princeton University Press.

Quimby, I. M. G., ed. 1971. *American Painting to 1776: A Reappraisal*. Charlottesville: University Press of Virginia.

Ransel, D. L. 1988. *Mothers of Misery: Child Abandonment in Russia*. Princeton, NJ: Princeton University Press.

Rapley, E. (2001). A Social History of the Cloister. Daily Life in the Teaching Monasteries of the Old Regime. Montreal/Quebec: McGill Queen's Press.

Rappaport, S. 1989. *Worlds Within Worlds: Structures of Life in Sixteenth-Century London*. Cambridge: Cambridge University Press.

Rawcliffe, C. 2006. *Leprosy in Medieval England*. Woodbridge: Boydell Press.

Razi, Z. 1980. Life, *Marriage and Death in a Medieval Parish: Economy, Society and Demography in Halesowen 1270-1400*. Cambridge: Cambridge University Press.

Reher, D. S. 1998. "Family Ties in Western Europe: Persistent Contrasts." *Population and Development Review* 24: 203–234.

Reis, J. 2005. "Economic Growth, Human Capital Formation and Consumption in Western Europe Before 1800." In *Living Standards in the Past: New Perspectives on Well-Being in Asia and Europe*, edited by R. C. Allen, T. Bengtsson, and M. Dribe, 195–225. Oxford: Oxford University Press.

Reis, J. 2007. "Institutions and Economic Growth in the Atlantic Periphery: The Efficiency of the Portuguese Machinery of Justice, 1870-1910." Paper presented at the conference on Law and Economic Development, Utrecht 2007.

Reis, J. 2008. "Is Education a Good Proxy for Human Capital? Measurement and Distributional Issues in Portugal During the 19th Century." Working Paper presented at the ESSHC, Lisbon.

Riddy, F., and P. J. P. Goldberg, eds. 2004. *Youth in the Middle Ages*. York: Medieval Press.

Rijpma, A., and S. G. Carmichael. 2016. "Testing Todd and Matching Murdock: Global Data on Family Characteristics." *Economic History of Developing Regions* 13(1): 10–46.

Romer, P. M. 1986. "Increasing Returns and Long-run Growth." *Journal of Political Economy* 94: 1002–1037.

Roxburgh, C., S. Lund, and J. Piotrowski. 2011. *Mapping Global Capital Markets*. McKinsey Global Institute.

Russell, J. C. 1948. *British Medieval Population*. Albuquerque: University of New Mexico Press.

Ruwet, J., and Y. Wellemans. 1978. *L'analphabetisme en Belgique (XVIIIème—XIXème Siècles)*. Louvain: Bibliothèque de l'Université.

Saito, O. 2005. "The Third Pattern of Marriage and Remarriage: Japan in Eurasian comparative perspectives." In *Marriage and the Family in Eurasia: Perspectives on the Hajnal Hypothesis*, edited by T. Engelen and A. P. Wolf, 165–195. Amsterdam: Aksant.

Sallares, R. 1991. *The Ecology of the Ancient Greek World*. Ithaca, New York: Cornell University Press

Saller, R. P. 1987. "Men's Age at Marriage and Its Consequences in the Roman Family." *Classical Philology* 82(1): 21–34.

Schellekens, J. 1995. "Poverty and Family Size in Two Eighteenth-Century Dutch Villages." *Continuity and Change* 10(2): 199–214.

Schlotheuber, E. 2004. *Klostereintritt und Bildung. Die Lebenswelt der Nonnen im späten Mittelalter.* Tübingen: Mohr Siebeck.

Schmidt, A. 2001a. *Overleven na de dood: weduwen in Leiden in de Gouden Eeuw* Amsterdam: Prometheus/Bert Bakker.

Schmidt, A. 2001b. "Touching Inheritance. Mannen, vrouwen en de overdracht van bezit in Holland in de 17e eeuw." *Holland, historisch tijdschrift* 33: 175–189.

Schmidt, A. 2007. "Survival Strategies of Widows and Their Families in Erly Modern Holland, c. 1580–1750." *History of the Family* 12: 268–281.

Schnapper, B. 1957. *Les rentes au XVIe siècle. Histoire d'un instrument de crédit.* Paris: Université de Paris, Faculté de droit.

Schweizer, T., and D. R. White, eds. 1998. *Kinship, Networks, and Exchange.* Cambridge: Cambridge University Press.

Schofield, R. 1985. "English Marriage Patterns Revisited." *Journal of Family History* 10: 2–33.

Schultz, T. P. 1997. "Demand for Children in Low Income Countries." In *Handbook of Population and Family Economics,* edited by M. R. Rosenzweig and O. Stark, 350–430. Amsterdam: Elsevier.

Sen, A. 1990. "More Than 100 Million Women Missing." *The New York Review of Books* 37(20): 61–66.

Service de la Propagande Artistique. 1952. Paris: Orangerie des Tuileries.

Sheehan, M. M. 1971. "The Formation and Stability of Marriage in Fourteenth-Century England: Evidence of an Ely Register." *Mediaeval Studies* 33: 228–263.

Sheehan, M. M. 1978. "Marriage Theory and Practice in the Conciliar Legislation and Diocesan Statutes of Medieval England." *Mediaeval Studies* 40: 408–460.

Sheehan, M. M. 1997. "Choice of Marriage Partner." In *Marriage, Family, and Law in Medieval Europe: Collected Studies,* edited by M. M. Sheehan and J. K. Farge, 362. Toronto: University of Toronto Press.

Simons, W. 1983. *Cities of Ladies: Beguine Communities in the Medieval Low Countries, 1200-1565.* Philadelphia: University of Pennsylvania Press.

Simons, W. 1991. "Een zeker bestaan: de Zuidnederlandse begijnen en de Frauenfrage." *Tijdschrift voor Sociale Geschiedenis* 17: 125–146.

Skolnick, A. 1993. "Changes of Heart: Family Dynamics in Historical Perspective." In *Family, Self, and Society, Toward A New Agenda for Family Research,* edited by P. A. Cowan, D. Field, D. A. Hansen, A. Skolnick, and G. E. Swanson, 43–68. Hillsdale, NJ: Lawrence Erlbaum.

Smith, J. E. 1984. "Widowhood and Ageing in Traditional English Society." *Ageing and Society* 4: 429–449.

Smith, R. M. 1979. "Some Reflections on the Evidence for the Origins of the 'European Marriage Pattern' in England." In *The Sociology of the Family: New Directions for Britain,* edited by C. Harris, M. Anderson, R. Chester, D. H. J. Morgan, and D. Leonard, 74–112. Sociological Review Monograph.

Smith, R. M. 1981. "The Structural Dependence of the Elderly as a Recent Development: Some Sceptical Historical Thoughts." *Ageing and Society* 4: 409–428.

Smith, R. M. 1983. "Some Thoughts on 'Hereditary' and 'Proprietary' Rights in land under Customary Law in Thirteenth and Early Fourteenth Century England." *Law and History Review* 1(1): 95–128.

Smith, R. M. 1984. "Some Issues Concerning Families and Their Property in Rural England 1250–1800." In *Land, Kinship and Life-Cycle,* edited by R. M. Smith, 1–86. Cambridge: Cambridge University Press.

Smith, R. M. 1986a. "Transfer Incomes, Risk and Security: The Roles of the Family and the Collectivity in Recent Theories of Fertility Change." In *The State of Population Theory: Forward from Malthus to Modern Times,* edited by D. A. Coleman and R. S. Schofield, 188–211. Oxford: Blackwell.

Smith, R. M. 1986b. "Women's Property Rights Under Customary Law: Some Developments in the Thirteenth and Fourteenth Centuries." *Transactions of the Royal Historical Society* 5: 165–194.

Smith, R. M. 1991. "The Manorial Court and the Elderly Tenant in Late Medieval England." In *Life, Death, and the Elderly: Historical Perspectives*, edited by M. Pelling and R. M. Smith, 33–51. London: Routledge.

Smith, R. M. 1992. "Geographical Diversity in the Resort to Marriage in Late Medieval Europe: Work, Reputation and Unmarried Females in the Household Formation Systems of Northern and Southern Europe." In *Woman Is a Worthy Wight: Women in English Society c. 1200-1500*, edited by P. J. P. Goldberg, 16–59. Wolfeboro Falls, NH: Alan Sutton.

Smith, R. M. 1999. "Relative Prices, Forms of Agrarian Labour and Female Marriage Patterns in England, 1350-1800." In *Marriage and Rural Economy: Western Europe Since 1400*, edited by I. Devos and L. Kennedy, 19–48. Turnhout: Brepols.

Smith, R.T. 1957. "The Family in the Caribbean." In *Caribbean Studies: A Symposium*, edited by V. Rubin, 67–74. Jamaica: Institute of Social and Economic Research, University College of the West Indies.

Smits, J.-P., E. Horlings, and J. L. van Zanden. 2000. *Dutch GNP and its Components, 1800-1913*. Groningen: Growth and Development Centre, Monograph Series no. 5.

Snell, K. D. M. 1981. "Agricultural Seasonal Unemployment, the Standard of Living, and Women's Work in the South and East, 1690-1960." *Economic History Review* 34(3): 407–437.

Spaans, J. 1997. *Armenzorg in Friesland 1500-1800: publieke zorg en particuliere liefdadigheid in zes Friese steden; Leeuwarden, Bolsward, Franeker, Sneek, Dokkum en Harlingen*. Hilversum: Verloren; Leeuwarden: Fryske Akademy.

Spaans, J. 2002. "Weduwen, wezen en vreemdelingen. Sociale zorg en tolerantie." In *Geschiedenis van Holland, deel II, 1572 tot 1795*, edited by T. de Nijs and E. Beukers, 255–286. Hilversum: Verloren.

Sparreboom, J. 1980. "Beroepsstructuur, vermogensstatistiek en taxatie van de schotplichtige bevolking van Edam." Unpublished manuscript, available at the Waterlands Archief.

Sparreboom, J. 1981. "Twee fiscale bronnen uit het stadsarchief van Edam, circa 1462." *Holland Historisch Tijdschrift* 13: 146–164.

Spierenburg, P. 1984. *The Spectacle of Suffering: Executions and the Evolution of Repression, from a Preindustrial Metropolis to the European Experience*. Cambridge: Cambridge University Press.

Spufford, M. 1976. "Peasant Inheritance Customs and Land Distribution in Cambridgeshire from the Sixteenth to the Eighteenth Centuries." In *Family and Inheritance: Rural Society in Western Europe, 1200-1800*, edited by J. Goody, J. Thirsk, and E. P. Thompson, 156–176. Cambridge: Cambridge University Press.

Stasavage, D. 2014. "Was Weber Right? The Role of Urban Autonomy in Europe's Rise." *American Political Science Review* 108(2): 337–354.

St. Clair, W. 2004. *The Reading Nation in the Romantic Period*. Cambridge: Cambridge University Press.

Stephens, W. B. 1990. "Literacy in England, Scotland, and Wales, 1500-1900." *History of Education Quarterly* 30: 545–571.

Stone, L. 1969. "Literacy and Education in England 1640-1900." *Past and Present* 42: 69–139.

Strubbe, E. I. 1923. "Het houden van de doorgaande waarheid in het Vrije van Brugge." *A.S.E.B.* 66: 249–253.

Struyck, N. 1753. *Beschrijving der Staartsterren en nader ontdekkingen omtrent den staat van het menselijk geslagt*. Amsterdam: Tirion.

Stuurman, S., and T. Akkerman, eds. 1998. *Perspectives on Feminist Political Thought in European History: From the Middle Ages to the Present*. London and New York: Routledge.

Summers, L. 1992. "Investing in All the People." World Bank Policy Research Working Papers 905.

Sylla, R. 2002. "Financial Systems and Economic Modernization." *Journal of Economic History* 62: 277–292.

Szoltysek, M. 2008. "Rethinking Eastern Europe: Household Formation Patterns in the Polish-Lithuanian Commonwealth and European Family Systems." *Continuity and Change* 23: 389–427.

Thane, P. 2000. *Old Age in English History: Past Experiences, Present Issues.* Oxford: Oxford University Press.

Tierney, B. 1959. *Medieval Poor Law: A Sketch of Canonical Theory and Its Application in England.* Berkeley: University of California Press.

Tilly, C. 1990. *Coercion, Capital, and European States, AD 990-1992.* Cambridge: Basil Blackwell.

Tilly, L. A., R. G. Fuchs, D. I. Kertzer, and D. L. Ransel. 1992. "Child Abandonment in European History: A Symposium." *Journal of Family History* 17(1): 1–23.

Todd, E. 1985. *The Explanation of Ideology: Family Structures and Social Systems.* Oxford: Blackwell.

Todd, E. 1987. *The Causes of Progress: Culture, Authority and Change.* Oxford: Blackwell.

Todd, E. 2011. *L'origine des systems familiaux.* NRF Essais Gallimard, Paris.

Tracy, J. D. 1985. *A Financial Revolution in the Habsburg Netherlands. Renten and renteniers in the County of Holland 1515-1565.* Cambridge: Cambridge University Press.

Uitz, E. 1990. *The Legend of Good Women: Medieval Women in Towns & Cities.* Mount Kisco, NY: Moyer Bell.

UN Development Program. 2006. *Assessing Age Heaping—Whipple's Index by Sex and Urban/ Rural Residence: Each Census, 1985 – 2003.* https://unstats.un.org/unsd/demographic/ products/dyb/DYBcensus/V1_Notes1c.pdf

UN Development Program. 2010. Human Development Report. United Nations. http://hdr. undp.org/en/content/human-development-report-2010.

UN Food and Agriculture Organization. 2011: *The State of Food and Agriculture 2010-2011. Women in Agriculture; Closing the gender gap for development.* Rome: FAO.

Van Bavel, B. 2006. "Rural Wage Labour in the 16th-Century Low Countries: An Assessment of the Importance and Nature of Wage Labour in the Countryside of Holland, Guelders and Flanders." *Continuity and Change* 21: 37–72.

Van Bavel, B. 2010. *Manors and Markets: Economy and Society in the Low Countries 500-1500.* Oxford: Oxford University Press.

Van Belle, R. 2006. "Vlakke grafmonumenten en memorietaferelen met persoonsafbeeldingen in West-Vlaanderen: Een inventaris, funeraire symboliek en een overzicht van het kostuum." Brugge: Exhibitions International NV.

Vandenbroeke, C. 1981. *Sociale geschiedenis van het Vlaamse volk. Beveren/Nijmegen:* Uitgeverij Orion/Uitgeverij B. Gottmer.

Van der Heijden, M. 2006. *Geldschieters van de stad. Financiële relaties tussen stad, burgers en overheden 1550-1650.* Amsterdam: Bert Bakker.

Van der Ree-Scholtens, G. F. 1993. *De grensgebieden in het noordoosten van Brabant ca. 1200–1795. Institutionele en juridische aspecten.* Assen: Van Gorcum.

Van der Woude, A. M. 1970. "De omvang en samenstelling van huishouding in Nederland in het verleden." *A. A. G. Bijdragen* 15: 202–241.

Van der Woude, A. M. 1972a. *Het Noorderkwartier. Een regionaal historisch onderzoek in de demografische en economische geschiedenis van westelijk Nederland van de late middeleeuwen tot het begin van de negentiende eeuw.* Wageningen: H. Veenman en zonen.

Van der Woude, A. M. 1972b. "Variations in the Size and Structure of the Household in the United Provinces of the Netherlands in the Seventeenth and Eighteenth Centuries." In *Household and Family in Past Times,* edited by Peter Laslett, 299–318. Cambridge: Cambridge University Press.

Van der Woude, A. M. 1980b. "De alfabetisering." In *Algemene Geschiedenis der Nederlanden,* 257–264. Bussum.

Van Dillen, J. G. 1940. "Summiere staat van de in 1622 in de Provincie Holland gehouden volkstelling." *Economisch-Historisch Jaarboek* 21: 167–189.

Van Dusen, R. A., & E. B. Sheldon. 1976. "The Changing Status of American Women: A Life Cycle Perspective." *American Psychologist* 31(2): 106–116.

Van Eeghen, I. H. 1941. *Vrouwenkloosters en begijnhof in Amsterdam van de 14e tot het eind der 16e eeuw*. Amsterdam: Paris.

Vangassen, H. 1964. *Bouwstoffen tot de historische taalgeografie van het Nederlands. Noordhollandse charters.* Tongeren: Belgisch Interuniversitair Centrum voor Neerlandistiek.

Van Gerwen, J., and M. H. D. van Leeuwen. 1998. *Studies over zekerheidsarrangement en: risico's, risicobestrijding en verzekeringen in Nederland vanaf de Middeleeuwen.* Amsterdam: Nederlandsch Economisch Historisch Archief.

Van Ham, W. A. 2000. *Macht en gezag in het Markiezaat. een politiek-institutionele studie van Stad en Land van Bergen Op Zoom (1477-1583).* Hilversum: Verloren.

Van Lottum, J., and J. L. Van Zanden. 2014. "Labour Productivity and Human Capital in the European Maritime Sector of the Eighteenth Century." *Explorations in Economic History* 53: 83–100.

Van Luijk, M. 2001. "Devote vrouwen tijdens de tweede religieuze vrouwenbeweging in de laatmiddeleeuwse Noordelijke Nederlanden," *Tijdschrift voor Sociale Geschiedenis* 27(1): 33–56.

Van Luyn, P. B. N. 1995. "Begijnstraat en Begijnhof." In *Historisch Jaarboek voor het Land Van Zwentibold,* 14–36. Sittard: Stichting Historisch Jaarboek voor het Land van Zwentibold.

Van Nierop, L. 1934. "De bruidegoms van Amsterdam van 1578 tot 1601." *Tijdschrift voor geschiedenis* 49: 136–160.

Van Zanden, J. L. 1985. *De economische ontwikkeling van de Nederlandse landbouw in de negentiende eeuw 1800-1914.* Wageningen: Universiteit Wageningen.

Van Zanden, J. L. 1993. *The Rise and Decline of Holland's Economy: Merchant Capitalism and the Labour Market.* Manchester: Manchester University Press.

Van Zanden, J. L. 2002a. "Taking the Measure of the Early Modern Economy: Historical National Accounts for Holland in 1510-1514." *European Review of Economic History* 6: 131–163.

Van Zanden, J. L. 2002b. "The Revolt of the Early Modernists: An Assessment." *Economic History Review* 55: 595–623.

Van Zanden, J. L. 2005. "De timmerman, de boekdrukker en het ontstaan van de Europese kenniseconomie." *Tijdschrift voor Sociale en Economische Geschiedenis* 2: 105–121.

Van Zanden, J. L. 2008. "The Road to the Industrial Revolution: Hypotheses and Conjectures About the Medieval Origins of the 'European Miracle.'" *Journal of Global History* 3(3): 337–359.

Van Zanden, J. L. 2009. *The Long Road to the Industrial Revolution: The European Economy in a Global Perspective, 1000-1800.* Leiden: Brill.

Van Zanden, J. L., E. Buringh, and M. Bosker. 2012. "The Rise and Decline of European Parliaments, 1188–17891." *Economic History Review* 65(3): 835–861.

Van Zanden, J. L., and M. Prak. 2006. "Towards an Economic Interpretation of Citizenship: The Dutch Republic Between Medieval Communes and Modern Nation-states." *European Review of Economic History* 10: 111–145.

Van Zanden, J. L., A. Rijpma, and J. Kok. 2017. *Agency, Gender and Economic Development.* London: Routledge.

Van Zanden, J. L., and B. van Leeuwen. 2010. "The Origins of Modern Economic Growth? Holland between 1347 and 1807." Unpublished manuscript. http://www.basvanleeuwen.net/bestanden/VanZandenVanLeeuwen21July2009Conference.pdf.

Vauchez. A. 1978. "Assistance et charité en occident, XIIIe-Xve siècles." In *Domande et consumi, livelli e strutturi XIII-XVIII,* edited by V. Barbagli Bagnoli, 151–162. Florence: Istituto Internazionale di Storia Economica "F. Datini" di Prato.

VerLoren van Themaat, L. M., and H. W. Dokkum. 1983. *Oude Dordtse lijfrenten: stedelijke financiering in de vijftiende eeuw*. Amsterdam: Verloren.

Viazzo, P. P. 2003. "'What's So Special About the Mediterranean?' Thirty Years of Research on Household and Family in Italy." *Continuity and Change* 18: 111–137.

Vogt, H. 2008. "Fledføring—Elder Care and the Protection of the Interest of Heirs in Danish Medieval Laws." *Legal History Review* 76(3-4): 273–281.

Voigtländer, N., and H.-J. Voth. 2011. "How the West 'Invented' Fertility Restriction." NBER Working Paper No. w17314, National Bureau of Economic Research.

Volkstelling. 1930. *Voorlopige uitkomsten. Het Departement van landbouw*, nijverheid en handel. Batavia.

Voth, H.-J. 2000. *Time and Work in England; 1750-1830*. Oxford: Clarendon Press.

Wall, R. 1983a. "Does Owing Real Property Influence the Form of the Household? An Example from Rural West Flanders." In *Family Forms in Historic Europe*, edited by R. Wall, J. Robin, and P. Laslett, 379–407. Cambridge: Cambridge University Press.

Wall, R. 1983b. "Family and Household as Work Group and Kin Group: Areas of Traditional Europe Compared." In *Family Forms in Historic Europe*, edited by R. Wall, J. Robin, and P. Laslett, 1–64. Cambridge: Cambridge University Press.

Weber, M. 1978. *Selections in Translation*. Edited by W. G. Runciman. Cambridge: Cambridge University Press.

Weir, D. R. 1984. "Life Under Pressure: France and England, 1670-1870." *Journal of Economic History* 44: 27–47.

Wilson, K. M. 1987. *Women Writers of the Renaissance and Reformation*. Athens:: University of Georgia Press.

Wintle, M. J. 1987. *Pillars of Piety: Religion in the Netherlands in the Nineteenth Century, 1813-1901*. Hull: Hull University Press.

Woodward, Donald. 1980. "The Background to the Statute of Artificers: the Genesis of Labour Policy, 1558-63." *Economic History Review* 33(1): 32–44.

World Bank. 2012. *World Development Report: Gender Equality and Development* . Washington, DC: World Bank.

Wrightson, K. 1982. *English Society, 1580–1680*. New Brunswick, NJ: Rutgers University Press.

Wrigley, E. A. 1983. "The Growth of Population in Eighteenth-Century England: A Conundrum Resolved." *Past & Present* 98: 121–150.

Wrigley, E. A., R. S. Davies, J. E. Oeppen, and R. S. Schofield. 1997. *English Population History from Family Reconstruction, 1580-1837*. Cambridge: Cambridge University Press.

Wrigley, E. A., and R. S. Schofield. 1981. *The Population History of England, 1541-1871: A Reconstruction*. Cambridge: Cambridge University Press.

Xu, D., C. Wu, and P. J. Curwen. 1999. *Chinese Capitalism, 1522-1840*. Basingstoke: Macmillan.

Yanigisako, S. J. 1979. "Family and Household. The Analysis of Domestic Groups." *Annual Review of Anthropology* 8: 161–205.

Youngs, D. 2006. *The Life Cycle in Western Europe, c.1300-c.1500*. Manchester: Manchester University Press.

Yunus, M. 2008. *Creating a World Without Poverty: Social Business and the Future of Capitalism*. New York: Public Affairs.

Zeitzen, M. K. 2008. *Polygamy, a Cross-Cultural Analysis*. Oxford and New York: Berg.

Zuijderduijn, C. J. 2008. "Conjunctuur in laatmiddeleeuws Haarlem: een eerste aanzet." *Holland Historisch Tijdschrift* 40: 3–18.

Zuijderduijn, C. J. 2009a. "Assessing a Late Medieval Capital Market: The Capacity of the Market for Renten in Edam and De Zeevang (1462-1563)." *Jaarboek voor Middeleeuwse Geschiedenis* 11: 138–164.

Zuijderduijn, C. J. 2009b. *Medieval Capital Markets: Markets for "Renten", State Formation and Private Investment in Holland (1330-1550)*. Leiden: Brill Academic.

Zuijderduin, J., and T. De Moor. 2010. "Spending, Saving or Investing: The Asset Management of Sixteenth-Century Holland Households." *Economic History Review* 66(1): 38–56.

Zurndorfer, H. T., ed. 1999. *Chinese Women in the Imperial Past: New Perspectives*. Leiden: Brill.

INDEX

Page references followed by *t* and *f* indicate tables and figures, respectively.

www.ingramcontent.com/pod-product-compliance
Lightning Source LLC
Chambersburg PA
CBHW052046101125
34603CB00019B/6
9780190847883